IDIOMS
OF
UNCERTAINTY

Peter J. Burgard

IDIOMS
OF
UNCERTAINTY

Goethe and the Essay

The Pennsylvania State University Press
University Park, Pennsylvania

Library of Congress Cataloging-in-Publication Data

Burgard, Peter J.
   Idioms of uncertainty: Goethe and the essay / Peter J. Burgard.
     p.   cm.
   Includes bibliographical references and index.
   ISBN 0-271-00845-8
   1. Goethe, Johann Wolfgang von, 1749–1832—Criticism and
interpretation. 2. Essay. I. Title.
PT2189.B8   1992
834'.6—dc20   91–38308
                                                            CIP

Published by The Pennsylvania State University Press,
Suite C, Barbara Building, University Park, PA 16802-1003

Printed in the United States of America

The typeface for this book is Sabon.

It is the policy of The Pennsylvania State University Press to use
acid-free paper for the first printing of all clothbound books.
Publications on uncoated stock satisfy the minimum requirements of
American National Standard for Information Sciences—Permanence of
Paper for Printed Library Materials, ANSI Z39.48–1984.

For Sylvia

Contents

Acknowledgments

Perhaps it is paradoxical, at the beginning of a book that concentrates on the subversion of systematic discourse and on intertextuality with its both traceable and untraceable citations, to acknowledge and thus define the sources and foundation of my work. But since the essay takes pleasure in paradox, I will allow myself the pleasure of discovering some of these traces.

This is a book about the essay, more specifically about Goethe's essays, and more specifically still about his essays on art. It also concerns community—textual community as well as the real community of which the text is part. And without my parents—a writer and a painter who create community in everything they do—I would never have happened upon my topic or written this book. To them, therefore, my greatest thanks.

After these and before all others I owe (more than) gratitude to Benjamin Bennett, a true critic and my friend and teacher, and to Josephine Trueschler, my first mentor and a fellow traveler in pursuit of the essay. The many readers of this text—Ernst Behler, Bernhard Greiner, Robert Leventhal, Peter Pütz, Richard Rorty, Thomas Sauer, Kenneth Weisinger, and especially Alice Kuzniar and Walter Sokel—were generous in their praise and enthusiasm and both discriminating and incisive in their criticism; I am grateful to all of them. Among the many friends and colleagues at Harvard, Virginia, and elsewhere who have provided support, challenge, and criticism in this endeavor, I would especially like to thank Stuart Barnett, Jones DeRitter, Neil Donahue, Leslie Gossage, Volker Kaiser, and Eva Knodt. Finally, I would like to express my appreciation to Philip Winsor

of Penn State Press for his consistent support of the project and
to Joseph Metz and Ann Reidy of Harvard University for their
help in the final preparation of the manuscript.

*   *   *

Some of the material presented here has appeared previously. A
brief summary of the argument on "The Collector and His Circle" in Part One originally appeared in my "Unlikely Affinities:
Warhol and Goethe," *MOSAIC: A Journal for the Interdisciplinary Study of Literature* 21, no. 1 (Winter 1988): 37–47. Another
summary, of my discussion of the Laocoön dialogue between
Lessing and Herder, appeared in "Dialogue and the Community
of Writing," *Studies on Voltaire and the Eighteenth Century* 264
(1989): 1178–82; this material is reproduced by permission of
the Voltaire Foundation. Finally, my argument in Part Two on
dialogue and truth in "The Collector and His Circle" and "On
Truth and Probability in Works of Art" appeared as "Goethe's
Transgressions," in *Fictions of Culture: Essays in Honor of Walter H. Sokel,* ed. Steven Taubeneck (New York: Peter Lang, 1992.
All rights reserved), 95–116, and is reprinted by permission of
the publisher.

Quotations from Goethe and from essays of Winckelmann,
Lessing, Herder, Hirt, and Kleist are presented both in translation
and in the original; all other quotations are presented in English
only. A number of Goethe's works have appeared recently in
English translation: *Goethe's Collected Works,* ed. Victor Lange
et al., 12 vols. ([Cambridge], New York: Suhrkamp/Insel, Suhrkamp, 1983–89), and *Goethe on Art,* ed. and trans. John Gage
(Berkeley and Los Angeles: University of California Press, 1980).
I use the Suhrkamp edition translations for texts included there
(with the exception of *Faust* and the poems), and my own translations for texts not included. Translations of quotations from
works other than Goethe's are my own except where noted. Page
references to published translations either immediately follow
the translation or precede references to the original. An asterisk
following the page number of a published translation indicates
emendation.

Cambridge, Massachusetts
August 1991

PREFACE

The Difficulty of the first Address, on any new Occasion, is felt by every Man in his Transactions with the World, and confessed by the settled and regular Forms of Salutation, which Necessity has introduced into all Languages. Judgment was wearied with the inextricable Perplexity of being forced upon Choice, where there was often no Motive to Preference; and it was found convenient that some easy Method of Introduction should be established, which, if it wanted the Allurement of Novelty, might enjoy in its place the Security of Prescription.

—Samuel Johnson, *The Rambler,* no. 1

Where can I begin to talk about Goethe's essays or about Goethe as an essayist? This question does not simply reveal the trepidation of an academic staring at the pristine blankness of the page in front of him, at the page that is to be the initiation of an extended study. The significance of beginnings in narrative art has been the topic of numerous critical endeavors. The very notion of a beginning, however, carries with it questions that deal specifically with essential characteristics of the essay *as a genre*.

Where does an essay begin? Not at the beginning, says Theodor Adorno. In his seminal study of the genre Adorno shows, in the manner of his expression as well as in his argumentation, the difficulty of ascertaining the point of departure in essayistic writing. To the question of the essay's beginning, as to the related question of its ending, one can only answer, definitively, in the negative: "The essay mirrors what is loved and hated instead of presenting the intellect, on the model of a boundless work ethic, as *creatio ex nihilo*. . . . It does not begin with Adam and Eve but with what it wants to discuss; it says what is at issue and stops where it feels itself at a loss to go further—not where nothing is left to say."[1] This statement is easily tested by looking at a few essays, and might be best tested by looking at the first of what are considered to be the first essays: Montaigne's "By diverse means we arrive at the same end."[2] Without preliminaries or a preceding history of the idea expressed in the title, Montaigne dives directly into the topic of his piece—at what must seem for the reader a random point—with claims expressing his opinion: "The commonest way of softening the hearts of those we have offended, when, vengeance in hand, they hold us at their mercy, is by submission to move them to commiseration and pity. However, audacity and steadfastness—entirely contrary means—have sometimes served to produce the same effect" (3). This is hardly an *ab ovo* development of an argument, not even a statement about the topic in general, but rather an example, a situation that enables the writer to reflect about a question that concerns him. Montaigne does not go on to produce a systematic study of the topic; he chooses, instead, to present a series of examples, in no necessary logical order, that

do not lead to a grand conclusion, but to yet another example
with which the essay then breaks off. The essay "says what is at
issue and stops where it feels itself at a loss to go further—not
where nothing is left to say."

In order to approach the context of the present study—the
essay in late eighteenth-century Germany—we can look at essays from Lessing and Herder. *Laocoön* is a reaction to Winckelmann's study of the imitation of Greek art, but Lessing does not
begin with Winckelmann's first points or with a history of the
problem; rather, he picks up points from his predecessor's work
as they suit his purpose. Lessing's beginning drops the reader
into the middle of a debate, and it is for the reader to find
her*his way, to reconstruct what might have come before. And
the same thing happens in Herder's reaction to *Laocoön*—his
first "Critical Grove" ["Kritisches Wäldchen"]; the essay begins
in the middle of a public/published critical dialogue, the "origin" of which goes back to Lessing, Winckelmann, and beyond.
The significance of these essays for my study of Goethe as an
essayist will become apparent later, but it will suffice for now to
see that they, too, are in accord with Adorno's description of
essayistic beginnings.

What about Goethe in this context? One need only (but not
solely) look at "The Collector and His Circle" ["Der Sammler
und die Seinigen"], which will be the topic of Part One, to see
that in his essays as well there is no pretense to beginning at the
beginning.[3] There, too, we are dropped into the middle of a
correspondence, not knowing who the writer is or who his correspondents are and having only a vague idea of what the correspondence is about. In the first letter of the essay the collector
begins to give a history of his collection, which he describes as
having started with his grandfather. But this seemingly absolute
starting point is then undermined by the mention of the *collections* of artists and art dealers from which the grandfather's
collection drew and grew. In other words, the point of inception
of the present collection is lost in the collection's dependence on
another collection; the starting point of that earlier collection,
we might expect, would then be just as difficult to determine.
Furthermore, in that Goethe's essay starts with a description of

an extensive collection, and in that the notion of a collection itself implies that something has already taken place (e.g., the act of collecting), that starting point loses its quality as an origin or beginning.

There seems nevertheless to be a way to begin an essay at the beginning, and that is to *talk about* beginning an essay. Dr. Johnson does this in the first of his *Rambler* pieces, the opening lines of which are quoted at the beginning of this preface.[4] Goethe does the same in "Diderot's Essay on Painting" ["Diderots Versuch über die Malerei"] when he reflects on the difficulty of starting to write, even when one has a fairly good idea of what one wants to say, and on the help afforded by conversation. The effect of such reflections, however, is paradoxically to undermine their own status as a beginning of the "topic" at the beginning. For what happens in the first *Rambler* essay is that the discussion of beginning to write an essay or essays becomes itself the topic of the essay, which does not then proceed to other, more "concrete" observations. The contemporary reader simply had to wait until the following Saturday for another, perhaps less self-reflective text. As it turns out, then, Johnson's first lines do not constitute a beginning at the beginning, but rather confront the reader with reflections that occur somewhere in the midst of considering the idea—that is, the topic—of beginning. Moreover, by beginning with reflections on beginning, Johnson makes a gesture of absolute originality that necessarily contradicts itself, inasmuch as writing has no single "origin." In the Diderot essay Goethe's remarks about the initiation of the act of writing have more practical ramifications: not only do those remarks themselves come to constitute an essay on the value of dialogue for the formulation of arguments, but they also lead to the abandonment of the study originally planned and thus to the elimination of their own status as an introduction.

Johnson speaks of prescription; in a literal sense, he pre-scribes his planned (and as yet largely undetermined) series of essays with this first essay that comes to be comprised almost entirely of reflection on the notion of introduction. In the course of this pre-scribing, ideas come to light that deal with the nature of his planned enterprise and serve to introduce it. Similarly, he pre-scribes my text and thus serves to introduce it; my pre-facing in turn should serve to introduce the essays that follow by bringing up, albeit in a less-than-systematic fashion, points about the essay as genre that will prove useful later on.

*   *   *

The unanswerable question of where Goethe's essays begin raises the question of where—with which essay—to begin a study of Goethe's essays. Uncertainty about which one came first renders questionable any attempt to start with the beginning of his career as an essayist; how can one perform the highly significant gesture of starting at the beginning if one cannot be absolutely sure where it is? And if one could decide on or prove a point of inception, the implications of starting there would be equally problematic. Goethe wrote hundreds of essays—the essays on art and literature alone comprise over two thousand pages in the Artemis edition of his works. An attempt to give a complete analysis or interpretation of this oeuvre would border on intellectual megalomania. And it is this pretense of completeness, inherent in the genre of the treatise and in systematic thought in general, that "beginning at the beginning" implies and that is, therefore, foreign to the essay. Adorno, in his discussion of beginnings, goes on to develop what had been a point about the *form* of the essay into a statement about its *intellectual character:* "Its concepts are neither deduced from any first principle nor do they come full circle and arrive at a final principle" (152; 10). It remains to be seen whether this characteristic has significance only for the essay genre in isolation from other forms of writing or rather reveals the essay to be implied criticism of all writing that pretends to achieve completion. At any rate, a desire for completeness in the present study would not only mean taking on the impossible, but would also belie the kind of writing I am trying to understand.

Perhaps more significant than the question of where to begin this study of Goethe as an essayist, however, is the question of why to undertake it at all. A stroll through the stacks of any university library confirms what we already know: Goethe's work has engendered an extraordinary amount of critical discourse. And there is no dearth of critical inquiry concerning his views on art, literature, and science. In other words, not only his poems, plays, and novels, but also his essays have occupied the center of attention in any number of studies. Thirty years ago Matthijs Jolles wrote a monumental work on *Goethe's View of Art* [*Goethes Kunstanschauung*], deriving that view almost entirely from a close analysis of "The Collector and His Circle." Especially in the last three decades there has been a steady stream of discussions of nearly everything Goethe ever wrote about—Hans Joachim Schrimpf's *Goethe's Concept of World Literature* [*Goethes Begriff der Weltliteratur*], Christoph Gögelein's *On Goethe's Concept of Science* [*Zu Goethes Begriff von Wissenschaft*], Heinz Hamm's *Goethe the Theorist* [*Der Theoretiker Goethe*], Victor Lange's excellent study of "Art and Literature: Two Modes of Goethe's Aesthetic Theory," and, most recently, a collection of essays on *Goethe as a Critic of Literature*.[5] And this to name just a few. From the titles of these studies alone one can already see a common thread in the analysis of Goethe's expository writing: the concern is always with a concept or theory that can somehow be hypostatized or divined from *what* Goethe says in different texts. With the possible exception of Jolles, critics tend to do what they would avoid at all costs when examining Goethe's literary works, namely to disregard the *way* in which he says what he says. Simply put, Goethe's essays are generally employed for the information that can be extracted or derived from them and are all too seldom treated as texts in their own right.

If we look for help to studies of the essay as a genre, we will be similarly disappointed. A number of good discussions of the genre appeared in the 1960s—perhaps instigated by Adorno's interest in the topic—and in the 1970s the *Jahrbuch für internationale Germanistik* published a long series of articles on essayism and journalism.[6] The last few years have witnessed yet another phase in this renaissance of scholarly interest in the essay, with the publication of three major studies—by Graham Good, John McCarthy, and John Snyder.[7] It is, however, extraordinarily rare to find more than *pro forma* or cursory mention of

Goethe in these various descriptions, histories, and definitions. And this despite the fact that Goethe wrote probably more essays than any of the "recognized" essayists, despite the fact that his essayism is apparent not only in the pieces collected under the heading of "writings on art and literature," but also throughout his scientific writing, his novels—especially *Wilhelm Meister's Journeyman Years* [*Wilhelm Meisters Wanderjahre*]—and his autobiography, and despite the significance of his reference to Montaigne as a "friend" in the autobiography, *Poetry and Truth* [*Dichtung und Wahrheit*] (IV, 356; X, 526). Max Bense, in an enumeration of "classic" German essayists, leaves Goethe out:

> In Germany we see Lessing, Möser, and Herder initiating this form of experimental literature and at the same time mastering it. And above all Herder, in the inexhaustible "Letters for the Promotion of Humanity," which certainly constitute the most significant classical collection of essays. Everyone knows what a plenitude of criticism they contain. Friedrich Schlegel, himself a master of criticism and the essay, calls Herder a pure critic and sees in him a protester in the broadest sense; and Adam Müller, in his lecture on the emergence of German criticism, calls Lessing one of the most definitive originary spirits of the German essay. ("On the Essay and Its Prose," 62)

In his introduction to *Deutsche Essays*—an extensive collection of essays as well as theoretical examinations of the genre (Grimm, Lukács, Bense, Adorno)—Ludwig Rohner goes so far as to call attention to Goethe's admiration of Montaigne, but then fails to discuss Goethe himself as an essayist. Lessing, Herder, Wieland, and Schlegel receive due attention; why not Goethe?

There is an apparent exception to the "rule" I have just been establishing. In the series in *Jahrbuch für internationale Germanistik* Joachim Wohlleben published five articles on "Goethe as a Journalist and Essayist" ["Goethe als Journalist und Essayist"] that were subsequently reprinted as a book.[8] Given the context in which these articles appeared and given the title of the study, one would expect a genre-specific treatment of Goethe's use of the essay. However, despite gestures indicating a concentration on the form of Goethe's essayistic writing, what Wohlleben actually produces is another study that for the most part focuses on the content, on the informational value of the texts it examines. We read that "the truly Goethean essay" is characterized by "its fundamentally fragmentary or, better said, mosaical presentation of a general world view, which, since it is not a 'system,' achieves partial expression in representatively valid 'eminent cases' or 'pregnant points' " (138). The words "fragmentary," "mosaical," and "partial expression" arouse expectations of a discussion of the rhetoric of Goethe's texts, but this direction is abandoned, and it turns out that the crucial words in that sentence are the ones that reveal the greatest content-orientation, namely "world view": "The extra-literary work is not a continuum, but rather a presentation of the world in the form of clearly perceivable fragments. . . . *Since all of these are only comprehensible within the context of Goethe's world view* . . . it is clear that we are dealing with a historical anomaly in the formation of the essay, which could not, therefore, constitute a model. Thus placing the Goethean essay in a generic history is . . . a delicate problem that I am not going to attempt to solve here" (138–39; my emphasis). This is less a study of Goethe's use of the genre than an exposition of how Goethe presents his world view, less an examination of the quality of those texts as texts, as essays, than a means of glorifying their author by denying the contextualization necessary in any study of genre and by consequently claiming that Goethe is great because he is unique. What Wohlleben ultimately tells us, even though he avoids the direct statement, is that Goethe did not write *essays* at all—that he had his very own, personal genre that he alone used. It is, therefore, fair to say that we still lack a study of Goethe's essays as essays.[9] My primary concern in these pages will not be to analyze or hypostatize Goethe's world view, or his theory of art or poetry, but rather to examine the genre he uses and the way he uses it, that is, to trace the rhetoric of the essay texts.[10]

I would like to return to the question: Why not Goethe? At the end of Book 13 of *Poetry and Truth* Goethe describes Möser's essays as follows:

We find that the objects of his serious and jocular observations are the changes in manners and customs, clothing, diet, domestic life, and education. One would have to rubricate everything that happens in the civil and moral world if one wanted to make an exhaustive list of the subjects he treats. And his treatment is an admirable one. A consummate public official is speaking to the people in a weekly gazette, in order to explain to each individual, from the proper perspective, the things undertaken or executed by a reasonable, benevolent government. But this is by no means done in a didactic way; on the contrary, the forms are so varied they could be called poetic, and at any rate are to be classified as rhetorical, in the best sense of the word. He is always elevated above his subject and manages to give a cheerful view of the gravest matters. Half hidden behind one mask or another, or speaking in his own person, he is always complete and detailed, but at the same time lighthearted, somewhat ironical, thoroughly capable, upright, well meaning, and sometimes even blunt and vehement. All this is done so judiciously that one has to admire the author's wit, understanding, facility, skill, taste, and character, all at the same time. (IV, 438–39*)

[Als Gegenstände seiner ernsten und scherzhaften Betrachtungen finden wir die Veränderung der Sitten und Gewohnheiten, der Kleidungen, der Diät, des häuslichen Lebens, der Erziehung. Man müßte eben alles, was in der bürgerlichen und sittlichen Welt vorgeht, rubrizieren, wenn man die Gegenstände erschöpfen wollte, die er behandelt. Und diese Behandlung ist bewunderns-

würdig. Ein vollkommener Geschäftsmann spricht zum
Volke in Wochenblättern, um dasjenige, was eine ein-
sichtige wohlwollende Regierung sich vornimmt oder
ausführt, einem jeden von der rechten Seite faßlich zu
machen; keineswegs aber lehrhaft, sondern in den man-
nigfaltigsten Formen, die man poetisch nennen könnte,
und die gewiß in dem besten Sinn für rhetorisch gelten
müssen. Immer ist er über seinen Gegenstand erhaben,
und weiß uns eine heitere Ansicht des Ernstesten zu
geben; bald hinter dieser bald hinter jener Maske halb
versteckt, bald in eigener Person sprechend, immer voll-
ständig und erschöpfend, dabei immer froh, mehr oder
weniger ironisch, durchaus tüchtig, rechtschaffen, wohl-
meinend, ja manchmal derb und heftig, und dieses alles
so abgemessen, daß man zugleich den Geist, den Verstand, die Leichtigkeit, Gewandtheit, den Geschmack
und Charakter des Schriftstellers bewundern muß. (X,
652–53)]

This passage has significance for a possible "definition" of the
essay and for my view of Goethe as an essayist, but for now it is
enough to see that Goethe displays great concern for and attention to the rhetorical and stylistic aspects of essayistic writing.
Given this demonstrable concern, along with the volume of his
production in the genre, it is disturbing that his own essayistic
writing has been largely ignored.

At the risk of inviting criticism for speculation (which, of
course, cannot be avoided on a question like this), I would like
to suggest a possible reason for the avoidance of Goethe the
essayist. In reading the essays, one is struck by their surprisingly
prattling and rambling quality. Consider the first paragraph of
"The Collector and His Circle":

Many thanks for your letter and the enclosed manuscripts which arrived so soon after you left. The two days
you spent with us were most enjoyable, yet much too
short, and I felt keenly the void caused by your departure. But your letter and the manuscripts lifted my spirits,

and I felt almost as happy as when you were here. The ideas expressed in your papers reminded me of our conversations, and I was as delighted then as I had been before to see that we agree in so many respects in our views on art. (III, 121–22*)

[Wenn Ihr Abschied, nach den zwei vergnügten nur zu schnell verfloßnen Tagen, mich eine große Lücke und Leere fühlen ließ, so hat Ihr Brief, den ich so bald erhielt, so haben die beigefügten Manuskripte mich wieder in eine behagliche Stimmung versetzt, derjenigen ähnlich, die ich in Ihrer Gegenwart empfand. Ich habe mich unsers Gesprächs wieder erinnert, ich habe die ähnlichen Gesinnungen in Ihren Papieren wieder angetroffen und mich jetzt wie damals gefreut, daß wir in so vielen Fällen als Kunstbeurteiler zusammentreffen. (XIII, 259)]

The first letter continues to ramble in this way, simply conversing and offering little in the way of theoretical statement or historical analysis, and it is not until well into the second letter that the collector begins to address his topic with any thoroughness. At the end of the first letter Goethe even has his "protagonist" call attention to the small talk that has displaced the direct treatment of a topic expected by his correspondents and by us as readers of the essay: "And now I am approaching the end of my letter without having carried out my intention. I prattled instead of telling my story" (III, 123*) ["Ich schließe diesen Brief, ohne meinen Vorsatz erfüllt zu haben. Ich schwätzte anstatt zu erzählen" (XIII, 262)]. Such levels of "discourse" are perhaps not overly surprising in a text comprised of letters, but the majority of Goethe's essays reveal a similar quality, even if they do not directly comment on it like "The Collector." In a French or English essayistic context this would not stand out as much as it does in the German context; rambling and a highly colloquial conversational tone are what we expect when we read Montaigne and Johnson, or at least that is the rhetorical *gesture* of their texts.[11] In Germany, where the blossoming of systematic philosophy and extensive aesthetic-theoretical endeavors did not occur until the eighteenth century, the situation is different. Goethe wrote the bulk of his essays during the age of Kant's greatest influence and Schiller's extensive theoretical tracts, during an intellectual age shaped by Christian Wolff and his followers. That context arouses expectations that are bound to be disappointed by the sense of a lack of theoretical substance with which Goethe's essays seem to leave us. Even where we might justifiably anticipate a thorough theoretical treatment of a topic, for example in "Simple Imitation of Nature, Manner, Style" ["Einfache Nachahmung der Natur, Manier, Stil"] or "On Truth and Probability in Works of Art" ["Über Wahrheit und Wahrscheinlichkeit der Kunstwerke"], we are disappointed.[12] Not only do the titles of these essays lead us to assume a certain systematic approach, but Goethe goes so far as to carry out in them what *appears* to be a systematic schematization of concepts; he abandons the discussion, however, before reaching any conclusions or completing those schemes. Considered in "friendlier," more essayistic surroundings, Goethe's essays still stand out in their highly conversational, less-than-theoretical quality; for example, Lessing's *Laocoön* and Herder's *Critical Forests* [*Kritische Wälder*], while they also ramble in parts (the title of Herder's work even thematizes this essayistic wandering), at least give more the appearance of serious and thorough theorizing, and they have certainly been treated as theoretical endeavors in most critical studies.[13] Thus one is puzzled when confronted with a Goethean essay. We can extract individual statements and ideas in order to support a general argument about the author's thoughts on a particular topic, but the essays, as texts, appear to render themselves inaccessible to the critical, organizing consciousness. However, especially in the context of Goethe, who always demonstrated great concern with genre, with the interplay of form and content (one need only compare *Götz von Berlichingen* with *Iphigenia in Tauris* or the early hymns with the later philosophical poetry), precisely this easy conversational tone of the essays, this undermining of the reader's expectations, must arouse interest, must have a reason.

My reason for writing about Goethe as an essayist is thus twofold: first, there is a large portion of his oeuvre—his entire treatment of the "fourth genre"—that has yet to receive sufficient attention; and, second, the rhetoric of his essays disconcerts the reader and therefore demands closer examination of *how* he writes and *why* he writes as he does.

*   *   *

Georg Lukács recognized the importance of examining how the essay does what it does, and also the necessary connection of this aspect to that of the genre's relationship to systematic inquiry, when he wrote: "The essay is a court, but it is not the judgment that is essential to it and that determines its value (as in the system), but rather the process of judging" (53). In other words, not *what* is said, but *how* it is said must principally concern both the essayist and us. Adorno also refers to this determining characteristic when he emphasizes the essay's concentration on "the *how* of expression" (160; 20).

Before I go into a more general discussion of characteristics of essayistic writing, let me reflect briefly on how I will proceed to write about Goethe's essays. As a point of contrast take Wohlleben's introduction to his section on "Goethe the Essayist": "It will be advisable not to proceed from a preconceived notion of the essay in the case of Goethe. Research into this literary genre has not yet been completed and is full of contradictions. . . . There can be no discussion of the history of the genre as long as it has not been determined exactly what the genre is" (40). Besides being especially foreign to the open-ended nature of this genre that does not begin at the beginning or end at the end, the notion of being able to discuss a genre, or any literary phenomenon for that matter, only when research on the topic has been "completed" and the context fully defined, would stifle critical inquiry from the outset. Requiring such precedence is equivalent to saying that, because the critical world has not yet *fully* determined what a drama or a novel or a novella *is*, no one should try to discuss Shakespeare's dramas, Flaubert's novels, or Hoffmann's novellas in their generic context. No genre is ever fully defined, the research on a genre is never completed. The only way to move closer to an understanding of a genre is to accept the paradox—that is, to examine its use by various writers as well as their writing in what will always be the incomplete and at most provisionally defined generic context. The other possibility, of course, is to treat only those texts as essays that are referred to as such by their authors. This would, however, restrict the field of inquiry dramatically and unnecessarily— eliminating Goethe from consideration, for example, which would please Wohlleben as little as it would me, since even with his determination not to place Goethe in the context of the essay genre he nevertheless refers to him as an essayist. Such limitations would also produce misleading results, as in the case of Bacon, whose "essayes" John Snyder has gone a long way toward portraying as questionable examples of the genre.[14]

Without contextualizing Goethe's essayism, that is, examining the essays against the background of a (tentative) concept of the genre, and without addressing the textuality of the essays in that context—their rhetoric, their style, their way of saying what they say—one can neither discuss Goethe's use of a genre nor contribute to a broader understanding of the genre itself. To call a piece of writing an essay is to have some understanding of what that designation means. In the present instance, readings of Goethe, Montaigne, Johnson, Lessing, Herder, and others, as well as of the more prominent theories of the genre, have resulted in a heuristic description or provisional outline of essayistic characteristics that will provide a useful context for discussing Goethe's essayistic endeavors.

In the 184th number of *The Rambler* Dr. Johnson discusses the difficulty of choosing topics for essays: "Every Day calls afresh upon him [the Writer of Essays] for a new Topick, and he is again obliged to choose without any Principle to regulate his Choice" (1098). (Here Johnson has also presented, in passing, one possible definition of the essay—as that genre which imposes *no* restrictions on content.) In my case the field of choice is already limited by the general topic of my study, but Dr. Johnson's remark does pertain to my project, in that the question of *which* essays to examine naturally arises. Since I have devised no system for ranking the importance of Goethe's essays and since I cannot treat all of them, there is necessarily some implied principle behind my choice. The most I can say, however, is that I will discuss those essays that seem to me to demonstrate most pointedly the characteristics of essayistic writing to which I am turning my greatest attention at a given point.

There is no need to provide a complete history or outline here of what has been written about the essay. Gerhard Haas has already performed this service, and I refer readers desiring a broader survey to his studies.[15] Instead, a look at three of the best known pieces on the essay will provide an introduction to some of the genre's most important features (many of which have already come up, in one way or another, in this preface). Georg Lukács, Max Bense, and Theodor Adorno all approach the essay from different perspectives, but in their examinations a number of points recur with sufficient frequency to suggest a certain validity.

In his essay "On the Essence and Form of the Essay" ["Über Wesen und Form des Essays"] of 1910, Lukács begins his attempt to locate the kind of writing that constitutes the essay by differentiating between art and science: "In science it is the contents that affect us, in art it is forms; science offers us facts and their interconnections, while art offers us souls and destinies" (34). He then separates the essay from the realm of art: "Poetry takes its motifs from life (and from art); for the essay art (and life) serve as a model" (44). By separating art and science so extremely, Lukács seems to place the essay on the side of science, since it belongs to the realm of "criticism" (40–41), but already in that differentiation of art and the essay we can see the separation breaking down, and he ends up by saying that the essay and art are intimately related inasmuch as they both assume the same attitude toward life (whatever that might mean). Furthermore, the place of the essay alongside scientific inquiry becomes doubtful as soon as Lukács begins comparing the two types of writing. The essay at first appears to bear a strong relationship to science in that both search for truth, but the point of divergence arises when one compares the respective *attitudes* to truth. While science makes claims to finally achieving truth, the essay must always be somewhere on the path toward truth, but never reaches it (hence also Lukács's emphasis on *process* in the essay—"not the judgment . . . but the process of judging" [53]). Out of this characteristic comes Lukács's main point, namely that because the essay can never achieve truth (without ceasing to be an essay), it is fundamentally unclosed, uncompleted, fragmentary, and is thus incommensurate with the closure of scientific, systematic discourse.

Four decades later Max Bense, in his study "On the Essay and Its Prose" ["Über den Essay und seine Prosa"], stated explicitly the conclusion one might draw from Lukács, but which Lukács avoids saying directly—that the essay occupies an area between poetry and prose (Bense's term for scientific discourse), between "creation" and "persuasion" [*Tendenz*]: "There is a strange border area . . . that forms between poetry and prose, between the aesthetic stage of creation and the ethical stage of persuasion. It is always somewhat enigmatic, ambivalent with regard to both creation and persuasion, literarily definable as the essay" (58). In his further attempt to define the concept, Bense introduces the traditional German translation of "essay"—"Versuch"—which allows him to develop his notion of the essay's most important generic distinction, its quality as experiment. Because of its experimental nature the essay's objects of inquiry and its thoughts can never find themselves in the condition of permanence or constancy, but must always be "relative," and thus the genre cannot be equated with that of the treatise: "Thus the essay is not a treatise. He writes essayistically who writes experimentally, who not only turns his subject [*Gegenstand*] this way and that, but also, in the course of writing, in the course of forming and communicating his thoughts, discovers and invents this object, who questions it, feels it, tests it, thoroughly reflects on it, and shows whatever can possibly be seen given the both aesthetic and ethical manual and intellectual conditions of the author" (59–60). Treatises operate in terms of completion and the making *absolute* of objects and thoughts; the treatise is never satisfied with relativity. In Bense much more than in Lukács this relativity receives approval; whereas Lukács believes that someday the grand aesthetic scheme ["die große Ästhetik"] will emerge and subsume the essay genre, Bense attributes far greater autonomy to the essay as a kind of writing that stands on its own in opposition to systematic endeavors and does not simply constitute a stage that eventually will be overcome: "The essay is an active category of the human mind per se" (69). To restate the difference between these views in terms neither uses but both imply, Lukács sees the essay as *un*systematic in the sense of distance from or lack of the system, while Bense emphasizes the quality of opposition that grants the essay its own territory where it need not fear elimination. He thus portrays the genre as essentially *anti*-systematic.

Adorno then explicates the implications of Bense's argument. In its reaction to Lukács, "The Essay as Form" reveals itself as a further development of Bense's main points. Adorno first differentiates the essay from art by pointing out that its conceptual medium and its "claim to truth" (153; 11) remove it from the aesthetic realm. (What Adorno means by "truth" here is apparently that the notion of truth is always present in conceptual discourse, even if there is no sense of being able to achieve it finally; he later speaks of truth as a game played in the context of the "untruth" of the essay [168; 29].) He then begins his main argument by comparing essayistic and scientific writing, and at this point the genre's anti-systematic nature becomes explicit: "With regard to scientific procedure and its philosophical grounding as method, the essay, in accordance with its idea, draws the fullest consequences from the critique of the system" (157; 16).[16] From this fundamental characteristic Adorno then derives the essay's other constitutive elements—its emphasis on the process of expression, on formulation, its predominantly open-ended quality, and its status as experimental writing.

Digression
Since the terms "system," "systematic thought," and "systematic discourse" will come up repeatedly in my consideration of the essay genre, it is perhaps appropriate to note briefly what I mean when I say "system." This is not the place to go through a detailed descriptive history of the term, which would entail discussion of and quotation from Descartes, Wolff, Kant, Hegel, and innumerable

other philosophers who used and defined it; for such detail I would refer my reader to some of the readily available and useful studies in the field.[17] Instead, let me simply present a list of characteristics that I have in mind when speaking of systems: completion, unity, absoluteness, certitude, claim to truth, coherence, consistency. What these various qualities amount to is what can be designated as perhaps the most general characteristic of the system, namely its *closure*.[18] And like the system in which it inheres, closure is a quality of both form and content. Without closure, that is without the self-sufficiency, structural integrity, immutability, and self-asssuredness into which that list of characteristics translates, there can be no system. In *Social Systems* [*Soziale Systeme*], Niklas Luhmann reinforces this view when he writes of the essential "differentiation of inside and outside" in the system and that "the preservation of the *boundary* [is] the preservation of the system."[19]

Some German discussions of so-called open systems would seem to draw my characterization into question. However, such expansions on the notion of system would not necessarily pertain to the eighteenth-century conceptions that constitute the backdrop to my discussion of the essay's situation with regard to systems. And if we consider what is meant by "open" in those discussions, we discover that "open" systems do *not* breach the closure of the system, that they represent an expanded notion of closure, but a notion of closure nonetheless. "Open" systems, according to Manfred Zahn, are divided into two types—self-regulating and self-organizing. Self-regulating systems are seen to have the capacity to maintain "their stability in the face of disturbances from 'outside' through compensatory countermeasures," while self-organizing systems maintain their stability "even when subjected to conditions of disturbance that are increasing in both extent and intensity."[20] In other words, "open" here does not mean "open to change" *as a result* of contrary evidence and disruptions in the system's "environment," but rather an ability to maintain validity, certitude, consistency, etc., *despite* that environment. Thus "open" systems actually represent a more extreme and more defiant immutability. Thus open systems are closed after all.

In Lukács's, Bense's, and Adorno's attempts to describe the essay genre, the reader can already begin to see that the same concerns arise again and again—albeit in different guises and with varying emphasis and evaluation. Moreover, it is not only in twentieth-century theories that such descriptions occur. In the first number of *The Rambler* Johnson introduces his essayistic project by concluding his procrastinative beginning with a description of the genre that intimates (with a great deal more humor and playfulness!) several of the main points in the theories I have just summarized:

He that questions his Abilities to arrange the dissimilar Parts of an extensive Plan, or fears to be lost in a complicated System, may yet hope to adjust a few Pages without Perplexity; and if, when he turns over the Repositories of his Memory, he finds his Collection too small for a Volume, he may yet have enough to furnish out an Essay. He that is afraid of laying out too much Time upon an Experiment of which he fears the Event, persuades himself that a few Days will shew him what he is to expect from his Learning and his Genius. If he thinks his own Judgment not sufficiently enlightened, he may, by attending the Remarks which every Paper will produce, inform himself of his Mistakes, rectify his Opinions, and extend his Views. If he suspects that he may with too little Premeditation entangle himself in an unwieldy Subject, he may quit it without confessing his Ignorance, and pass to other Topicks less dangerous, or more tractable. And if he finds, with all his Industry, and all his Artifices, that he cannot deserve Regard, or cannot attain it, he may let the Design fall at once, and, without Injury to others, or himself, retire to Amusements of greater Pleasure, or to Studies of better Prospect. (6)

Johnson thus introduces the notions of the essay's distance from systematic discourse (and its concomitant playfulness and tendency not to take things all too seriously), its relationship to experiment, the absence of completion or closure, and the importance of the process of thought.

Dr. Johnson also suggests an aspect of essayistic writing largely ignored by Lukács, Bense, and Adorno—its dialogic quality.[21] Lukács only implies the dialogic aspect by presenting his essay in the form of a letter; Bense denies dialogism outright, calling the essay a reflecting monologue; and the closest Adorno comes to indicating the importance of dialogue for the essay is in his discussion of the genre's communicative intentions. In stating that the essayist can adjust his views and correct his mistakes by "attending the Remarks which every Paper will produce," Johnson emphasizes that the essay, because it is not a system, enters into or initiates a dialogue that can be productive not only for those who respond to the essay, but also for the essayist who responds, whether in writing or not, to that response. In the passage quoted above from Book 13 of *Poetry and Truth* Goethe, too, adduces a dialogic consciousness in the essay—on a different, intratextual, we might even say Bakhtinian level—when he describes Möser's essays as being the product of the interplay of different voices assumed by the writer within the text.

The notion of dialogue, especially the kind Johnson suggests, reminds us of another side of essayistic writing that requires consideration and that is conspicuously absent in Lukács and Adorno and only briefly introduced in Bense. What distinguishes a play from a novel is not only its different textual composition and structuring or the relative immediacy or mediation of presentation, but also that which makes it possible to think in terms of such mediation in the first place, namely the reader or audience. Montaigne, in his preliminary note "To the Reader," addresses his audience directly, in the second person, and thus gives a strong intimation of the significance of the reader of his essays (2). In any examination of genre the situation of the recipient in relation to the work must be considered, and so we must attempt to determine the place the reader assumes (or is implied or forced to assume) in essayistic writing.[22]

There is, however, yet another aspect of the genre that has received even less attention than the situation of the reader, namely the essay's predilection for self-reflection.[23] Self-reflection occurs on two levels, the first of which can be called authorial self-reflection, by which I mean the tendency of the essay to approach autobiography. Montaigne states this autobiographical bent directly: "Thus, reader, I am myself the matter of my book" (2). Although Goethe does not demonstrate autobiographical intentions or concerns so openly, he nonetheless implies them in a number of his essays. Conversely, what he presents as his autobiography reveals an essayistic consciousness—not only in the passage describing Möser, but also in the innumerable essay-like passages that practically constitute the work. The second type of essayistic self-reflexivity is what I would call textual self-reflection and is more difficult to detect and demonstrate; it is what Adorno refers to when he criticizes positivism for tending toward a "rigid separation of form and content" and thus failing to recognize that "it is scarcely possible to speak of the aesthetic unaesthetically, stripped of any similarity with its object, without succumbing to philistinism and *a priori* losing touch with the aesthetic object" (153*; 11). A relatively simple example of textual self-reflexivity would be the first number of *The Rambler,* where Johnson *talks about* beginning a work (here a series of essays) while at the same time *doing* just that. Textual self-reflection emerges when a text performs, as a whole or specifically in its structures, what it talks about, or in more complex instances, when qualities of the text's performance implicitly modify or nullify its apparent content and thus lead the reader to conclusions that contradict what the writer might be saying explicitly. Here, again, Johnson provides an example, in that he ultimately *fails* to begin at the beginning by implicitly thematizing the problematical nature of the "origins" of writing.

* * *

Anti-systematic, skeptical, process-oriented, experimental, mindful of the reader, dialogic, self-reflective, open-ended. These are the characteristics we can derive not only from theories of the

genre, but also from consideration, albeit still brief and preliminary, of the writings of Montaigne, Johnson, Lessing, Herder,
and, of course, Goethe.[24] With particular attention to the anti-
systematic and the dialogic, those characteristics will both guide
my readings of Goethe's essays and will, I hope, make more
sense as a result of these readings. Some apparently paradoxical
alignments, such as that of self-reflexivity and open-endedness,
will cease to appear quite so paradoxical, and some additional
characteristics and new alignments will emerge, such as intertextuality and its association with the dialogic. Examination of
Goethe's essays will provide insight into the textual community
that the essay as a genre implies, as well as into Goethe's notion
of community in general. This examination will be a close textual analysis of rhetorical and discursive strategies, for it is only
in this way that we can move beyond the current state of research on the genre—where there is fairly widespread agreement that the essay *is* anti-systematic, dialogic, self-reflective,
and open-ended—and *show* in detail what has yet to be shown
sufficiently, especially in the case of Goethe, namely: *how* the
essay is all these things; *how* the texts themselves, and not just
the statements they contain, are all those things; that is, *how* the
texts *work*. My hope is thus that the book will serve two pur-
poses, that in addition to contributing to our understanding of
Goethe and a significant component of his work, it might also
supply a broader foundation for our understanding of the genre
of the essay and perhaps even add a story or two.

Part One

THE SERIOUS GAME

System and Irony in "The Collector and His Circle"

And now, to our distress, he has come back a philosopher! . . . He is not interested in things we understand, and we do not understand the things he is interested in.

[Nun kommt er zu unserer größten Betrübnis als Philosoph zurück. . . . Was wir verstehen, interessiert ihn nicht, und was ihn interessiert, verstehen wir nicht.]
— "The Collector and His Circle" (III, 123–24; XIII, 262–63)

Suffice it to say I succeeded . . . by transforming the apparent seriousness into a clever and cheerful jest, in satisfying the mind and in leaving material to provide the imagination with new images and the mind with further reflection.

[Genug mir gelang, . . . durch Umwendung eines scheinbaren Ernstes in geistreichen und heitern Scherz das Gemüt zu befriedigen, der Einbildungskraft Stoff zu neuen Bildern und dem Verstande zu fernerm Nachdenken zu hinterlassen.]
— *Poetry and Truth* (IV, 330*; X, 488–89)

Context

There has been little or no agreement among critics on the genre of "The Collector and His Circle."[1] Almost all, however, treat the text as a kind of hybrid that inhabits a space somewhere between literature and philosophy, but is neither exclusively one nor the other. As we can gather from the more prominent theorists of the genre, this is itself one definition of the essay. Further encouragement for considering the piece an essay can be derived from an examination of the context in which it appeared—in the collection of essays that was Goethe's journal, the *Propyläen*.

Propylaea

Goethe wrote an introduction to his journal that appeared in the first number and was later published as an essay in its own right. This "Introduction to the *Propylaea*" has served as a basis for the deduction of the so-called Weimar Art Program [*Weimarer Kunstprogramm*]. Indeed, critics have employed this text as a "Classicist Art Manifesto," as a programmatic statement of the position of the "Weimar Friends of Art," Goethe, Schiller, and Meyer, and have filled in the details of that program with information from the various essays that appeared in the journal during its brief existence (1798–1800). If we restrict ourselves to the explicit conceptual-theoretical statements that can be isolated in the text, such an attitude can be justified. On this level, the main concerns are nature and art and their relationship to one another. In the context of discussing nature and the importance of the artist's adherence to it (inasmuch as s*he must learn from its processes and select her*his objects from its material), Goethe simultaneously claims the radical *divergence* of art from nature. In other words, although the artist draws inspiration and her*his objects from nature's "treasury of materials" and learns from nature about the laws (e.g., of tone and color, of the functioning of the body) that will inform her*his artistic activity, that activity itself is essentially different from the processes of nature. It is the artist's *treatment* of some raw material that constitutes art itself and along the way that raw material, nature, is subsumed. The *organic* procedure of nature stands in opposition to, or on a different plane from, the *organizing* procedure of the artist. In the most direct statement of his claim Goethe says that "nature is separated from art by an enormous chasm, which even genius cannot bridge without resorting to external means" (III, 81) ["die Natur ist von der Kunst durch eine ungeheure Kluft getrennt, welche das Genie selbst, ohne äußere Hülfsmittel, zu überschreiten nicht vermag" (XIII, 141)]. It is this statement about the autonomy of the work of art that has consumed almost entirely the attention and interpretive energies of the critical world.

I do not wish to deny the significance of Goethe's remarks in the "Introduction" about the relationship between art and nature or that they might constitute a central aspect of their author's understanding of the art form he always desired to master, but never could. Nor do I deny that those remarks are central to what has been hypostatized as the "Weimar Art Program." (Whether they are central in the way they are assumed to be is another question; the discussion of the *Propyläen* essay "On Truth and Probability in Works of Art" in Part Two will show, for example, that Goethe himself undermines what critics have taken to be the centerpiece of his "classical aesthetics"—the autonomy of the work of art.) Exclusive concentration on the information that can be derived from Goethe's text, however, leads to a failure to consider its quality *as text*. By treating the "Introduction" as a manifesto or a summary of Goethe's aesthetic program, critics implicitly assume that the piece has the quality of a theoretical system, of a treatise that presents the *results* of a thought process, and thus fail to give credence to its status *as an introduction*. Goethe is very careful throughout this introduction to emphasize that as yet there is no certainty about what will come of his planned journalistic endeavor, that it is just that—a plan. At the beginning he speaks of the editors' "intention" and in discussing the implications of the title *Propyläen* he uses both the subjunctive and terms of equivocation to suggest what his readers *might* expect to find in the pages that follow: "What we wish to convey by this title is at most something that might have taken place there: discussions and conversations which perhaps would not have been unworthy of those hallowed halls" (III, 79) ["Unter dem Namen des Ortes verstehe man das, was daselbst allenfalls hätte geschehen können, man erwarte Gespräche, Unterhaltungen, die vielleicht nicht unwürdig jenes Platzes gewesen wären" (XIII, 137)]. He does not say what the contributions *will* contain, but what they *should* contain: "The present work . . . [is to] contain remarks and observations on nature and art by a like-minded group of friends" (III, 79*) ["Gegenwärtiges Werk . . . (soll) Bemerkungen und Betrachtungen harmonisch verbundner Freunde über Natur und Kunst enthalten" (XIII, 137)]. And discussing the plan further he uses such expressions of implied uncertainty as "propose" [*gedenken*], "hopefully," and "perhaps." Finally, he states directly that the results of the journal are undeterminable: "May our undertaking be guided by a cheerful mood; where our efforts will take us, only time can tell" (III, 80*) ["Eine heitere Stimmung möge unsere Unternehmungen begleiten, und wohin wir gelangen, mag die Zeit lehren" (XIII, 140)]. Thus we can hardly justify treating this introductory piece as a summary of the essays it introduces, as the result of extended theorizing. Not the least of the reasons for this is that it introduces essays that had not yet been written.

*　　*　　*

The language of uncertainty and equivocation in the "Introduction," which demonstrates its introductory vis-à-vis an implic-

itly assumed summarizing quality, also reveals the essayistic attitude or consciousness of its author. Treatises employ deductive
arguments in order to prove a point and establish a systematic
context of conceptual understanding. Ideally, if not actually,
they are sure of themselves at every step and know from the
beginning what direction they will take, since their results are
more important than the individual stages of their argumentation (that is, their essentially teleological character subsumes
any autonomous significance of their various means). This is
Adorno's recognition when, in arguing the anti-systematic nature of the essay, he emphasizes the genre's concentration on
"the *how* of expression" as opposed to the treatise's overriding
concern for *what* is achieved.

In the "Introduction to the *Propylaea*" Goethe shows his own
overriding concern for the *process* of inquiry as opposed to a
simple preoccupation with concluding or completing it: "Thus it
is our intention to address the means [of the artistic rendering of
the human form]. And although we do not anticipate being able
to complete the necessary work ourselves, we still plan to present
a general survey and also to introduce the discussion of specific
topics" (III, 82*) ["Deshalb ist unsere Absicht, hier ins Mittel zu
treten, und, wenn wir gleich nicht voraussehen, die nötige Arbeit
selbst vollenden zu können, dennoch, teils im ganzen eine Übersicht zu geben, teils im einzelnen die Ausführung einzuleiten"
(XIII, 142)]. When discussing the advantages of conversation for
intellectual inquiry, he states directly his concern for the *means*
by which one achieves the results that then, we are given to
understand unfortunately, receive too exclusive attention: "How
well conversation serves in communicating ideas! Yet, conversation is transitory, and while the outcome of such an exchange is
permanent, the means by which we arrive at it are soon forgotten" (III, 80) ["Wer hat nicht erfahren, welche Vorteile in solchen
Fällen das Gespräch gewährt! allein es ist vorübergehend, und
indem die Resultate einer wechselseitigen Ausbildung unaus-
löschlich bleiben, geht die Erinnerung der Mittel verloren, durch
welche man dazu gelangt ist" (XIII, 138–39)]. Because of the
tendency to forget those means, Goethe favors written correspon-

dence, which is more suited to preserving the "stages" of inquiry and enables us, after having reached some conclusion, to look back at those stages and once again become involved in the process of thought. Here Goethe even goes so far as to say that this look back engenders "an indefinite continuation" (III, 80) ["ein künftiges, unabläßiges Fortschreiten" (XIII, 139)], and he thus implies that *the process of thought itself actually undermines the significance of its apparent results.* Concentration on the stages of our analysis forces us to see *all* results as only provisional, as always subject to change the moment we become involved in the process again.

In my introduction I presented processuality, dialogue, and open-endedness as three of the foremost characteristics of essayistic writing. In introducing a series of essays yet to be written (the writings that will comprise the *Propyläen* are referred to as "Aufsätze," a common translation of "essay"), Goethe also concentrates on the significance of dialogue (in the form of conversations and correspondences) and of the process of thought and writing, and by indicating the consequent sublation of the results of the process he implies that the essays in his journal will be open-ended. Also implied in these characteristics is an adversarial attitude toward systematic thought, since such thought, in that it operates under the mandate of completion and closure, insists above all else on the results of inquiry. Goethe further reveals his anti-systematic intent when he envisions his journal as a series of "observations" and "remarks" that will not and cannot be entirely dependable: "Yet we should attribute importance to these observations only to the extent that we can trust the nature and training of our mind as a basis for them" (III, 79*) ["Betrachtungen . . . auf die wir kein größer Gewicht legen dürfen, als insofern wir uns auf die Natur und Ausbildung unseres Geistes einigermaßen verlassen möchten" (XIII, 138)]. And his claim that "everything is subject to constant change" (III, 84) ["alles ist einem ewigen Wechsel unterworfen" (XIII, 146)] undermines the very notion, the very possibility of final truths; this statement also recalls Adorno's description of the essay's opposition to scientific, systematic discourse—"more than the procedure of defining, the essay urges the reciprocal interaction [*Wechselwirkung*] of its concepts in the process of intellectual experience" (160*; 20–21).

This sense of the absence of the system's certainty and its attendant closure or finality is then reflected again in statements that reveal further aspects of the essayistic consciousness. In the discussion of colors we find the following remark: "Perhaps the supposition will be proven that all color effects in nature—like magnetic, electric or other effects—are based on reciprocity, on polarity" (III, 83) ["Vielleicht bestätigt sich die Vermutung, daß die farbigen Naturwirkungen, so gut als die magnetischen, elektrischen und andere, auf einem Wechselverhältnis, einer Polarität . . . beruhen" (XIII, 144)]. In addition to the apparent importance of this thought, on its explicit level, for the discussion of the way in which the artist learns to use colors, there are at least two levels of implicit meaning. First, it shows Goethe's well-known preoccupation with polarities, and, second, it reveals the essentially *experimental* character of his planned enterprise—he starts with suppositions, but it is the job of the various essays to test them, and there is no assurance that he will find what he thinks he might find. Near the end of the introduction, he then expresses the wish that his journal might stimulate rather than satisfy the desire of its readers (III, 87) ["das Verlangen der Leser mehr zu reizen als zu befriedigen" (XIII, 152)]. This wish implies not only an aversion to a system's tendency to complete its inquiry, to conclude it, and thus to present results that then satisfy a reader's desire for certainty, for concrete knowledge or understanding, but also the essayistic gesture of involving the reader in the process of thought, of forcing her*him to carry on incomplete arguments and not allowing her*him to fall into the passivity that such satisfaction engenders.

Process-oriented, open-minded, dialogic, anti-systematic, skeptical, experimental, involving the reader—this is how Goethe envisions the texts that will constitute the *Propyläen*. In considering the essayistic predilection for textual self-reflection, however, it becomes apparent that in the "Introduction to the *Propylaea*" we find not only an introduction to a series of essays, but also an essay in its own right.

At the beginning of the introduction Goethe discusses how the artist appropriates her*his experiences and observations and later communicates them (in her*his art):

Anyone with an artistic calling will show a lively interest in everything around him. Objects and their component parts will attract his attention, and by applying what he learns from his new interest he will gradually become more and more discerning. In the beginning he will work almost exclusively for himself, but later gladly share what he does with others. (III, 79)

[Derjenige, der zum Künstler berufen ist, wird auf alles um sich her lebhaft acht geben, die Gegenstände und ihre Teile werden seine Aufmerksamkeit an sich ziehen, und indem er praktischen Gebrauch von solchen Erfahrungen macht, wird er sich nach und nach üben, immer schärfer zu bemerken, er wird in seiner frühern Zeit alles soviel möglich zu eignem Gebrauch verwenden, später wird er sich auch andern gerne mitteilen. (XIII, 137–38)]

Immediately following this is a statement of how Goethe and his friends will approach their current critical endeavor: "We, too, want to share with our readers certain things we consider instructive and agreeable, ideas and observations we have collected under various circumstances over the past several years" (III, 79) ["So gedenken auch wir manches, was wir für nützlich und angenehm halten, was, unter mancherlei Umständen, von uns seit mehrern Jahren aufgezeichnet worden, unsern Lesern vorzulegen und zu erzählen" (XIII, 138)]. In other words, the methods to be discussed, inasmuch as they are presently known, coincide with the method of their presentation. The structure of the author's own critical development that will reveal itself in his promised critical writing parallels the proposed content of that writing.

This subtle introduction of the notion of textual self-reflection into critical writing then encourages the reader to consider the relationship between the content of the "Introduction" it-

self and its form. I have attempted to show that the significance of the "Introduction" lies not so much in the various
remarks about questions of art and nature, but rather in the
introduction to aspects of the way the author approaches such
questions and what the discursive character of that approach
might be. Upon closer examination, we can see that the "Introduction" itself performs much of what it talks about. It states
the intention of presenting a series of "observations" and "remarks" and is itself a series of observations and remarks. It
concentrates on the notion of process versus final results, thus
opposing systematic inquiry along with its accompanying closure and implication of achieving truth. And at the same time
it is itself unsystematic and open-ended and offers no final
truth. The last discussion—on the contemporary state of the
arts and art collections in various countries—is broken off
suddenly, and we read only that this is all the writer is prepared to say at this point: "So much for the general intent of
our publication, which we hope will find many serious and
benevolent participants" (III, 90*) ["So viel im allgemeinen
von der Absicht eines Werkes, dem wir recht viel ernsthafte
und wohlwollende Teilnehmer wünschen" (XIII, 156)]. By ending so abruptly, practically in the middle of a thought, the
piece also involves the reader—it excites rather than satisfies
our curiosity. Moreover, the use of the word "participants"
rather than "readers" emphasizes that the reader is expected to
become actively involved and not simply "receive" passively
the ideas brought forth. Finally, as these instances of self-
reflective performance demonstrate, the "Introduction" introduces the notion of textual self-reflexivity while at the same
time being textually self-reflective.

Returning to the beginning of Goethe's introduction, we find
an explanation for the name of his journal:

A young man who feels attracted to nature and art expects, by striving vigorously, to gain immediate entrance
to the inner sanctum. As an adult he discovers that after a
long and arduous pilgrimage he is still in the vestibule.
This consideration prompted the selection of a title for

our periodical. The place where we will converse with our friends can only be a stairway, a gate, an entrance, an antechamber, an area between the inside and the outside, between the sacred and the profane. (III, 78–79*)

[Der Jüngling, wenn Natur und Kunst ihn anziehen, glaubt mit einem lebhaften Streben bald in das innerste Heiligtum zu dringen; der Mann bemerkt, nach langem Umherwandeln, daß er sich noch immer in den Vorhöfen befinde.
   Eine solche Betrachtung hat unsern Titel veranlaßt. Stufe, Tor, Eingang, Vorhalle, der Raum zwischen dem Innern und Äußern, zwischen dem Heiligen und Gemeinen kann nur die Stelle sein, auf der wir uns mit unsern Freunden gewöhnlich aufhalten werden. (XIII, 136–37)

This, however, is not only an explanation of the title as such; rather, it already serves as an introduction to the kind of writing the reader can expect. The location Goethe describes—the area between the outside and the inside—recalls the position and progression of the essay, which neither starts at the beginning nor ends at the end, but rather concentrates on the thought processes in between. The outside, where the essay does not start, might be seen as the absent origin and the inside—the center, conclusion, culmination, end—as the final truth the essay never achieves nor pretends to achieve. In other words, Goethe's opening remarks themselves are already a textually self-reflective moment in the introduction of an essayistic enterprise.

The title of the *introduction* also calls forth the essay's concentration on process and its recognition of the impossibility of ever reaching a true end. Since the propylaeum itself is a locus of introduction, and we are thus informed that the essays in the journal will all in a sense be introductions—Goethe also says that the purpose of the journal as a whole is "to introduce" (III, 82) ["einzuleiten" (XIII, 142)]—the title "Introduction to the *Propylaea*" could be translated as "Introduction to the Introductions." This not only conveys an appropriate and stronger sense of constant deferral, of the process of always moving toward something that will never be achieved, it also demonstrates, by implication, that the texts that follow will resemble the text that pre-scribes them—that is, they will be essays.

The View from the Vestibule

From my introduction and from my interpretation of Goethe's "Introduction," it should be clear that as I read Goethe's essays and examine them *as* essays my attention will be devoted more to what we might call the "sub-text" of his writings than to their more immediately apparent "super-texts." In the "Introduction" itself Goethe presents what can be seen as a metaphor for this approach to texts. One of the problems the artist will face upon returning from an educational journey to Italy, he says, is that this artist will find "few people who are inclined to see, enjoy, and think the work of art. Most viewers will only look at a work superficially, thinking random thoughts and enjoying their own feelings" (III, 85*) ["wenig Personen . . . die das Gebildete eigentlich sehen, genießen und denken mögen, sondern meist nur solche, die ein Werk obenhin ansehen, dabei etwas Beliebiges denken, und nach ihrer Art etwas dabei empfinden und genießen" (XIII, 148)]. On one level, this statement reflects Goethe's conviction that the reception of any work of art is determined by what he called "supplying" (*supplieren*—a complex notion to which I will return in Part Two). It also, however, shows Goethe's criticism of the tendency to concentrate on the explicit "statement" of a work; in order truly to appreciate and understand a work, he says, we must cut through this upper level of meaning and attempt to discover its implicit level, that is, its sub-text. (Goethe uses a somewhat peculiar expression here—"to think the work"—but one that effectively evokes the essay's performative criticism and its concentration on process.) We find a similar criticism in *Poetry and Truth* when Goethe describes the reception, by his teacher Clodius in

Leipzig, of an occasional poem his parents asked him to write
for his uncle's marriage:

> I was not at all dissatisfied with my work. I received a
> nice congratulatory letter from home about it . . . and
> hoped to wring some praise from my teacher too. But
> here I had badly miscalculated. He took the thing seri-
> ously, and, paying no regard whatever to the clearly
> parodistic aspect of the idea, he declared it to be ex-
> tremely reprehensible to make such great use of divine
> means for such petty human ends. (IV, 227)

> [Die Arbeit mißfiel mir keineswegs. Ich erhielt von Hause
> darüber ein schönes Belobungsschreiben . . . und hoffte
> meinem Lehrer doch auch einigen Beifall abzunötigen.
> Allein hier hatte ich's schlecht getroffen. Er nahm die
> Sache streng, und indem er das Parodistische, was denn
> doch in dem Einfall lag, gar nicht beachtete, so erklärte er
> den großen Aufwand von göttlichen Mitteln zu einem so
> geringen menschlichen Zweck für äußerst tadelnswert.
> (X, 331)]

Professor Clodius failed to read Goethe's sub-text, the rhetoric
of his text, and it is this that enrages the author; indeed, he even
goes so far here as to suggest that this kind of superficial reading
is typically the work of pedants.

As I have indicated, the "explicit meaning" of Goethe's essays
on art has received extensive consideration in the secondary
literature; as a means of coming to terms with the textuality
(and thus the generic quality) of the essays, I will approach them
always with an eye toward their sub-texts and toward the effects
of these sub-texts. This is not to say that the "super-text" can be
seen as being simply subsumed when confronted with the sub-
text. Rather, the explicit is affected in various ways—subverted,
enacted, or emphasized—by the implicit. Indeed, the explicit/
implicit dichotomy collapses as such as soon as the implicit is
brought to the fore—as in the present study—and thus made

explicit. Nevertheless, the dichotomy is useful, perhaps even inescapable—at least as a heuristic device.

*   *   *

"The inconspicuous wealth of interrelated motifs, the witty and hidden ironies, and the humanistic concern for presenting, within the context of the contemplation of art and conversations about it, a cornerstone for friendship, reconciliation, and civilized social life—all this renders 'The Collector' an unrecognized little masterpiece" (115–16). Thus Hans Rudolf Vaget praises Goethe's essay. I would agree that the work is a masterpiece, not so much because of its significance for the program of Goethe, Schiller, and Meyer, but rather because of what it reveals about Goethe's use of a genre and about the way he thinks. And some twenty years after Vaget's study, "The Collector" is unfortunately still very much unrecognized. For this reason it seems appropriate, before developing my argument about the (sub-)text, to discuss what it appears to be on its surface—the first view, so to speak, from the propylaeum.

"The Collector" comprises a correspondence in eight letters between a practicing physician/art collector (and, later, others in his family as well) and the editors of a journal, the *Propyläen.* We, however, read only the letters written to the editors and never their responses. The editors, who have visited the collector recently, have requested of him a contribution to their journal. He is prepared to oblige them, but not with a theoretical study; he chooses instead to present them with the history of his collection. The composition of this history over the first four letters and the collector's accompanying reflections about his forebears' varying attitudes toward art lead to a typology of the possible incarnations of artists and art lovers. The main categories of this scheme are the nature-imitators (his father and his brother-in-law), the "dotters" or miniaturists (his uncle), the sketchers (the collector himself), and the lovers of the soft, pleasant, and graceful (his niece Caroline, whose objection prevents him from generating a nickname for this type). Further but subordinate categories are occupied by the caricaturists, the improvisers, the scholar-artists, and the scholar-art-lovers. The collector presents all of these types as examples of an unfortunate one-sidedness, an obsession that undermines any balanced appreciation of art. He thus criticizes himself as well, but also indicates that he has found a way of overcoming his bias for the "boldly casual patterns, exuberant use of ink, strong strokes" (III, 131) ["das kühn Hingestrichene, wild Ausgetuschte, Gewaltsame" (XIII, 274)] of sketches, namely by discovering the transition from such an outline to its execution.

The end of the fourth letter brings with it the end of the collector's historical outline, and in the fifth letter another phase in his correspondence with the editors begins. This "second half" of the essay does not, however, represent a break from the first, since the topic remains the same and the attempt to understand the different attitudes toward art continues. The fifth letter reports, and in part reproduces, a debate with an art connoisseur who visits the physician in order to see the collection. The argument arises out of the visitor's extreme hatred of all "mannerists," whom he sees as positing a surface beauty as the ultimate goal of art, and out of his insistence on an intellectualized, conceptual foundation of art—what he calls "the completely characteristic" (III, 138*) ["das vollkommen Charakteristische" (XIII, 286)]. The collector defends the notion of beauty as the final criterion for judging art; one of the dangers he sees in the visitor's limiting attitude is that it would undermine the artistic value of large parts of his collection.

The collector's young friend, whom he calls "the philosopher," becomes interested in the debate and then displaces the collector as the visitor's opponent; in the sixth letter the young friend reproduces the continued debate. The philosopher's argument centers around artistic creativity. With his definition of art in terms of the productive activity, the handling of a given material by the artist, he undermines the visitor's insistence on the underlying concepts of a particular object, which is then seen as simply the raw material to which the artist imparts form and thereby creates a work of art. The philosopher's defense of the collector and his newfound activity in the dialogue about art draw him more solidly into the circle of the collector's family. Whereas previously his divergent interest in philosophy resulted in a tense relationship with the collector and distance from his concerns, his involvement in the debate with the "characterist" leads to participation in their communal endeavor to classify the types of artistic activity and art lovers. The seventh letter narrates their observation of a group of visitors to the collection and the failed attempt to fit them into the categorization; this difficulty shows them that while the categories represent a perhaps dangerous one-sidedness, these biases are not as threatening as those of such philistines.

The essay closes with the eighth letter, in which Julie presents as the culmination of the preceding reflections and observations the philosopher's schematization of the types of art and art lovers. In that scheme the collector's typology of the fourth letter surfaces again, but this time in greater detail and in the context of theoretical definitions and relationships. The philosopher's system opposes the "imitators" to the "imaginers" (those of Julie's persuasion), the "characterists" to the "undulators" (Caroline's category; one notices that she has not been able to escape the categorizing, systematizing, naming consciousness of the philosopher), and the miniaturists, the "small artists," to the "sketchers" (III, 159; XIII, 319). He then produces another scheme to show how the combination of these opposites leads to truth, beauty, and completion in art and artistic production. This system, presented as the culmination of the family's reflections, takes on the appearance of the essay's explicit goal and tangible theoretical result. And along with the debate on artistic production in the sixth letter, which Vaget calls the "climax" of the text, this culmination has indeed represented for critics what the text *means*.

Goethe and Systems

Johann Caspar Lavater's *Physiognomical Fragments* [*Physiognomische Fragmente*] consumed Goethe's interest, and much of his energy, in the early 1770s and left such an impression on him that forty years later, in *Poetry and Truth,* he would devote seemingly disproportionate attention to it. At its outset Lavater declares "that we by no means either want to, or can, provide a systematic whole."[2] We can assume that Goethe would have been pleased with Lavater's avoidance of systems, even though he might have preferred that it not be quite so explicit. (At least, such a conviction suggests itself when one considers that Goethe disapproved of Kant's critiques in many ways, but nevertheless was distraught as a result of Herder's outspoken reaction against them.) Indeed, we have already seen a kindred attitude implied in the introduction to his *Propyläen*.

This opposition to systems has not escaped critics entirely. Notably, Victor Lange, who at points speaks of Goethe's "aesthetic system" (165) and of the "systematic criteria" of the *Theory of Color* [*Farbenlehre*], concludes his study of Goethe's aesthetic theory with insights into the essentially anti-systematic character of his critical thought. In terms of literature we learn of Goethe's view that "the poet should not aim at conveying anything like a coherent philosophical system" (173) and that, in general, "any abstract discussion of aesthetic matters for the sake of constructing a precarious system was for Goethe profoundly suspect and distasteful" (175). In much more direct terms than Lange's, Arseni Gulyga's article "Goethe as Aesthetician and Theorist of Art" ["Goethe als Ästhetiker und Kunsttheoretiker"] begins with the proclamation, "Goethe left us no systematic textbook of aesthetics and produced no generalizing works on the theory of art."[3] Gulyga does not, however, proceed to examine thoroughly why this might be the case, but rather attempts to reconstruct what is perceived as the "missing" or latent system of Goethe's thought. A similar problem arises in Wohlleben's study. Although he occasionally admits that no system is to be found in an essay or that Goethe "shied away from systematic explanation" (153), systematic thought actually becomes a desideratum in his view of Goethe. When discussing the essay fragment, "On Dilettantism" ["Über den Dilettantismus"], which he calls "the axis of the work on the *Propyläen*" (105), he reveals his need to find a system: "It is hard to say what form the finished essay would have had. One would have to expect it to have been a theoretical treatise with

polemical intentions. The systematic part would have been followed by a historical part with names and examples" (107). In
treating essays in the natural sciences Wohlleben again conveys
this sense that the system is always "really" the goal of Goethe's
thought and writing: "One can hardly say that Goethe's works
in natural science established a system. His General Morphol-
ogy strove for something of the kind. But since it, like so many
other projects, could not be completed, he let the unity of his life
take the place of . . . the unattainable unity of the system" (130).
The recognition of Goethe's extreme reluctance to complete
what might have appeared to be a system should have led to a
different conclusion. The question of systems in Goethe's essayistic writing thus emerges occasionally in the work of critics;
and although there seems to be an awareness that Goethe wrote
little that can be unequivocally construed as systematic, a tendency remains to *want* to see his writing as a prelude to or
outline of an absent system, that is, to impose upon him the
systematic consciousness that the *critic* desires.

   If one wanted to find explicit testimony to Goethe's attitude
toward philosophy and its systems, one need only consult his
autobiography. We cannot take for granted that *Poetry and
Truth* presents an accurate picture of the years in his life it
describes, but we can be fairly certain that it reveals a great deal
about the way Goethe thought when he wrote it—in the years
after Schiller's death and the failure of their so-called classicist
program. Goethe's greatest essayistic production occurred in
that period of intense intellectual activity; thus we might be
justified in assuming that the intellectual development and formation of those "classical" years influenced the memory of his
youth and the way he portrays his thoughts of the earlier forma-
tive period.

   Throughout *Poetry and Truth* Goethe repeatedly states that
philosophy is incommensurable with his own way of thinking
and he quite often mocks the philosophers' orderly, systematic
approach to knowledge. His first exposure to strict philosophical
reasoning, provided by the tutor sent to help him overcome the
Gretchen episode, calls forth that difference: "But, alas, these
matters [the mysteries of philosophy] refused to fit together *in*

this way in my brain. . . . However, our main difference of opinion concerned my assertion that there was no need for a separate philosophy, since it was already completely contained in religion and poetry" (IV, 171*; my emphasis) ["Aber leider wollten diese Dinge (die philosophischen Geheimnisse) in meinem Gehirn *auf eine solche Weise* nicht zusammenhängen. . . . Unsere wichtigste Differenz war jedoch diese, daß ich behauptete, eine abgesonderte Philosophie sei nicht nötig, indem sie schon in der Religion und Poesie vollkommen enthalten sei" (X, 245; my emphasis)]. (This passage also reveals once again Goethe's sense of the importance of implicit signification, of sub-texts.) In the description of his early days in Leipzig we read of his distaste for the systematic processes of philosophy:

At first I attended my lectures diligently and faithfully, but philosophy refused to make sense to me. The odd part about logic was that, if I wanted to learn the correct use of mental processes which I had performed with the greatest ease since childhood, I was supposed to dissect, isolate, and virtually destroy them. (IV, 189)

[Meine Kollegia besuchte ich anfangs emsig und treulich: die Philosophie wollte mich jedoch keineswegs aufklären. In der Logik kam es mir wunderlich vor, daß ich diejenigen Geistesoperationen, die ich von Jugend auf mit der größten Bequemlichkeit verrichtete, so auseinander zerren, vereinzeln und gleichsam zerstören sollte, um den rechten Gebrauch derselben einzusehen. (X, 273)]

Later, in Book 12, the narration of his association with a journal, the *Frankfurter Gelehrten Anzeigen,* presents us with an even more pronounced image of Goethe's unsystematic way of thinking and its perceived divergence from the systematic modes of history and philosophy, of his "objective thinking" [*gegenständliches Denken*] vis-à-vis the subjective abstraction of philosophy:

My historical knowledge lacked coherence, for the history of the world, of science, and of literature had attracted me

only by individual epochs, and the topics themselves only
in part and in bulk. My ability to breathe life into things
and visualize them out of context allowed me to feel completely at home in a century or branch of science without
having any information about antecedents or successive
events. Further, I had developed a certain theoretical-
practical sense which enabled me, without real philosophical coherence but with sporadic accuracy, to describe
things more as they ought to have been than as they were.
(IV, 406)

[Mein historisches Wissen hing nicht zusammen, die
Geschichte der Welt, der Wissenschaften, der Literatur
hatte mich nur epochenweis, die Gegenstände selbst
aber nur teil- und massenweis angezogen. Die Möglich-
keit, mir die Dinge auch außer ihrem Zusammenhang
lebendig zu machen und zu vergegenwärtigen, setzte
mich in den Fall, in einem Jahrhundert, in einer Abtei-
lung der Wissenschaft völlig zu Hause zu sein, ohne daß
ich weder von den Vorhergehenden noch von dem Nach-
folgenden irgend unterrichtet gewesen wäre. Ebenso war
ein gewisser theoretisch praktischer Sinn in mir aufge-
gangen, daß ich von den Dingen, mehr wie sie sein
sollten als wie sie waren, Rechenschaft geben konnte,
ohne eigentlichen philosophischen Zusammenhang, aber
sprungweise treffend. (X, 602)]

These represent just a few examples of Goethe's expressed opposition to the philosopher's approach to knowledge and
understanding.

Specific criticisms of systematic thought can be found in other
contexts as well. When discussing his literary interests in the
Leipzig years, he takes the occasion to condemn Gottsched,
whose systematic categorization of the types of poetry he sees as
the destruction of the very notion of poetry: "This columbarium, which really destroys the conception of what poetry intrin-
sically is, had been quite completely constructed by Gottsched in
his *Critical Poetics,* where he had also pointed out that German

poets had already succeeded in filling all the niches with excellent works" (IV, 207*) ["Von Gottsched war schon dieses
Fächerwerk, welches eigentlich den innern Begriff von Poesie zu
Grunde richtet, in seiner kritischen Dichtkunst ziemlich voll-
ständig zusammengezimmert und zugleich nachgewiesen, daß
auch schon deutsche Dichter mit vortrefflichen Werken alle
Rubriken auszufüllen gewußt" (X, 300)]. With a great deal of
humor Goethe describes his relief—" . . . what a stone his exhor-
tation had rolled from my heart" (IV, 352) [". . .welchen Stein
mir sein Zureden vom Herzen wälzte" (X, 520)]—at the Strasbourg law dean's rejection of his dissertation (the "treatise" he
had hated writing and hoped would not pass) and at the suggestion that he take the option of the less thorough and less systematic "disputation on theses." Finally, in Book 15, Goethe includes in a brief essay on "the epoch in which we lived" a
lampoon against the systematic preoccupations of the age:
"Meanwhile reason also intervened; everything was supposed
to be reduced to clear concepts and presented in logical form"
(IV, 482*) ["Der Verstand mischte sich indessen auch in die
Sache, alles sollte auf klare Begriffe gebracht und in logischer
Form dargelegt werden" (X, 718)]. In their pervasiveness, these
various instances of un- or anti-systematic thought taken together constitute, I think, a statement of the writer's fundamental way of thinking.

Yet another passage from the autobiography reveals, more
forcefully than any of those I have introduced so far, Goethe's
extreme distancing of himself from systematic discourse. In
Book 16 we find the famous discussion of Spinoza's philosophy
and the influence it had on the young poet. At first, this might
seem to contradict my argument, but such doubt dissolves when
we examine the nature of that influence. Goethe's summary of
Spinoza's philosophy *seems* to imply subscription to the philosopher's system, but we then read that "my confidence in Spinoza
was based on the peaceful effect he produced in me" (V, 523*)
["mein Zutrauen auf Spinoza ruhte auf der friedlichen Wirkung, die er in mir hervorbrachte" (X, 732)] and that we, the
readers, should not assume that it is a case of endorsing that
system: "Let no one imagine, however, that I wanted to sub-

scribe to his writings and literally profess them" (V, 524)
["Denke man aber nicht, daß ich seine Schriften hätte unter-
schreiben und mich dazu buchstäblich bekennen mögen" (X,
733)]. This statement, by itself, would simply reveal an unwillingness to accept a particular system. It is the *reason* he gives
for that unwillingness that shows a distancing from systems *as
such:* "For I had already seen all too clearly that no individual
understands any other, that the same words have different meanings for everyone, that a conversation or a reading prompts
varying trains of thought in various people" (V, 524) ["Denn
daß niemand den andern versteht, daß keiner bei denselben
Worten dasselbe, was der andere, denkt, daß ein Gespräch, eine
Lektüre bei verschiedenen Personen verschiedene Gedanken-
folgen aufregt, hatte ich schon allzu deutlich eingesehen" (X,
733)]. This remark obviously carries with it great significance
for Goethe's views on dialogue and on reading and will thus
necessarily be of concern in later discussions. For the current
context its significance is equally great. Goethe does not question the validity of Spinoza's system *for Spinoza*. Within the
individual subject the system is always possible; indeed, the
subject, by itself, *is* system. The problem arises when that system is set down in a *text,* that is, when it enters the context of
intersubjectivity. For once the system becomes text, it is exposed
to the uncertainties of language. Goethe describes this uncertainty in one of his essays, the short "scientific" text entitled
"Symbolism," as follows: "With words we fully express neither
things nor ourselves. Through language something like a new
world emerges, one consisting of the necessary and the accidental" (XII, 26*) ["Durch Worte sprechen wir weder die Gegenstände noch uns selbst völlig aus. Durch die Sprache entsteht
gleichsam eine neue Welt, die aus Notwendigem und Zufäl-
ligem besteht" (XVI, 855)]. (Contrary to the conventional understanding, Goethe treats the individual subject here as the
"necessary" [the systematic] and the intersubjective or collective as the "accidental" [and thus non-systematic].)[4]

Goethe's notion of what happens on the textual, linguistic
level could also be understood in Peircean terms—as an infinite
semiosis, as the infinite multiplication of interpretants. And this

view of language has a direct bearing on the very possibility of the system as a textual entity, which must operate with clear and distinct concepts in a logically consistent order. ("Especially with *Descartes* and ever since, the notion of a demonstrative science has gotten its bearings from the system as *perfectum et absolutum*. As a result, this science has had to be complete and orderly in its scope, clear and distinct in its content, and rigorous and univocal in its reasoning" [Zahn, "System," 1463].) Given the infinite multiplication of interpretants, given the impossibility of the univocal, the possibility of conceptual clarity is lost and with it that of distinct concepts; this loss, in turn, removes the possibility of strict logical analysis and relationships. In the absence of those prerequisites, strictly valid systems become impossible and those who believe in them and attempt to produce them are revealed as the victims of a fantasy.

To understand Goethe's remarks as a rejection of the system, of course, it is necessary that we take those remarks as presenting clear concepts, that we limit the interpretants so as to be able to complete a logical progression. Thus Goethe's rejection and our contribution to his argumentation fall victim to the kind of paradox that created such great problems for Herder in his rejection of Kant—that is, to argue directly against something, we must participate in the same discourse we attempt to undermine. In more recent philosophical criticism, the problem has been formulated as one of not being able to question the tradition of logocentrism without assuming its vocabulary and inhabiting its conceptual structures. In "Structure, Sign and Play in the Discourse of the Human Sciences," when challenging the history of metaphysics, Derrida says: "There is no sense in doing without the concepts of metaphysics in order to shake metaphysics. We have no language—no syntax and no lexicon—which is foreign to this history; we can pronounce not a single destructive proposition which has not already had to slip into the form, the logic, and the implicit postulations of precisely what it seeks to contest."[5] The paradox seems inescapable, and in order to continue our investigations and our criticism, we must simply acknowledge it and live with it—"We cannot give up this metaphysical complicity without also giving up the cri-

tique we are directing against this complicity" ("Structure, Sign
and Play," 281).

*   *   *

Poetry and Truth provides especially extensive documentation
of Goethe's aversion to systematic thought, of what we might
call his "way of thinking," but we need not restrict ourselves to
the autobiography. *Faust,* for example, includes several vigor-
ous critiques of systems. The most explicit of these appears in
Mephistopheles' conference with the student in the second
"Study" scene. Mephistopheles first pokes fun at philosophy in
general by describing how its foundation in the strictures of
logic distances it from reality:

> So, Friend, (my views to briefly sum,)
> First, the *collegium logicum.*
> There will your mind be drilled and braced,
> As if in Spanish boots 't were laced,
> . . . .
> Days will be spent to bid you know,
> What once you did at a single blow,
> Like eating and drinking, free and strong,—
> That one, two, three! thereto belong.
> Truly the fabric of mental fleece
> Resembles a weaver's masterpiece,
> Where a thousand threads one treadle throws,
> Where fly the shuttles hither and thither,
> Unseen the threads are knit together,
> And an infinite combination grows.
> Then, the philosopher steps in
> And shows, no otherwise it could have been:
> The first was so, the second so,
> Therefore the third and fourth are so;
> Were not the first and second, then
> The third and fourth had never been.
> The scholars are everywhere believers,
> But never succeed in being weavers.[6]

[Mein teurer Freund, ich rat Euch drum
Zuerst Collegium Logicum.
Da wird der Geist Euch wohl dressiert,
In Spanische Stiefeln eingeschnürt,
. . . .
Dann lehret man Euch manchen Tag,
Daß, was Ihr sonst auf Einen Schlag
Getrieben, wie Essen und Trinken frei,
Eins! Zwei! Drei! dazu nötig sei.
Zwar ists mit der Gedankenfabrik
Wie mit einem Webermeisterstück,
Wo Ein Tritt tausend Fäden regt,
Die Schifflein herüber-hinüberschießen,
Die Fäden ungesehen fließen,
Ein Schlag tausend Verbindungen schlägt.
Der Philosoph, der tritt herein
Und beweist Euch, es müßt so sein:
Das Erst wär so, das Zweite so
Und drum das Dritt und Vierte so,
Und wenn das Erst und Zweit nicht wär,
Das Dritt und Viert wär nimmermehr.
Das preisen die Schüler aller Orten,
Sind aber keine Weber geworden.
(Part 1, lines 1910–35)]

In general, he equates systems with reduction: "When you have learned, all things reducing, / To classify them for your using" (78) ["Wenn Ihr lernt alles reduzieren / Und gehörig klassifizieren" (Part 1, lines 1944–45)]. He then goes on to draw other realms of traditionally systematic inquiry and discourse—metaphysics and theology—into question and even indicates that what makes them questionable is their systematic character, insofar as their goal is certitude:

On *words* let your attention centre!
Then through the safest gate you'll enter
The temple-halls of Certainty.
(79)

[Im ganzen: haltet Euch an Worte!
Dann geht Ihr durch die sichre Pforte
Zum Tempel der Gewißheit ein.
(Part 1, lines 1990–92)]

In his next speech, Mephistopheles even mentions systems, again in the context of language: "With words 't is excellent disputing; / Systems to words 't is easy suiting" (80) ["Mit Worten läßt sich trefflich streiten, / Mit Worten ein System bereiten" (Part 1, lines 1997–98)].[7] While we might otherwise take Mephistopheles' parody of systems with a grain of salt, since it comes from the "Spirit that always denies," the text includes a signal to the reader that these comments are to be taken straightforwardly: *after* finishing his polemic, Mephistopheles says "I'm tired enough of this dry tone,— / Must play the devil again, and fully" (80) ["Ich bin des trocknen Tons nun satt, / Muß wieder recht den Teufel spielen" (Part 1, lines 2009–10)].

The problematization of systems in *Faust* is not restricted, however, to Mephistopheles' remarks. The play opens with Faust on the verge of despair—a despair that arises out of his inability to find or create a *system* that can explain the world or his existence. His search for the system, for the absolute knowledge of "the inmost force / Which binds the world, and guides its course" (18) ["was die Welt / Im Innersten zusammenhält" (Part 1, lines 382–83)], has led him to the realm of magic and mysticism. But even though he finds in Nostradamus's book the *sign* of that system, "the sign of the Macrocosm" (19), he must ultimately realize the inadequacy of what is *only* a sign of "How each the Whole its substance gives" (20) ["Wie alles sich zum Ganzen webt" (Part 1, line 447)]: "How grand a show! but, ah! a show alone" (20) ["Welch Schauspiel! Aber ach! ein Schauspiel nur!" (Part 1, line 454)]. His desire for system and despair over the apparent impossibility of ever finding it nearly leads him to suicide, but the Easter bells and chorus keep him from drinking the poison. What saves him is neither some realization that the search for an ultimate system is an inessential kind of striving nor simply a sudden loss of desire for system, but rather

an intimation of the *possibility* of finding in religion the systematic certitude he requires:

Ye choirs, have ye begun the sweet, consoling chant,
Which, through the night of Death, the angels ministrant
Sang, God's new Covenant [certainty—P.B.] repeating?
(31)

[Ihr Chöre, singt ihr schon den tröstlichen Gesang,
Der einst um Grabesnacht von Engelslippen klang,
Gewißheit einem neuen Bunde?
(Part 1, lines 746–48)]

Only after he has escaped from the realm of pure abstraction
and broken the spell of his radical interiority through his love
for another human being, only then does he see without despair
the impossibility of system, of ever achieving certitude and complete knowledge: "That nothing can be perfect unto Man / I
now am conscious" (148) ["O daß dem Menschen nichts Voll-
kommnes wird, / Empfind ich nun!" (Part 1, lines 3240–41)].

*   *   *

Goethe's autobiography and his best known work reveal his
attitude toward systems, and his remarks on language provide
an explanation for that attitude. It is in his essays, however, that
we discover the true extent of his opposition to systematic
thought and discourse. And it is in the essays that he *acts* against
such discourse—by formulating systems, playing with them,
and ultimately subverting them.

Text

At first glance there might seem to be a contradiction in my method. I argue the anti-systematic quality of the essay and of Goethe's thought, but I have chosen as the basis of this argument what seems the most systematic essay Goethe wrote. In the middle of "The Collector and His Circle" the collector presents the systematic categorization of the types of art lovers described above. The piece then culminates in the philosopher's system of relationships between these types. Closer examination of these systems themselves, however, reveals irony in their presentation and slippage within the structure and language of the schemes that make this essay particularly well suited to showing that anti-systematic tendency.

The first system we encounter in "The Collector"—the collector's typology—degenerates to the point that it ceases to exist as a system as soon as we begin to consider it as such. The collector presents his classification in an off-the-cuff manner, portraying it as the result of occasional observation and casual conversation, rather than as the product of strict theoretical intellection (III, 135; XIII, 280–81). The first sign of the categorization's unsoundness comes when he describes the kind of art his niece Caroline prefers: "When we came to the class where the soft, the pleasing, the graceful predominate, Caroline immediately declared herself an adherent and protested solemnly against giv-

ing it a nickname" (III, 136*) ["Für die Rubrik, in welcher das
Weiche, das Gefällige, das Anmutige herrschend ist, hat sich
Karoline sogleich erklärt und feierlich protestiert, daß man
dieser Klasse keinen Spitznamen geben möge" (XIII, 283)]. The
collector does not resist Caroline's wish and thus undermines
the systematic quality of his endeavor. To name is to define,
limit, set fast. The omission of the name undermines the opera-
tive means of schematic categorization—the establishment of
identity and its consequent immutability, the elimination of difference and of play. One could argue, on the other hand, that the
absence of a name for this category *alone* reflects and thus
names the category itself. But by indicating a (possibly infinite)
multiplication of interpretants—"the soft, the pleasing, the
graceful . . ."—the collector draws into question the possibility
of conceptual clarity and distinction and thus the consistency of
the system. This breach is immediately followed by a further
breach—that of logical form: "After discussing the soft styles
we naturally came to speak of woodcuts and engravings of the
early masters, whose works, in spite of a harsh, severe, and rigid
style, still delight us because of their rough-hewn, solid quality"
(III, 136–37) ["Von den Weichlichen kamen wir natürlicher-
weise auf die Holzschnitte und Kupferstiche der frühern Meister, deren Werke, ohngeachtet ihrer Strenge, Härte und Steif-
heit, uns durch einen gewissen derben und sichern Charakter
noch immer erfreuen" (XIII, 283–84)]. There is, however, nothing "natural" or logical about this progression. Caroline's class
was described as that of the soft, pleasant, and graceful, whereas
the woodcuts and engravings of the old masters represent precisely the opposite—harshness, severity, and rigidity. Only if the
classification had operated throughout on the basis of a progression through opposites could we consider this step "natural."
But since this is not the case, any apparent logical progression is
drawn into question. For those who have failed to recognize the
implied ironic attitude toward the system he presents the collector then provides explicit directions: at the beginning of the fifth
letter he does not refer to his categorization in terms that would

indicate he takes it seriously, but rather writes only of his "curious classifications" (III, 137) ["wunderlichen Klassifikationen"
(XIII, 284–85)]. The ultimately unsystematic quality of this system is therefore fairly easy to discern; it is openly ironized and is
not presented with any gesture of finality.

The ironization of the second system is a matter of far greater
subtlety and complexity. The philosopher claims that his scheme
is pure and thorough—"But foreign elements, the false, and the
lopsided are not provided for in my system. My six categories
designate the qualities which, all combined, would describe the
true artist as well as the true connoisseur" (III, 154*) ["Das
Falsche, Schiefe, fremd Eingemischte aber findet hier keinen
Platz. Meine sechs Klassen bezeichnen die Eigenschaften,
welche, alle zusammen verbunden, den wahren Künstler, sowie
den wahren Liebhaber, ausmachen würden" (XIII, 311)]—and
he attributes to it a sense of completion by introducing it as "the
whole thing" (III, 159*; XIII, 319). The system then acquires
the quality of finality when Julie remarks, "So there you have a
complete overview! I am finished with my assignment" (III,
159) ["Hier haben Sie nun die ganze Übersicht! Mein Geschäft
ist vollendet" (XIII, 319)]. The philosopher summarizes his treatise with a table that presents the system he has developed in its
entirety:

Seriousness	Seriousness and Play	Play
Alone	Combined	Alone
One-sidedness	Development to-ward diversity	One-sidedness
Manner	Style	Manner
Imitators	Artistic Truth	Phantomists
Characterists	Beauty	Undulators
Miniaturists	Completion	Sketchers
		(III, 159*)

[*Ernst*	*Ernst und Spiel*	*Spiel*
allein	verbunden	allein
Individuelle	Ausbildung ins	Individuelle
Neigung,	Allgemeine	Neigung
Manier	Stil	Manier
Nachahmer	Kunstwahrheit	Phantomisten
Charakteristiker	Schönheit	Undulisten
Kleinkünstler	Vollendung	Skizzisten
		(XIII, 319)]

This table not only transforms the system into a concrete image, but also contains elements that draw attention to its status *as a system*. The combination of the "imitator" and the "phantomist" results in "artistic truth," that of the "miniaturist" and the "sketcher" in "completion"; thus the philosopher thematizes in his system two central characteristics of systematic thought itself—the goals of truth and completion. The effect of this thematization for the reader is to emphasize that s*he is witnessing the formation of a system. Whether or not we accept this relational scheme as the final statement of the essay must then depend on a close examination of the context in which it occurs, of the manner in which it is presented to us, of the soundness of its terms and structure, and of the figure who composes it.

Presentation

When we first learn that the philosopher has completed his scheme and that Julie will present it to the *Propyläen* editors, we are encouraged to adopt a skeptical attitude toward it. Julie says that her uncle and the philosopher have forced an unpleasant duty on her and she feels incapable of performing it. She calls it

> a task that was literally forced on me. I feel neither qualified nor able to do it. . . .

I am supposed to report to you what happened yesterday and describe the people who visited our gallery. And then, I am to explain that delightful scheme which in future will pigeonhole and label all artists and art lovers who focus on one particular aspect and are unable to embrace the whole. (III, 148)

[eine Pflicht . . . die mir im eigentlichsten Sinne aufgedrungen worden: denn ich fühle mich weder dazu bestimmt noch fähig. . . .

Die Geschichte des gestrigen Tages soll ich aufzeichnen! die Personen schildern, die gestern unser Kabinett besuchten, und zuletzt Ihnen Rechenschaft von dem allerliebsten Fachwerk geben, worin künftig alle und jede Künstler und Kunstfreunde, die an einem einzelnen Teile fest halten, die sich nicht zum Ganzen erheben, eingeschachtelt und aufgestellt werden sollen. (XIII, 302)]

As if her doubt about her ability to do this were not enough to make the reader wonder about the endeavor, she then says that she will try to find a way to avoid reproducing that system. In the course of the seventh letter our suspicion grows as we learn of the uncle's and the philosopher's unwillingness to perform the task they have unloaded on Julie, and of the philosopher's unwillingness to present his system even to his close circle of friends in conversation, much less make it public. At the conclusion of her narration of the previous day's events Julie reiterates her intention to shirk the unwelcome responsibility: "Also, I want to see if I can't get out of this obligation" (III, 153) ["Auch muß ich sehen ob ich nicht etwa dieses Geschäft von mir abschütteln kann" (XIII, 310)]. By this point, the reader, who knows that the system exists, realizes that s*he is witnessing the *avoidance* of the system, or at least a sense of inappropriateness connected to writing it down for the editors of a journal and thus possibly lending it a quality of permanence or greater validity through its "publication."

Julie nonetheless does present the system to the editors and to us. At the beginning of the eighth letter her aversion to the task has vanished and she suddenly appears to relish the opportunity. But the *reason* she gives for her change of heart again draws the content of her writing—the system—into question: she performs her duty out of a "spirit of contradiction" (III, 153*) ["Geist des Widerspruchs" (XIII, 310)]. This notion had emerged earlier in the essay when the collector was narrating the history of his collection; his love for sketches arose out of a "spirit of contradiction" (III, 131*; XIII, 274) in relationship to his father's and uncle's extreme mimetic drives. In that his preference for this form of art helped to balance the collection and eventually provided him with a better sense of what constitutes great art, that spirit of contradiction reveals itself as productive.

Our horizon of expectation when we read the word "contradiction" is usually determined by a sense of disfavor or negativity; in analyzing any sort of discourse—scientific, literary, philosophical, psychological—we learn to avoid contradiction at all costs. We might thus be surprised to find a favorable attitude toward it in "The Collector," but this view should not come as a surprise to readers of Goethe, who repeatedly demonstrates his interest and the pleasure he takes, not only in oppositions and polarities, but explicitly in contradiction and paradox. In his autobiography he makes the strong pronouncement that "the spirit of contradiction and the taste for paradox are latent in us all" (IV, 261) ["der Geist des Widerspruchs und die Lust zum Paradoxen steckt in uns allen" (X, 385)]. But in Goethe it was stronger than in most. He sees the literary period in which he was born as one that emerged through contradiction to the preceding period (IV, 197; X, 285), and he writes of how at an early age he learned the importance of choosing the topics for his art and of conciseness in their treatment "from many conflicts of opinion" (IV, 214) ["durch so manche widerstreitende Meinung" (X, 311)]. He remembers the time of his return to Frankfurt from Strasbourg as one in which a friend, Riese, exercised and sharpened his mind as well as (happily) undermined his tendency to dogmatic enthusiasm "with his persistent contradiction" (IV, 374) ["durch anhaltenden Widerspruch" (X, 552)]. And in arguments with Basedow he used the "weapons of paradox" (IV, 453) ["Waffen der Paradoxie" (X, 674)], which in turn brought him renewed intellectual excitement. We need not restrict ourselves to the autobiography in order to discover that contradiction represented for Goethe anything but a threat; in the essay "On Granite" ["Über den Granit"], for example, he reveals his advocacy of contradiction: "I do not fear the accusation that a spirit of contradiction has led me away from my consideration and depiction of the human heart . . . and has brought me to the observation of the oldest . . . son of nature" (XII, 132*) ["Ich fürchte den Vorwurf nicht, daß es ein Geist des Widerspruchs sein müsse, der mich von Betrachtung und Schilderung des menschlichen Herzens . . . zu der Beobachtung des ältesten . . . Sohnes der Natur geführt hat" (XVII, 480)]. Indeed, we would be hard pressed to discover an instance in which Goethe looks unfavorably upon contradiction or sees in it anything but a productive manner of thought that makes progress possible.

The notion of contradiction, however, is not only important for the productiveness Goethe attributes to it, but also in what it implies for systematic thought. In summarizing *Poetry and Truth* Goethe speaks of his spiritual development as a young man as something that one can only understand in terms of contradiction and not in terms of straightforward concepts: "He believed that he perceived something in nature (whether living or lifeless, animate or inanimate) that manifested itself only in contradictions and therefore could not be expressed in any concept, much less in any word" (V, 597) ["Er glaubte in der Natur, der belebten und unbelebten, der beseelten und unbeseelten etwas zu entdecken, das sich nur in Widersprüchen manifestierte und deshalb unter keinen Begriff, noch viel weniger unter ein Wort gefaßt werden könnte" (X, 839)]. Here we are back at the basic notion of the clear and distinct concepts and univocal language indispensable to systematic thought; Goethe shows the incommensurability of contradiction, which he favors, even advocates, with systems. (As always, here too Goethe is playful and attentive to the performative aspect of writing, for a few lines after the passage just quoted, he contradicts his own statement. He names the one word that designates that which cannot be expressed in one word: "This essence, which appeared to infiltrate all the others, separating and combining

them, I called *daemonic*" (V, 597; my emphasis) ["Dieses
Wesen, das zwischen alle übrigen hineinzutreten, sie zu sondern,
sie zu verbinden schien, nannte ich *dämonisch*" (X, 840; my
emphasis)].)

Recognizing the implications of the word "contradiction" in
Goethe, we can then return to Julie's decision to reproduce the
philosopher's scheme out of a spirit of contradiction. Her state
of mind is incommensurable with what she will write. By informing the reader of her revised intention, she reveals her inability
to identify with, to subscribe to that which will come out of her
quill. Yet she is the one from whom we receive the system. Thus
the text's attitude to the system it presents is an ironic attitude.
Thus the context of presentation forces us to question what is
presented. Thus the rhetoric of the text challenges the apparent
meaning of the text.

Slippage

The form itself of the philosopher's system thematizes its status as
a system in that it presents systematic thought in its most straightforward and obvious, if most reductionist, manifestation—as a
schematic categorization. As such, it is already the subject of
ironization: not only did Goethe make fun of categorizations
when he spoke of the destructive effect for poetry of Gottsched's
"columbarium" [*Fächerwerk*], but in "The Collector" Julie distances herself from what she humorously terms the philosopher's
"delightful scheme" [*Fachwerk*], and she implicitly questions its
value by using the pejorative "pigeonhole" to describe the way in
which it deals with the various types of artist and art lover. Furthermore, the categorization itself reveals a less-than-serious attitude toward itself. Before examining other levels of irony in the
way it is presented to us, we should concern ourselves with the
operation of this inner ironization.

Perhaps the first thing that strikes us as questionable when we
consider the scheme is its purported goal. The philosopher
claims that the combination of all six biases—those of the "imi-

tators," "characterists," "miniaturists," "imaginers," "undulators," and "sketchers"—will result in the "true" artist or art
lover. The possibility of this synthesis ever occurring, however,
is remote if not nonexistent, especially since many of the categories have been described as mutually exclusive. Vaget calls attention to this weakness when he mentions "the obvious objection
that in reality a great artist would never emerge from the pre-
scribed synthesis of those six one-sided manners" (124); because of the playful context of the system's presentation, however, he is not disturbed by the weakness and so does not pursue
its implications. Since his study concerns itself primarily with
Goethe's view of dilettantism, it is understandable that he
would not pursue this point. But it is an important point for an
attempt to come to terms with Goethe's treatment of systems in
his essayistic writing, because it is the first sign that something is
amiss in the system itself. Moreover, the view that the system is
"consistent and complete" (Vaget, 119) is difficult to reconcile
with the recognized impossibility of its culminating synthesis
and its less-than-serious presentation.

   In order to be able to say that the system is complete, we
would have to accept the exclusion of those who visited the
collector before it was composed. The philosopher defends his
exclusion by saying that his scheme has no room for "the foreign elements, the false, and the lopsided" that these philistine
visitors seem to represent. The reader is inclined at first to agree
with him. But on closer consideration, we must recognize that
these people, too, are art lovers of a sort, and although their
appreciation is determined by *more* extreme biases and informed by *more* foreign elements, they are nevertheless interested in art and visit the collector in order to contemplate it.
Moreover, they differ from the types included in the scheme
mainly in the degree of their one-sidedness. The very foundation
of the system is the desire to provide a means for overcoming
one-sidedness and the types that make up the scheme's categories are examples, strictly speaking, of "lopsidedness" and of a
view of art that is false because of its bias. The types included
are also not entirely free of "foreign elements"—one need only
think of the "poeticizers" whose fault consists in their tendency

to mix poetic desires or intentions with their sense of the visual arts. We can thus justifiably conclude that the system is *not* as complete as its creator claims, since its categories cannot or at least do not account for all of the phenomena that, in its own terms, it should be able to encompass.

When we consider the supposed consistency of the system, we encounter even greater difficulty. Before producing his summarizing table, the philosopher had stated the three central oppositions as occurring between the "imitators" and the "imaginers," between the "characterists" and the "undulators," and between the "miniaturists" and the "sketchers." The transferral of these oppositions into the table then reveals an inconsistency, in that no longer the "imaginers" but the "phantomists" represent the opposition to the "imitators." The "phantomists" earlier had been a subset of the "imaginers" category and one of the more derogatory designations within that category; using this term thus creates an oppositional imbalance since "imitator" is the more generic, less judgmentally colored term. Even if we were to conclude that both terms—"phantomists" and "imaginers"— indicate essentially the same thing, we would nevertheless be confronted with indecision or uncertainty in the choice of terms and thus a lack of distinctness in the system's constituent concepts.

A related inconsistency occurs in the alignment of categories within the table. Here we find the "imitators" and the "characterists" placed within the more general category of "manner." In the fifth and sixth letters, however, we had the opportunity to observe the visiting characterist's extreme opposition to, even hatred of, mannerists. Given his bias, this opposition is understandable; both the imitator and the characterist concentrate exclusively on the object to be depicted, find the meaning and significance of the work of art in that object, whereas those whom the characterist calls mannerists lose sight of the original object in their devotion to its treatment by the artist. That the two are then equated, without explanation or justification, must lead us to doubt the consistency of the scheme. Were we willing, nonetheless, to accept that in one sense all of the types of one-sidedness represent a kind of mannerism, as the final table implies, we would still be faced with an element of conceptual confusion, since we would have to conclude that "manner" itself has essentially different meanings, and that its unqualified use is therefore inconsistent.

The syntheses of oppositions do not compensate for the lack of conceptual clarity in some of the scheme's individual terms. That the combination of "imitators" and "phantomists" results in "artistic truth" is justifiable in the terms the philosopher has laid out. Of the "imitator" we learn that "he lacks artistic truth as beautiful appearance" (III, 154*) ["es fehlt ihm die Kunstwahrheit als schöner Schein" (XIII, 312)], whereas the "imaginers" lack "artistic truth as beautiful reality" (III, 155*) ["Kunstwahrheit als schöne Wirklichkeit" (XIII, 313)]. Inasmuch as the imitators are seen to provide the "beautiful reality" and the imaginers the "beautiful appearance," the combination of the two would eliminate the lack of each individually and thus produce "artistic truth." Already here, though, a certain doubt arises *because* of the conceptual indistinctness introduced into the opposites that are to be synthesized. And if we accept the characterist's argument that "beauty" [*Schönheit*] derives from "appearance" [*Schein*], "beautiful reality" ["schöne Wirklichkeit"] might represent a contradiction in terms and "beautiful appearance" ["schöner Schein"] a tautology.[8] The other two syntheses—that of "characterists" and "undulators" to achieve "beauty" and that of "miniaturists" and "sketchers" to achieve "completion"—are even less comprehensible. How, for example, can the "miniaturist," whose art is characterized by the possibility of an infinite process of adding detail—"that matter can be divided ad infinitum" (III, 136) ["daß man die Materie ins Unendliche teilen könne" (XIII, 282)]—combine with the "sketcher," for whom the ideal work of art is also never completed, to achieve completion? The philosopher's treatise contains nothing that even approaches sufficient explanation of these combinatory results.

It is possible to make this argument in different, perhaps simpler terms. Take, for example, the "imitators" and the "phantomists." The former are seen to be lacking in the subjective aspect, whereas the latter lack attention to the object. If we

bring them together, then we would have that ideal combination
of subject and object that is called "artistic truth." But if we
pursue the implications of the categorization, we must see that
already in isolation from one another, the categories would have
to possess "artistic truth" in order to exist. The subjective side
must include the object to some degree in order to be even
recognizable as art, indeed in order to be recognizable at all to
an other. And the objective side must include the subject's consciousness, since all experience involves perception, and without
some degree of subjectivity, the simple imitation would not be
art, would not be imitation, but the object itself. If the opposing
sides of the scheme already constitute, at least in part, their ideal
synthesis, then they cannot exist as those distinct extremes in the
first place.

We have now seen the weakness of individual terms of opposition and of their combination. The terms that designate the
supposed achievement of those combinations provide us with
further difficulty. Even though we can extrapolate the meaning
of "artistic truth" as the ideal combination of the subjective and
objective (and then must see that it does not only fulfill the
function of a synthesis, but is also already present in the antitheses), it never receives close attention or description in the treatise, and the philosopher does not succeed in undermining the
characterist's problematization of the term "beauty" before including it in his table. Furthermore, the concepts "completion"
and "style" are introduced here for the first time and receive no
explanation or definition. We can, perhaps, infer what the philosopher might mean by "completion" as a higher goal of art,
but there is nothing in the treatise, or in the essay as a whole,
that can provide us with an insight into the meaning of "style."
The word itself has occurred only once before this point, in
passing and without discussion or definition (III, 145; XIII,
296), and suddenly we find it at the geometric center of the
system.

One effect of using this undefined, unprepared term is to
undermine the supposed closure of the system. The philosopher has told us we are being given "the whole thing," and

Julie reinforces his claim by saying that her job is completed once she has committed the "complete overview" to paper. But undefined terms contradict any such impression, because they leave the recipient nonplussed, wondering what they might mean and *unable* to understand the system they might otherwise complete.

The ending of the essay as a whole—the last lines of Julie's letter—reflects this breach of apparent closure and the open-endedness that results from it. She hurries to finish her letter and send it off to the editors because of her conviction "that discussions both pro and con must start at the very place where I leave off" (III, 159) ["daß ein beistimmendes oder abstimmendes Gespräch eben da anfangen muß, wo ich aufhöre" (XIII, 319)]. In one sense, however, this remark can be seen to result, paradoxically, in closure, can be seen to reveal itself as only an apparent breach of closure. We could say that Julie's letter as a whole includes both the system and its possible criticism and that the system is thus closed precisely *by* concluding with this sort of criticism of itself, by establishing a structure of possible theoretical alternatives, that it is self-reflexively closed by accounting for such possibilities, that its stability *as* a "complete overview" will maintain itself even in the face of a "dissenting" judgment by virtue of its ability to subsume that criticism into its "entirety" (much in the way an "open" system maintains its stability despite disturbances in its environment). But, on the other hand, this particular system does not give us any indication of *how* it would compensate for possible criticisms (such as the argument that the antitheses already include the syntheses); it is not even an "open" system. The *tour de force* of declaring it "the whole thing" does not make it so. Furthermore, by positing another beginning *in the very moment* of completing—"start at the very place where I leave off"—the gesture of non-closure asserts itself with at least equal force. It seems to me that the paradoxical simultaneity of these gestures, the combination of closure and non-closure, must result in non-closure. We might also say that the *question* of closure, especially since it is raised at the "end" of the text, produces a *mise-en-abîme*, which is itself non-closure.

Searching for Style

Another way to try to understand the use of the word "style" in the center of the philosopher's scheme would be to view it as a kind of intertextual bait. Especially since the term occurs in conjunction with the concepts of manner and imitation, it seems we are encouraged to look back to an essay Goethe wrote ten years earlier: "Simple Imitation of Nature, Manner, Style." Indeed, in that piece Goethe had already prepared for such a possible future intertextuality: "We will have occasion to recall these pages whenever discussing the visual arts" (III, 72*) ["Wir . . . werden, sooft von bildender Kunst die Rede ist, Gelegenheit haben uns dieser Blätter zu erinnern" (XIII, 69)]. This together with the opening lines of the essay—"It seems advisable to give a clear indication of what we mean by these terms, for we will refer to them frequently" (III, 71) ["Es scheint nicht überflüßig zu sein, genau anzuzeigen, was wir uns bei diesen Worten denken, welche wir öfters brauchen werden" (XIII, 66)]—seems to indicate that the essay is meant to constitute a programmatic statement on the terms of its title. Outwardly the essay does just that. Goethe describes the terms under separate headings and by arranging his text like a dictionary emphasizes the quality of a systematic definition. The systematic quality of the procedure also consists in the notion that the three terms represent a progression from origin to conclusion: one moves from simple imitation through manner and then, given the proper talent and quality of mind, on to the highest degree of art—style. But whereas the definitions of simple imitation and manner contain a sufficient amount of detail to make relatively clear what Goethe means by them, under the rubric of "style" we learn only that if one has gone through the development of imitation and finally mastered manner, then the possibility of achieving the degree called style emerges. The brief "definition" he gives of style turns out not to be a definition at all, but rather only a statement of the foundation of style, and an extraordinarily abstract and nebulous one at that: "Style . . . rests on the most fundamental principle of cognition, on the essence of things—to the extent that it is granted us to perceive this essence in visible and tangible form" (III, 72) ["Der Stil (ruht) auf den tiefsten Grundfesten der Erkenntnis, auf dem Wesen der Dinge, insofern uns erlaubt ist es in sichtbaren und greiflichen Gestalten zu erkennen" (XIII, 68)]. And if we consider that in the preface to the *Theory of Color* Goethe says that "the essence of a thing" (XII, 158*) ["das Wesen eines Dinges" (XVI, 9)] cannot be expressed, then the very possibility of ever defining style would seem to be drawn into question.

At two later points in the essay we read what we might take to be definitions of "style." In discussing the advantages for an imitator of also being a learned botanist, Goethe says that through choosing her*his objects with intelligence and properly portraying their characteristics, this imitator will show us her*his taste, earn our respect, and teach us something. This in turn will mean s*he has achieved "style": "Here we could say that he has formed his own style. But it is also obvious that if such a master were not so conscientious and only concerned with the easy expression of the striking and dazzling, he would soon become a mannerist" (III, 73) ["In diesem Sinne würde man sagen können, er habe sich einen Stil gebildet, da man von der andern Seite leicht einsehen kann, wie ein solcher Meister, wenn er es nicht gar so genau nähme, wenn er nur das Auffallende, Blendende leicht auszudrücken beflissen wäre, gar bald in die Manier übergehen würde" (XIII, 70)]. This only tells us what style is not and is thus a non-definition. Near the end of the piece we read that "Our only concern is to assure the word 'style' a position of the highest honor in order to have available a term to designate the highest level that art has ever reached or can reach" (III, 74) ["Es ist uns bloß angelegen, das Wort Stil in den höchsten Ehren zu halten, damit uns ein Ausdruck übrigbleibe, um den höchsten Grad zu bezeichnen, welchen die Kunst je erreicht hat und je erreichen kann" (XIII, 71)]. This, again, is a non-definition. Nowhere in this essay on style do we learn what style really is; by employing such non-definitions, the text modifies its apparent original enterprise. Thus Goethe has disappointed the expectations he engendered in his readers and has undermined his initially apparent systematic intentions.

(We could, of course, pursue the implications of Goethe's text and generate a definition of "style" in extrapolation from the text. Style is seen as the combination of imitation and manner, of recognizing that which is outside of us, but also understanding it from within us [as the botanist understands the plant and can thus paint it with "style"]. Style would thus be roughly equivalent to the category of "artistic truth" in the final scheme of "The Collector," that is, an ideal combination of object and subject. By thus involving the subject, however, this definition undermines itself as such, since then only the "stylist" her*himself could make a strictly valid assertion concerning the presence or absence of style in her*his work; it would remain unrecognizable to us. Furthermore, in trying to understand that work of art, we would bring our own inner perception to it and then would have changed the work's ideal combination of object and subject.)

Those initially apparent systematic intentions of "Simple Imitation of Nature, Manner, Style" have already been implicitly called into question in the first paragraph of the essay and are not only undermined in the final analysis, but throughout the text. Just after expressing the necessity of defining the terms of the title, Goethe explains why he sees this need: "They have long been in use, and although they seem to have been sufficiently defined in theoretical works, everyone employs them according to his own understanding" (III, 71) ["Denn wenn man sich gleich auch derselben schon lange in Schriften bedient, wenn sie gleich durch theoretische Schriften bestimmt zu sein scheinen, so braucht denn doch jeder sie meistens in einem eignen Sinne" (XIII, 66)]. To my reader this should recall the very similar statement in *Poetry and Truth* concerning Spinoza's system and how such an attitude essentially renders systematic thought impossible. Midway through the 1789 essay Goethe cuts off the systematic progression and arrangement of his definitions and expresses doubt about the very possibility of defining style in the present context: "A more detailed discussion of the above would fill entire volumes" (III, 72*) ["Die Ausführung des oben Gesagten würde ganze Bände einnehmen" (XIII, 68)]. He then says that "the concept itself [style] can be studied only in nature and in works of art" (III, 72) ["der reine Begriff aber ist allein an der Natur und den Kunstwerken zu studieren" (XIII, 69)]. Thus even those "entire volumes" could not possibly define the term. Furthermore, at this point we must begin to wonder whether style can be a valid and employable concept at all. The other concepts—imitation and manner—function systematically because they can be defined, can be seen as sufficiently clear and distinct; style, on the other hand, is portrayed here as a phenomenon that can only be experienced, never defined.

The very next line of the text—"We would like to add a few observations" ["Wir fügen noch einige Betrachtungen hinzu"]—calls our attention, as does the implied reflection here within the text about the process of writing, to the more essayistic quality of what we will now read. The text thus also thematizes the divergence of essayistic writing from systematic discourse. It is in this essayistic context that we then find those non-definitions of style cited above and it is here that the text begins to play more obviously with contradictions. "It is quite obvious that the three ways of producing works of art described here as separate categories are closely related and can sometimes overlap imperceptibly" (III, 72) ["Es läßt sich leicht einsehen, daß diese drei hier voneinander geteilten Arten, Kunstwerke hervorzubringen, genau miteinander verwandt sind, und daß eine in die andere sich zart verlaufen kann" (XIII, 69)]. Here Goethe blatantly contradicts what the "systematic" part of the text had attempted to demonstrate—that "simple imitation," "manner," and "style" represent a progression from the lowest to the highest level of art. That sense of progression is subverted the moment he admits of the possibility of style, the supposed pinnacle of artistic production, running over into simple imitation, the realm of comfortable limitation in art. Later we read that simple imitation can immediately precede style—"Thus simple imitation operates in the vestibule of style" (III, 73) ["Die einfache Nachahmung arbeitet also gleichsam im Vorhofe des Stils" (XIII, 70)]; "manner" has been eliminated from the progression (Goethe reinserts it in the next paragraph!) and, in that through the proper or "ideal" practice of imitation it *becomes* style, we again lose sight of any clear distinction between the terms. The final contradiction comes when Goethe says that he uses the word manner "positively and in a respectful sense" (III, 74) ["in einem hohen und respektablen

Sinne" (XIII, 71)], and this just after he has said that if the mannerist does not strive for faithful imitation of nature on the one hand or style on the other, in other words if s*he does not cease to be a *mannerist*, s*he will distance her*himself from the foundation of art and her*his art will become ever emptier and less meaningful.

"Simple Imitation of Nature, Manner, Style" does on a smaller scale what "The Collector and His Circle" does on a large scale and more complexly. While it makes the obvious gesture of presenting a system, it ultimately undermines that system in the context of essayistic writing. It does not reach a conclusion, but remains open at the end. The last lines reinterpret what was originally designed as a finite, closed treatise as only the beginning of a continuing dialogue: "Merely recognizing this level [style] is a great reward, and discussing it with knowledgeable people a rare pleasure which we trust we will have many opportunities to enjoy in the future" (III, 74*) ["Diesen Grad auch nur erkennen, ist schon eine große Glückseligkeit, und davon sich mit Verständigen unterhalten ein edles Vergnügen, das wir uns in der Folge zu verschaffen manche Gelegenheit finden werden" (XIII, 71)]. By emphasizing the *pleasure* of such open dialogue, Goethe includes one last subtle but damning criticism of the serious business of systems.

* * *

In "The Collector" Goethe implicitly encourages us to embark on intertextual exploration, but then leads us to frustration. The positive effect of that exploration lies in the fact that it forces *us* to perform the act (rather than simply to receive the idea in a relatively passive manner) of breaking the boundaries of his text and breaching the feigned closure of the system it contains. The positive effect of that frustration lies in our consequent realization—a strong realization in that it issues from our own interpretive activity—that hard as we may try we cannot repair the breach in the system's closure. This search itself produces a model of nonclosure. After having recognized the incoherence and inconsistency of the system (in "The Collector"), we look for another system, a context that would solve the problem of the first system. We then recognize the weaknesses of this second system ("Simple Imitation of Nature, Manner, Style") and search for another context that might explain away its problems. This third system (the "text" of our attempt to generate a systematic definition of "style") fails as well, and by this point we can see that an infinite regress has begun. Once it has begun, it can no longer be stopped. In that infinite regress lies fundamental non-closure.

Fritz Mauthner describes systems as a function of human desire: "Order is a human concept. In real nature there is neither order nor the desire for order. There is no order in the human brain either, since it is real nature; but there is certainly a *sense* of order there, a longing to order methodically first the knowledge of a particular discipline and then *all* knowledge, a longing to have everything together in a system" (*Dictionary of Philosophy*, 251). "The Collector" plays with our desire for systematic understanding and its inherent closure. By undermining the system itself from within, within the bounds of the one text, and by then inducing us to enter into a frustrating search for its completion and validation, Goethe achieves a very subtle but very forceful ironization of systematic thought.

Presentation₂

We have seen how the context of the system's presentation— Julie's narration—ironizes the philosopher's scheme. That narration, however, does not account for the context of presentation in its entirety, since it is not Julie, but the philosopher, who composes the system. The first we learn of the collector's young friend is that his newfound devotion to philosophy causes his mentor great consternation and makes communication between them impossible: "And now, to our distress, he has come back a philosopher! He has devoted himself primarily, nay, exclusively to philosophy, and . . . the members of our little circle . . . do not really know what to talk about with him. He is not interested in things we understand, and we do not understand the things he is interested in" (III, 123–24) ["Nun kommt er zu unserer größten Betrübnis als Philosoph zurück. Der Philosophie hat er sich vorzüglich, ja ausschließlich gewidmet und unsere kleine Sozietät . . . ist sämtlich um Unterhaltung mit ihm verlegen; was wir verstehen, interessiert ihn nicht, und was ihn interessiert, verstehen wir nicht" (XIII, 262–63)]. The collector's attitude is less inexplicable if we recall the attitude toward philosophy and its systems disclosed throughout Goethe's autobiography. Within the text of the essay the divergence between the collector's way of understanding the world and the "philosopher's" explains that displeasure. In the first letter the collector had explained his unwillingness to produce for the editors of the *Propyläen* a systematic treatise on art with the statement, "Theory has never been my forte" (III, 122) ["Theorie ist nie meine Sache gewesen" (XIII, 260)], and had instead offered them the benefits of his "experience" and what he has observed. To him, the conceptual abstraction of philosophy seems incapable of explaining the phenomena he has experienced, which can only be known through that experience, through observation. These are the grounds on which he criticizes the philosophy to which his young friend subscribes, a philosophy that gives little or no credence to the validity of outer experience: "What a strange subject philosophy is, especially the new philosophy! Delving into the self, spying on your mind at work, wrapping yourself completely in yourself to understand better what the world is all about!" (III, 124*) ["Was ist das mit der Philosophie und besonders mit der neuen für eine wunderliche Sache! In sich selbst hineinzugehen, seinen eignen Geist über seinen Operationen zu ertappen, sich ganz in sich zu verschließen, um die Gegenstände desto besser kennen zu lernen!" (XIII, 263)]. The explicit connection of this philosophy—of what in its extreme subjectivity constitutes a rejection of the phenomena of the outside world—to systematic thought emerges at the beginning of the third letter, where we learn specifically of those interests of the philosopher that the collector does not understand:

> His main pursuit is ethics, a topic about which I know very little, except what my heart tells me. Some of his scholarly zeal is also directed toward natural law, for

which I see no need because our courts are fair and our
police active. His ultimate goal is constitutional law, a
subject which my uncle ruined for me when I was still
quite young. (III, 130*)

[Die Sittenlehre, von der ich außerhalb meines Herzens
wenig weiß, beschäftigt ihn besonders; das Naturrecht,
das ich nicht vermisse, weil unser Tribunal gerecht und
unsere Polizei tätig ist, verschlingt seine nächsten For-
schungen; das Staatsrecht, das mir in meiner frühesten
Jugend schon durch meinen Oheim verleidet wurde, steht
als das Ziel seiner Aussichten. (XIII, 272)

The common denominator of these interests lies in the fact that
they all represent systems or the attempt to systematize something, for example morals, that the collector holds to function
best without the imposition of an abstract scheme or set of laws.
The collector then implies the incommensurability of such systematic preoccupation with the understanding and appreciation
of art by informing us of the result of his friend's interests: "My
engravings leave him silent, my paintings leave him cold" (III,
130) ["Meine Kupfer lassen ihn stumm, meine Gemälde kalt"
(XIII, 272)].
    The collector's critique of systematic philosophy—that it
looks inward rather than outward for all explanations—suggests
that the "school" referred to is Kantian idealistic philosophy, as
does the phrase "the new philosophy," which was one of the
standard ways of referring to the work of Kant and his followers.
The debate between the philosopher and the characterist in the
sixth letter provides further justification for this view. The philosopher argues that "the human mind" (III, 143*) ["das mensch-
liche Gemüt" (XIII, 293)] is the point at which the effects of all art
are collected and from which its laws flow. The characterist recognizes this standpoint and proceeds to ridicule its proponents, the
new idealistic philosophers: "Ah yes! You and your new breed of
philosophers always want to play according to your own rules.
Of course, it is more convenient to shape the world in accordance
with an idea than to subordinate ideas to things as they are" (III,

143*) ["Ja! ja! es ist die Art der neuen Herren Philosophen alle
Dinge auf ihren eignen Grund und Boden zu spielen, und
bequemer ist es freilich die Welt nach der Idee zu modeln, als seine
Vorstellungen den Dingen zu unterwerfen" (XIII, 293)].[9] The
debate in the sixth letter contains yet another allusion to the
philosopher's Kantianism: the characterist defends "understanding" ["Verstand"] as the ultimate criterion for knowledge of the
world, whereas the philosopher claims that only "reason"
["Vernunft"] can "light our path" (III, 143–44; XIII, 294–95).
The case for seeing the collector's criticism of systematic philosophy as a more-or-less veiled attack on the Kantians receives additional support when we consider Goethe's own reaction to Kant:
"I have critical, idealistic philosophy to thank for drawing my
attention to myself; that is an enormous gain. But it never addresses the object" ["Ich danke der kritischen und idealistischen
Philosophie, daß sie mich auf mich selbst aufmerksam gemacht
hat, das ist ein ungeheurer Gewinn; sie kommt aber nie zum
Objekt"].[10] This blunt remark—especially blunt in following the
ironic, thus questionable, praise—indicates that Goethe, even
thirty years later, held the same view as the collector of Kant and
of the failure of his inwardly turned philosophy to account for the
phenomena we experience.

   We can, then, justifiably see the young friend as a Kantian. A
critique of him as such would already imply a critique of systematic philosophy, but Goethe goes even further to make that
critique explicit. Thus the system with which "The Collector"
culminates would seem to emerge from the context of systematic philosophy, and the young friend has indeed been taken to
be a systematic philosopher at the moment of the system's composition.[11] However, if we consider the process that leads to his
acceptance into the circle of the collector's "little society," it
becomes apparent that his philosophical stance has been undermined and that by the time he composes the system he is no
longer that same philosopher at all.

   It is the debate with the characterist that leads to the young
man's acceptance and participation in the endeavors of the collector and his nieces. The collector himself informs his correspondents of this change before we receive his friend's report of

the debate: "His participation in yesterday's conversation suddenly broke the barriers, and the first signs of a blossoming friendship are beginning to appear" (III, 140) ["Seine Teilnahme an dem gestrigen Gespräch hat auf einmal die Schalen unserer wechselseitigen Entfernung abgestoßen und ein paar hübsche Pflanzen im Garten der Freundschaft zeigen sich" (XIII, 290)]. His participation in the debate is itself the first visible step in the deterioration of his status as systematic philosopher. In his prefatory remarks to the editors he asks them to excuse him for having acted in a manner that contradicts his principle of thoroughness and clarity of understanding: "Last night I interjected myself rather forcefully into a discussion on the visual arts without having much first-hand information on the subject, what knowledge I possess having come from literature" (III, 141) [" . . . daß ich gestern abend mich in ein Gespräch über bildende Kunst lebhaft einmischte, da mir das Anschauen derselben fehlt, und ich nur einige literarische Kenntnisse davon besitze" (XIII, 291)].[12] In closing his report of the debate, the philosopher then admits to Julie that he has undermined himself: "Today I committed a grievous sin. I acted contrary to my principles when I spoke about a subject I had not studied thoroughly" (III, 147) ["Ich habe heute sehr gesündigt, ich handelte gegen meinen Vorsatz, indem ich über eine Materie sprach, die ich nicht ergründet habe" (XIII, 300)]. By jumping into the middle of a debate, by experimenting with thoughts and by writing them down before he knows where they might lead—that is, by abandoning the predictability indispensable to the system—he has acted *essayistically*. It is precisely this aspect of his participation, not so much what he said or the fact that he defended his friend, that the collector appreciates and praises: "He [the collector] was kind enough to praise what I had criticized in myself" (III, 147) ["Er war freundlich genug das an mir zu loben was ich an mir tadelte" (XIII, 300)]. The collector then asks him to join the family in its attempt to classify the types of artists and art lovers, and it is out of this endeavor that his scheme emerges.

The philosopher does not subsequently recover his previous stance on intellectual inquiry. Rather, the systematic foundation of his thought continues to crumble. That he "improvises" (III,

148*; XIII, 301) his scheme and thus composes it in the absence of concentrated and serious theoretical abstraction, belies its seemingly systematic grounding; moreover, he characterizes the scheme as "not very thorough, but at least amusing" (III, 148) ["nicht gründlich, doch wenigstens lustig" (XIII, 301)]. The young friend himself recognizes his continued "degeneration"—"I don't know what it is these days that causes me to make one mistake after another" (III, 149) ["Ich weiß nicht, was mich diese Tage von einem Fehler zum andern verleitet" (XIII, 303)]—as well as the divergence of what he has produced from what he could justifiably call a theory. As a result of his recent actions and the radical change they reveal in the nature of his thought, he requests that he no longer be called a philosopher (III, 149; XIII, 302). We have to agree with him—he is no longer what he was.

By undermining this representative of systematic thought, the essay has set the stage for undermining systematic thought itself. When we read the "philosopher's" claims for his system—that it is complete and presents the means by which "true" art is achieved—we should already know better than to accept those claims at face value. Coming as they do from this *ex*–systematic philosopher, they must be viewed ironically. In that the systematic context for the production of the scheme has been undermined, and in that the system is then nonetheless presented straightforwardly *as a system* (at least on the surface of the text, where the "philosopher's" qualms are quickly forgotten, even suppressed), that presentation once again proves to be ironic.

The Irony of Truth

Whatever perspective we take, the system in which "The Collector and His Circle" culminates is undermined. Both aspects of its presentation—the young man's composition and Julie's report—are determined by a high level of irony, as is the system itself. What we face in the essay, however, is not merely the ironization of one particular system, but an implied attempt to undermine systematic thought as such. Because this particular system thematizes systems in general by employing "truth" and "completion" as two of its central terms, undermining the specific system has the effect of undermining those central concepts and their supposed attainability through conceptual argumentation and formulation, and thus the effect of subverting the validity of all systems. This subversion is repeated, and thus emphasized, in the arguments that lead up to the final tabular scheme. In the description of the categories of artistic bias we find a further thematization of the systematic consciousness. We learn of the characterists' "method of abstracting, of reducing matters to concepts" ["Abstraktion, ihre Reduktion auf Begriffe"] and of their "merely logical existence" ["bloß logisches Dasein"] (III, 156*; XIII, 314–15); in that these are portrayed as some of this type's main qualities, we can easily draw the connection to systematic thought, which operates on the basis of abstraction and requires clear and distinct concepts and logical form. We must then recall that this type represents an unhealthy one-sidedness that as such can never achieve the ultimate goals of art. And if we recall that those goals include "truth" and "completion" and that reaching the pinnacle, achieving "style," means becoming a "true" artist, we can formulate the implication as a statement that the systematic approach can never lead to truth and completion. Since truth and completion are the reason for the existence of systems, the pretense of systematic thought to achieving those goals is revealed as a delusion. We can then discern further irony in the essay. Not only is the system ironized from without and within, but its final goal—truth—is ironized both in this specific instance and in general. By revealing an ironic attitude toward truth vis-à-vis the system's belief in the achievability of truth through its formulation, the essay itself stresses its incommensurability with systematic thought.[13] By thematizing systems and systematic thought in general and then subverting them, the essay questions the very grounds of their possibility.

Metatext

Irony pervades "The Collector and His Circle." Beyond the ironies of presentation and the inner irony of the system itself we
find a more general irony in the essay as a whole, a textual irony,
which resides in the subversive relationship of implicit to explicit
statement, of latent to manifest discourse. It is in addressing this
fundamental irony in Goethe's text, these fundamental discrepan-
cies, that one recognizes the affinity of Goethe's textual strategies, his textual "work," to the work of deconstruction.[14]

Turn-Styles

Incommensurate levels of signification draw into question the
possibility of the system in Goethe's essay. In her introduction to
Derrida's *Dissemination* Barbara Johnson describes the critical
process of deconstruction as "a form of what has long been
called a *critique*. A critique of any theoretical system is not an
examination of its flaws or imperfections. It is not a set of
criticisms designed to make the system better. It is an analysis
that focuses on the grounds of that system's possibility" (*Dissemination*, xv). Uncovering flaws and imperfections in Goethe's text has not been an end in itself, but rather a means of
approaching a more acute insight into the operation of Goethe's
text, a means of performing what Johnson describes as the "careful teasing out of warring forces of signification *within the text*

itself," which "signifies in more than one way, and to varying
degrees of explicitness" (xiv). She goes on to describe how dis-
crepancies in levels of signification such as those we have traced
in Goethe's essay can often be produced "by a double-edged
word, which serves as a hinge that both articulates and breaks
open the explicit statement being made" (xiv–xv). The aspect of
Goethe's text that most forcefully reveals the warring forces of
signification is just such a double-edged word: "style."

What renders the use of the word "style" in Goethe's essay
especially significant is not simply the discrepancy between its
apparent, explicit articulation of the system's goal and its actual inability to do so, nor its implicit breach of the system's
closure. Other terms perform a similar task—"phantomists" as
a replacement for "imaginers," "imitators" under the heading
of "manner," "completion" as a synthesis of "miniaturists"
and "sketchers." The deconstructive force of "style" lies in the
position it assumes at the *center* of the system. In "Structure,
Sign and Play in the Discourse of the Human Sciences" Derrida
examines the traditional function of the "center" in systematic
structures. He argues that the structurality of structure "has
always been neutralized or reduced, and this by a process of
giving it a center" (278) and that the main function of the
center has been "to make sure that the organizing principle of
the structure would limit what we might call the *play* of the
structure" (278). A certain confusion arises in the reader when
s*he sees the next sentence—"By orienting and organizing the
coherence of the system, the center of a structure permits the
play of its elements inside the total form" (278–79)—and then
again—"Nevertheless, the center also closes off the play which
it opens up and makes possible. . . . At the center, the permuta-
tion or the transformation of elements . . . is forbidden" (279).
In order to understand the notion of structures that are not
structural and of play that restricts play, we must see that two
notions of structure, two notions of play are in operation. The
traditional structure, the structure organized and made coherent by a center—the system—lacks the ability, because it is
frozen by that center and its need for certitude, to realize the
possibilities of its own form; its play is not play because that

same drive for certainty and immutability restricts play to such a degree that it is no longer recognizable as such. By threatening certitude and thus closure, play, in the more general sense, threatens the coherence of the system; for this reason, play is "allowed" in the centered structure only within the structure's own strict boundaries and thus only in a *re*stricted sense. The "play" of the centered structure thus bears a resemblance to the supposed openness of "open" systems, which are open only to the extent that they claim the power to maintain their closure despite contrary evidence outside themselves. This kind of play and this kind of openness thus represent an extremely restricted (and non-essential) mobility and shifting, rather than the possibility of *change*. "The concept of centered structure is in fact the concept of a play based on a fundamental ground, a play constituted on the basis of a fundamental immobility and a reassuring certitude, which itself is beyond the reach of play" (279).

We now recall that the main headings of the system at the end of "The Collector" are "seriousness" and "play," separate and in conjunction, but that the culmination of Goethe's essay does not advocate play *alone* (for play cannot exist in the complete absence of structure). We can then see that Goethe has introduced into that system yet another element that problematizes it, since the system, on one level, is designed to show the necessity of play, and this play necessarily interferes with the ostensibly systematic structure.[15] The play of the system consists in the mobility that results from its various logical and conceptual shortcomings—it is the play of irony. And this play cannot be separated from the seriousness, the playful seriousness that lies in the system's self-reflexivity, in the way it calls attention to itself *as* system and undermines itself, that is, in the implied statement about systems as such.[16]

Derrida associates the center with a "full presence which is beyond play" and proceeds to discuss the effects of "decentering," of the *absence* of the center *qua* center. In addition to undermining certitude, the absence of the center, of the "transcendental signified," "extends the domain and the play of signification infinitely" (280). In terms of systems this would

mean the breach of closure and the resulting open-endedness of
discourse. The locus in history of this decentering, we learn, is
represented by critiques of traditional realms of systematic
thought, of areas of thought that operate on the basis of centered structure: "the Nietzschean critique of metaphysics, the
critique of the concepts of Being and truth, for which were
substituted the concepts of play, interpretation, and sign (sign
without present truth); the Freudian critique of self-presence,
that is, the critique of consciousness, of the subject, of self-
identity and of self-proximity or self-possession; and, more radi-
cally, the Heideggerean destruction of metaphysics, of onto-
theology, of the determination of Being as presence" (280).
Goethe would find good company here, since he criticizes not
just an area of thought determined by centered structures, but
rather those centered structures themselves, systematic thought
as such. Moreover, Goethe performs this critique *by means of a
decentering*. The non-definition and incomprehensibility of
"style" within the context of the system and the essay, and also
in the context of its intertextual allusion, decenters that system
by rendering its center effectively *absent*. To be more specific,
the center is absent in its function as a systematic element; it
remains present, however, insofar as it fulfills an apparently
indispensable communicative function in the discussion and understanding of art. The immediate consequences of this "absenting" are the subversion of the system's certitude and the breach
of its closure. The absence of the center extends the domain of
signification beyond the immediate text to an essay written ten
years earlier; its absence *there* then extends that domain into
unknown territory, perhaps infinity. We might then also see the
numerous instances of irony in the text, because they prob-
lematize the seemingly authoritative signification of the system,
as an extension (perhaps infinite) of the play of signification.[17]

    We might now take yet another approach to "style," might
attempt once more to discover a way in which it functions as
something other than a moment of subversion. The intertextual
search for a definition of style that would heal the wound it
created in the structure of the system and the closure of the text
proved futile; if anything, the search aggravated the wound. But

one might object that the search was misguided to begin with, that the desire to find a definition of style blinded us to the possibility that style is not something that can be defined in the same way that other constituent concepts in the system can be defined: we might see style as a concept that cannot operate in isolation as such, but only in the process of a text, whether verbal or visual. Since every text necessarily has a style, we might then say that in "The Collector" "style" is *in effect* defined in that it is *at work* throughout the text. There is already slippage here, however. Understanding style in this way would mean granting it a conceptual status and systematic function separate from the other terms of the system; in other words, this difference would force us to discern yet another rupture in the system. Furthermore, we would be extending the domain of the term's application to the entire text of "The Collector" and thus separating it, at least in part, from its function within the systematic structure of the philosopher's scheme at the end of the text. And even if we were to allow this extension in order then to be able to explain the concept within the bounds of the system, we would encounter a problem that arises for that system as a result of the subsequent attempt to describe what the style of the text is. In that this style can be characterized as primarily *dialogic*—more on this in Part Two—we would have to acknowledge once again that the system is undermined. Placing dialogism at the center has the effect of subverting its quality *as center,* inasmuch as the presence of at least two equally privileged elements eliminates the possibility of a center by dis-integrating its requisite unity. Again, the ostensible center renders itself absent *as such.* The breach of closure in the system, and in Goethe's text, survives.

"Style" is the hinge that breaks open the text, that provides ingress and egress, that allows movement between texts. It is a textual turnstile in that it makes *and* breaks the system: from the center, "style" both structures the boundaries of the text *and* opens them.

* * *

Goethe's ironic, essayistic treatment of systematic thought and discourse is not restricted to "The Collector" and "Simple Imitation of Nature, Manner, Style." For example, we find at least one fairly obvious instance of and perhaps a precedent for his play with centers and their absence in the early piece, "Shakespeare: A Tribute" ["Zum Schäkespears Tag"] (1771).[18] The text contains a number of passages that can be seen to refer to important concerns of essayistic writing: the opposition to systems implied in the criticism of French neoclassical drama; the unwillingness to formulate thoughts in systematic order—"Do not expect me to write much or in an orderly way" (III, 163) ["Erwarten Sie nicht, das (*sic*) ich viel und ordentlich schreibe" (IV, 122)]; the sense of the necessary incompletion of and the indeterminacy of the boundaries of writing—"Now let me finish—though I haven't even started yet" (III, 165) ["Und nun zum Schluss, ob ich gleich noch nicht angefangen habe" (IV, 125)]; and the conviction that "no one attains the goal he has so ardently sought" (III, 163) ["dass keiner sein Ziel erreicht" (IV, 122)]. More striking than these aspects of the essay, however, is the famous statement on the essence of Shakespeare's plays: "Each [of his plays] revolves around the secret point |: which no philosopher has discovered or defined :| where the characteristic quality of our being, the pretended freedom of our will, collides with the necessary course of the whole" (III, 165*) ["Seine Stücke, drehen sich alle um den geheimen Punckt, |: den noch kein Philosoph gesehen und bestimmt hat :| in dem das Eigenthümliche unsres Ich's, die prätendirte Freyheit unsres Wollens, mit dem nothwendigen Gang des Ganzen zusammenstösst" (IV, 124)]. In the terms of my study, what these lines convey is that the *center* of our existence in the world is unnameable and undiscoverable. In that it is a secret especially to the philosophers (whom Goethe, as we have seen, identifies as systematizers), the center would be effectively absent for the purposes of any attempt to formulate the system of that existence. Since the center, as a systematic element, is absent, no such system can be devised or articulated. (We might even see the notion of system inscribed in the way Goethe draws special attention to the philosophers' inability to gain access to the secret point: rather than using the usual sign for parentheses, which we would not notice, he uses the "punctuation" of one of the most systematic of all "languages"—music. In addition, he uses "punctuation marks" that dictate repetition for the sake of emphasis.)

Montaigne's Center

"Structure, Sign and Play" also gives us cause to return, at least momentarily, to a more general discussion of the essay genre. Not only does Derrida's text, in conjunction with Goethe's, reinforce the essay's opposition to systematic thought by way of showing the function of centers and their absence, it also brings up additional notions closely related to the genre and even reveals an admiration for the essay by invoking the "authority" of some of the great essayists.

Derrida discusses Lévi-Strauss's "search for a new status of discourse" and its "stated abandonment of all reference to a *center,* to a *subject,* to a privileged *reference,* to an origin, or to an absolute *archia*" (286). He then ties this project into Lévi-Strauss's belief that it is necessary to forgo "scientific or philosophical discourse, to renounce the *episteme* which absolutely requires . . . that we go back to the source, to the center, to the founding basis" (286). The affinity to the essay of this rejection of the operations of systematic discourse lies not only in the basic opposition to systems, but also in what their dependence on the center implies. The center can also be called "the origin or end, *archē* or *telos*" (279). With the displacement, the absenting of the center, the archeological and teleological aspects of systematic discourse are dispelled, and we are faced with writing that does not claim to go back to an absolute beginning or origin, nor to reach a final conclusion or end, or, to quote Adorno on the essay, writing that starts where it wants and finishes where it feels itself at a loss to go further. In Goethe's essay we hear an echo of this attitude toward thought and writing (here on the topic of art) when the collector subtly warns the editors not to make the mistake of striving for "the ultimate" ["das Vollkommenste"] and attempting to discover "the source" ["die Quelle"] (III, 133*; XIII, 278).[19]

If we consider two of the historical instances of decentering Derrida cites, the affinity to the essay of the writing he advocates becomes clear. In addition to the significance of what they wrote about, of the critiques themselves, Nietzsche and Freud distinguished themselves through the *process* of their writing, through the *way* they composed their critiques, through their essayistic writing. (Indeed, their achievements in this area receive attention in most studies of the genre and their essays are considered sufficiently exemplary to be included in anthologies.[20]) But Derrida also draws a much more direct connection to the essay by choosing an epigraph for his text—"We need to interpret interpretation more than to interpret things"—from *Montaigne*. He thus accords essayistic writing a textually privileged position, the position of pre-scription. Furthermore, the content of Montaigne's statement not only reflects Derrida's focus on *critique de la critique,* but also ties Montaigne into the decentering activity that is Derrida's main concern here. Montaigne had planned his essays as a frame that would surround the posthumous publication of a text written by his close friend, Etienne de La Boétie. The text—*La servitude volontaire*—was controversial and before Montaigne could carry out his project, opposing forces managed to publish the work in a context that would serve their condemnatory purpose. As a result, the center of his enterprise vanished, and it was this "decentering" that, at least in one sense, brought about what we know as the Montaignean essay, the deep self-probing and the advocacy of interpreting interpretations.[21]

It would be tempting to conclude from this aspect of Montaigne's work that the absence of the center is an originary moment and thus a determining characteristic of all essayistic writing. Inasmuch as the essay genre opposes systematic thought and discourse, we could say that there must always be some kind of decentering at work in its texts, that the "absence" of the center is somehow always implied. To explicate this implication, of course, would then require individual textual analysis. But to treat it as an absolutely privileged characteristic because it has been discovered at the assumed inception, birth, origin of the genre would be to attribute primacy to an aspect that is one of many interrelated aspects. It would also mean *re*-placing the center that we have just recognized as *dis*-placed and thus reinforcing the tradition of origin-orientation, of logocentrism, that the essay challenges.

Intertext

Intertextual exploration aided us in our attempt to understand the implications of Goethe's use of the term "style." "The Collector and His Circle" provides us with a further intertextual allusion that, in more general terms, gives a background for Goethe's own manipulation and rejection of systematic thought, and more specifically, shows that Goethe perhaps sensed a similar means of such rejection, a similar decentering gesture, in what he considered the most important critical text of his age: Lessing's *Laocoön: An Essay on the Limits of Painting and Poetry* [*Laokoon oder über die Grenzen der Malerei und Poesie*]. Goethe's essay does not name Lessing's text, but does refer to it with what approaches explicitness when the characterist, in his conversation with the collector, first condemns Lessing for his exaggerated concentration on the Greek ideal of beauty and then, in his argument against treating beauty as the goal of Greek art, uses the Laocoön group as his primary example (III, 139; XIII, 287–88). In his debate with the characterist, who is portrayed as the systematic thinker par excellence in that he reduces everything to concepts and is a merely logical being, the "philosopher" of Goethe's essay derives his points about the visual arts from his knowledge of ancient poetry, which reminds us of Lessing's attempts to explain the Laocoön group by referring to Virgil and Sophocles. And while the characterist brushes aside the notion of beauty with a reductive etymological definition of the word, those who depend on beauty for their understanding of art—the collector and his young friend—never come close to defining the term; challenged by the characterist, the collector even declares his inability to do so: "Can you tell me what beauty is? he exclaimed. Perhaps not! I said, but I can show you beauty" (III, 138*) ["Können Sie mir sagen was Schönheit sei? rief er aus. Vielleicht nicht! versetzte ich, aber ich kann es Ihnen zeigen" (XIII, 286)]. This again recalls Lessing's work, where the crucial notion of beauty is never defined ("I wanted simply to establish that among the ancients beauty was the supreme law of the visual arts" ["Ich wollte bloß festsetzen, daß bei den Alten die Schönheit das höchste Gesetz der bildenden Künste gewesen sei"]).[22]

Lessing presents his study of the boundaries of painting and poetry as an anti-systematic enterprise when he describes his strategy as one that will diverge from that of systematic argumentation. In his preface he calls the chapters that will follow "essays"—"Aufsätze"—and claims that they neither emerged in the context of a systematic endeavor nor unite to constitute a system: "They were written as chance dictated and more in keeping with the sequence of my reading than through any systematic development of general principles. Hence they are to be regarded more as unordered notes for a book than as a book itself" (5*) ["Sie sind zufälliger Weise entstanden, und mehr nach der Folge meiner Lektüre, als durch die methodische Entwickelung allgemeiner Grundsätze angewachsen. Es sind also mehr unordentliche Collectanea zu einem Buche, als ein Buch" (VI, 11)]. This image of a disorderly collection of thoughts that proceeds without a particular goal in mind evokes the meandering, open-ended quality of the essay. Lessing repeats his essayistic gesture in the first chapter when, after quoting a passage from Winckelmann, he declares that his investigations will start from this point and follow the process of the developing order of his ideas (8*; VI, 13). We cannot help but recall Adorno's description of the essay: "It does not begin with Adam and Eve but with what it wants to discuss; it says what is at issue and stops where it feels itself at a loss to go further—not where nothing is left to say." That Lessing perceives the divergence of this essayistic consciousness from that of the systematic thinker becomes clear when he follows his first statement on the way he will proceed with the remark, "We Germans suffer from no lack of systematic books" (5) ["An systematischen Büchern haben wir Deutschen überhaupt keinen Mangel" (VI, 11)], and places such books in direct opposition to his own writing. He then reinforces this opposition when he says that his reasoning may not be as logical or conclusive as that of a Wolffian thinker like Baumgarten. That he opposes Baumgarten by invoking the notion of "the source" ["Quelle"]—"My examples will at least smack more of the source" (5) ["so werden doch meine Beispiele mehr nach der Quelle schmecken" (VI, 11)]—does not negate that opposition; "source" in this context does not mean "origin" and thus imply the systematic consciousness, but rather is used in the sense of close textual analysis, of attention to the object as opposed to a sole concern for the subject's organizing consciousness. Lessing goes on to tell us that his collection of essays will contain a number of reflections that have nothing to do with his main point and that therefore, we must conclude, necessarily demonstrate the impossibility of considering his study a system. Our first and strongest impression of *Laocoön* is thus its essayistic rejection of systematic thought.

Our first suspicion about these anti-systematic gestures arises when we realize that they seem to be concentrated in his preface and therefore might be nothing more than a posture the author assumes. On consideration of the genesis and the structure of the text, it becomes apparent that his main essayistic gesture, his emphasis on the meandering process of his writing, is a fiction. Lessing composed several drafts of his text before it went into print; the first two drafts reveal a plan to write what would have amounted to a systematic, deductive study. As a result, our trust in the claim that *Laocoön* did not emerge from a "systematic development of general principles" is shaken and the fact that the Winckelmannian framework was not introduced until later leads to the conclusion that Lessing did *not* just read Winckelmann's work and then sit down to write *Laocoön*. In other words, his essays did not follow the course of his reading.

The discussion of Winckelmann's *History of Ancient Art* [*Geschichte der Kunst des Altertums*] is designed to support the claim that Lessing wrote down his thoughts in the order in which they developed. But the discussion fails to provide such support, for it contains yet another fiction—one that reinforces the conclusion that Lessing created a fiction in the preface. At the end of chapter 19 we read: "But I shall spare myself the trouble of collecting my scattered observations on a point which I hope to find fully treated in the art history which Mr. Winckelmann has promised us" (103*) ["Doch ich entlasse mich der Mühe, meine zerstreuten Anmerkungen über einen Punkt zu sammeln, über welchen ich in des Herrn Winckelmanns versprochener Geschichte der Kunst die völligste Befriedigung zu erhalten hoffen darf" (VI, 129)]. Chapter 26 then begins with the words, "Mr. Winckelmann's *History of Ancient Art* has appeared" (138*) ["Des Herrn Winckelmanns Geschichte der Kunst des Altertums ist erschienen" (VI, 166)]. Lessing, however, was familiar with the *History,* which appeared in 1763, long before *Laocoön* went into print. And in the context of just having read and responding to the *History* Lessing discusses points—such as Winckelmann's use of the term "parenthyrsos"—that actually refer to arguments in Winckelmann's earlier text, *Thoughts on the Imitation of Greek Works in Painting and Sculpture* [*Gedanken über die Nachahmung der griechischen Werke in der Malerei und Bildhauerkunst*]. Thus, again, *Laocoön* is *not* composed according to the sequence of Lessing's readings.

That the apparently anti-systematic strategy of not writing according to a strictly logical method proves to be a fiction does not mean that the strategy that "remains" is a systematic one. The care Lessing took to establish these elaborate fictions, to inscribe them in his text over the course of many chapters, points rather to the great degree of attention he paid to questions of textual strategy. Such concern with strategy makes it impossible for the reader, even when s*he has recognized the fictional quality of the anti-systematic gesture, to disregard the process of the text, to abstract from the form of the text some systematic argument as its "core." Those fictions resist, as such, any attempt to read *Laocoön* as a systematic treatise.

One could, perhaps, read Lessing's compositional fictions conversely and claim that his insistence on a kind of writing that follows the "natural" order of ideas from beginning to end, and that introduces new ideas only as they become possible in the course of investigation, is evidence of a basic systematic, an archeo-teleological impulse—of a desire to "begin with Adam and Eve and stop where nothing is left to say." From this perspective, the undermining of Lessing's systematic strategy would be apparent as soon as the declaration of an intention to write in such an archeo-teleological way reveals itself as a fiction. Regardless, therefore, of how we interpret these fictions, they constitute a rhetorical strategy that renders it impossible to see the text as a systematic presentation of a systematic differentiation of the arts.[23]

But only if we disregard chapter 16. It is here, at the midway point of his study, that Lessing presents his main argument on the fundamental differentiation of visual and literary art. By thus giving his work a center and creating a sense of symmetry and balance, he seems to belie the initial impression of essayistic exploration, experimentation, and disjointedness. This centering gesture is particularly surprising after we have just discovered the playful subversion of the apparently archeo-teleological orientation of his writing.

Chapter 16 begins with the statement, "But I shall attempt now to derive the matter from its first principles" (78) ["Doch ich will versuchen, die Sache aus ihren ersten Gründen herzuleiten" (VI, 102)]. "Derive" introduces the language of the system (continued in the repeated use of the word "accordingly" [*folglich*]) as well as the systematic endeavor of definition and differentiation that follows. Furthermore, the notion of explaining the differentiation "from its first principles" reveals an "archeological" intention, a desire to make the origin present, that would achieve the centered structure's interdiction of play. The crucial distinction—the description of poetry as the realm of "action" [*Handlung*]—then implies the other centering aspect of this chapter: an "action" is a movement toward an end or goal, and thus a teleological concept. Lessing had made this point already in his "On the Essence of the Fable" ["Von dem Wesen der Fabel"] of 1759: "I call an *action a sequence of changes, which together constitute a whole. This unity of the whole is founded on the coming together of all parts for an ultimate goal"* ["*Eine Handlung* nenne ich, *eine Folge von Veränderungen, die zusammen Ein Ganzes ausmachen.* Diese *Einheit des Ganzen* beruhet auf der *Übereinstimmung aller Teile zu einem Endzwecke*" (V, 367)]. Chapter 16 therefore not only introduces systematic thought into Lessing's text, but also emphasizes this new aspect by *thematizing* the operation of systems.

It is this ostensibly systematic quality of *Laocoön* on which critics have concentrated and that has led to the work's acquisition of the status of a treatise. This would undermine the significance I attribute to Goethe's allusion to Lessing's text in "The Collector." But already in recognizing the fictionality of Lessing's essayistic gesture we must wonder why he would make such a false gesture if he had already composed the arguments of *Laocoön,* in the drafts, in a systematic fashion. And once we have seen systematic thought *thematized,* we must also begin to suspect a simultaneous divergence from such thought, since in order to thematize a form of thought or discourse—especially when, as in *Laocoön,* it stands in such stark contrast to the rest of the text—one must stand at some distance from it. Further investigation of the "central" argument of chapter 16 shows that Goethe's intertextual allusion *is* appropriate in the context of essayistic, de-systematizing writing.

Our doubts about the systematic project of chapter 16, already awakened by the divergence implied in thematization, increase when we examine Lessing's use of the systematic word "action." In one of the earliest drafts we read: "Imitating signs *that follow one another* can express only objects or parts of objects that follow one another. Such objects are called *actions.* Accordingly, actions are the true subject of *poetry*" ["*Nachahmende Zeichen auf einander* können auch nur Gegenstände ausdrücken, die auf einander, oder deren Teile auf einander folgen. Solche Gegenstände heißen überhaupt *Handlungen.* Folglich sind Handlungen der eigentliche Gegenstand der *Poesie*" (VI, 565)]. Moses Mendelssohn, in his comments on the draft, objected strenuously to Lessing's use of the word "action" and pointed out that what

Lessing "really meant to say" was "movement" ["Bewegung" (VI, 565)]. As it turns out, this *is* what Lessing really meant to say; he realized his mistake and in the next draft we then read: "Poetry depicts movements and, by suggestion through movements, bodies" ["Die Poesie schildert Bewegungen, und andeutungs Weise durch Bewegungen, Körper" (VI, 594)]. That Lessing understood why Mendelssohn objected becomes clear when he explains the fundamental difference between the two terms by referring to the teleological character of "action." Mendelssohn had not provided this explanation, but Lessing only had to think back to his 1759 study of the fable, and he recalls the earlier definition of action when he writes, "A series of movements that aims at an ultimate goal is called an *action*" ["Eine Reihe von Bewegungen, die auf einen Endzweck abzielen, heißet eine *Handlung*" (VI, 594)]. This correction did not interfere with his argument, since he was able to incorporate it without difficulty by then differentiating between "simple actions" ["einfachen Handlungen"], which are the business of poetry, and the "collective actions" ["kollektiven Handlungen"] that painting employs (VI, 594). But when we then look at the final version of the study, we are more than a little astonished to read that "objects or parts of objects which follow one another are called actions. Accordingly, actions are the true subject of poetry" (78*) ["Gegenstände, die auf einander, oder deren Teile auf einander folgen, heißen überhaupt Handlungen. Folglich sind Handlungen der eigentliche Gegenstand der Poesie" (VI, 103)]. Here, at the center of his argument, Lessing places a concept—moreover a concept that evokes the very notion of the center—that he knows is questionable in this context. The center disappears, since as a result of its instability it can no longer function as a central element that would anchor the system; the center is rendered absent, insofar as it can no longer support the coherence and stability of the systematic structure. By thus decentering an apparently centered structure Lessing undermines the systematic quality of his study. As in "The Collector," that which ostensibly creates the coherence of the system *at the same time* ironizes it; like "style," "action" functions as a double-edged word.

We could describe Lessing's textual strategy as one of double reversal. First the stated anti-systematic intention is reversed by the systematics of chapter 16, but then that reversal is reversed, and we realize that the piece is anti-systematic after all. Lessing first makes the essayistic gesture of writing according to the as yet undeterminable sequence of his thoughts and reading; this gesture is cancelled both by the discovery that it is a fiction and by the systematic symmetry and closure we discern in chapter 16. We then discover, however, that systematic coherence does not come about, that the piece does not come to a conclusion (also since the planned second part is missing) and that the fictionality itself is in a sense annulled—insofar as the text does not demonstrate the logical linearity of movement from *archē* to *telos*.

Lessing's textual strategy has a subversive effect on the supposed theoretical goal of his text. Since "action," now recognized as a questionable concept or at least a questionably employed concept, takes the position of the center of the project of differentiating painting and poetry, this center—that is, the differentiation itself—becomes questionable. Put another way, Lessing's play with systematic structures is at the same time a play with what is, after all, the systematic quality of a strict differentiation—a playful subversion of the explicit goal of his text.

That we can expose Lessing's statement on the way he will write as a fiction does not mean that the essayistic foundation of and impetus for that statement is a fiction. By building extreme slippage into the center of his study, Lessing opens up the text to the structurality of structure, to the essayistic play of the process and form of writing. As in "The Collector," systematic discourse itself becomes the object of essayistic play.

*   *   *

Laocoön proceeds from an explicit anti-systematic stance to the manifest centrality, certitude, and closure of a system and then on to implicit ironization of that system. This process is mirrored in "The Collector and His Circle"; we can see the reflection by looking back at the collector's statement in the first letter that "theory has never been my forte" and considering its implications for the essay as a whole. The collector's remark echoes Goethe's own attitude toward theory, which in its identity with philosophy he saw as superfluous, in that whatever theory we might need is already completely contained within religion and poetry (IV, 171; X, 245). "All theorizing," he says in *Poetry and Truth,* "is an indication either that one's creative powers are deficient or that they are at a standstill" (IV, 398) ["Alles Theoretisieren (deutet) auf Mangel oder Stockung von Produktionskraft hin" (X, 590)]. In the *Theory of Color,* however, he comments on the *unavoidability* of theorizing: "Merely glancing at a thing gets us nowhere. Looking at an object inevitably merges into contemplation, contemplation into reflection, reflection into association, and so one can say that with every attentive gaze into the world we are already theorizing" (XII, 159*) ["Denn das bloße Anblicken einer Sache kann uns nicht fördern. Jedes Ansehen geht über in ein Betrachten, jedes Betrachten in ein Sinnen, jedes Sinnen in ein Verknüpfen, und so kann man sagen, daß wir schon bei jedem aufmerksamen Blick in die Welt theoretisieren" (XVI, 11)]. When he does declare an intention to theorize, in the "Announcement of the *Propylaea*" ["Anzeige der Propyläen"], he is careful to distinguish his project from what one would normally assume to find under the heading of "theory":

> Turning now from description to theory, we must first explain that we do not take theory in the strict sense demanded by the philosopher. In everyone who is capable of thinking about what he does something general gradually takes root, something that has helped or hindered him. In this way principles emerge; we could call these principles, as it were, the beliefs of the artist, which he follows and which he wishes others might follow.

> [Wenn wir nun auch von der Darstellung zur Theorie übergehen, so müssen wir vorerst erklären, daß wir Theorie nicht in dem Sinne nehmen, wie sie der Philosoph auf strenge Weise aufzustellen verlangt. Jeder, der über das Geschäfte, das er treibt, zu denken fähig ist,

setzt bei sich nach und nach etwas Allgemeines fest, wo-
durch er sich gefördert oder gehindert gefunden hat; so
entstehen Grundsätze, die gewißermaßen Konfessionen
des Künstlers genannt werden können, wornach er sich
richtet, und wornach er wünscht, daß andere sich richten
mögen. (XIII, 195)]

In *The World, the Text, and the Critic,* Edward Said discusses a
traditional opposition between the study of literature as that of
"aesthetic instances of every variety of experience" and theory
as that which is "associated with abstraction and ideas."[24] It is
this dichotomy of experience and abstraction that operates in
the "Introduction to the *Propylaea,*" where Goethe advocates a
different kind of theory, like that mentioned in the "Announcement," that does not function through abstraction, but rather
through observation. He first criticizes theory and its inability to
lead to a general understanding of art, and then proposes that
"principles for the education of the artist" (III, 86*; XIII, 150)
emerge from the observation of works of art themselves. In
other words, the theory of the systematic philosopher remains
fruitless, and if there is to be any theory at all it should be a
modified notion of theory, a theory that arises out of experience.
The theory that the collector rejects is the first kind, in place of
which he offers the insights gained through his experience and
observation of art.[25]

"The Collector and His Circle" proceeds on the basis of this
notion of the greater validity of experience. The collector composes his typology from what he has observed in his family, in his
collection, and in the visitors to the collection. Once the scheme is
completed, however, it acquires at least a quality of conceptual
abstraction. Perhaps in recognition of this danger, the collector
quickly ironizes it by speaking of his "curious classifications."
This treatment of that which has become or threatens to become
hypostatized as a theory is in line with Goethe's statement in the
Theory of Color on how we should approach the theorizing in
which we inevitably find ourselves involved whenever we observe
phenomena: "If the abstraction we fear . . . is to be rendered
harmless, then we will have to be able to do this [theorize] con-

sciously, with self-knowledge, freely, and (if I may venture to put it so) *with irony*" (XII, 159*; my emphasis) ["Dieses (theoretisieren) aber mit Bewußtsein, mit Selbstkenntnis, mit Freiheit, und um uns eines gewagten Wortes zu bedienen, *mit Ironie* zu tun und vorzunehmen, eine solche Gewandtheit ist nötig, wenn die Abstraktion, vor der wir uns fürchten, unschädlich . . . werden soll" (XVI, 11; my emphasis)]. The experiential, observational attitude continues to determine the thoughts on art and art lovers in "The Collector" and is even the initial basis of the philosopher's categorization. But the moment that categorization is produced, a scheme arises that, in its establishment of interrelationships, its projection of syntheses, and its use of notions such as "artistic truth," "beauty," and "completion," reveals that the text—in the voice of the "philosopher"—has succumbed to conceptual, theoretical (in the derogatory sense) abstraction. However, as we have seen, the rhetorical strategies of the text—the context of this system's presentation and its structural ironies— deconstruct the system. As in *Laocoön*, we find a movement from explicit anti-systematic (that is, anti-theoretical) intention to system (theory) and then on to implicit ironization of the system.[26] Thus, on the level of the essay's process, we gain insight again into how systems become the object of play.

Reader-Text

In order to formulate the ironization of systems in Goethe's and Lessing's texts—that is, to make (logical) sense of the texts' performances, to make them clear—it is necessary to participate, at least to some extent, in the kind of systematic discourse those texts undermine. Readings of the texts that articulate their critiques of system, making them explicit, thus succumb to the complicity Derrida says cannot be avoided.

Texts like "The Collector and His Circle," however, seem to escape such complicity, precisely because their critiques are *not* explicit, but rather occur in the texts' rhetorical strategies, in their self-deconstruction. Through its blatant, but ironized, participation in systematic discourse, "The Collector" effects the deconstruction of that discourse. That is, by operating through explicit complicity, the essay seems to avoid successfully the final paradox of critical complicity. (It is tempting to make the same claim for *Laocoön,* but Lessing's essay does not go as far as Goethe's in that the implied subversion of the system does not reside so much within the text itself as in its connection to its preliminary stages.) We might then understand the difference between what a reading of the text that articulates its deconstruction does and what the text itself does as follows: the reading that makes the implicit critique explicit is, by virtue of the necessarily logical explanation of the critique, implicitly complicitous, whereas the text's explicit complicity renders implicit and non-complicitous critique possible. A careful reading of the performance of such a text, and of the effects of that performance on the text's explicit statement, thus forces the reader into this complicity. However, if the reader *considers* this effect, s*he confronts her*his own systematic tendencies and desire for systematic understanding, and is thereby drawn into a self-critique that prevents at least complete complicity. There is, however, one more (ironic) turn of the screw: in recognizing the complicity in which our reading involves us, we must also recognize that Goethe's text, in that it *requires* our interpretive work, is complicitous after all—complicit in our complicity. The text's critique of the system, its self-deconstruction, takes place only when it is read, only when the reader teases out and traces the textual strategies that constitute that critique.

Supplement

I mistrust all systematists and I avoid them. The will to system represents a lack of honesty.

[Ich misstraue allen Systematikern und gehe ihnen aus dem Weg. Der Wille zum System ist ein Mangel an Rechtschaffenheit.]
                                                —Friedrich Nietzsche, *Twilight of the Idols*

My introduction is detailed, and you will have to help me formulate my conclusion.

[Meine Einleitung ist ausführlich und meinen Schluß sollen Sie mir selbst ausführen helfen.]
                                  —"The Collector and His Circle" (III, 135*; XIII, 282)

The belief in and advocacy of systems, systematic thought, and systematic discourse have of course survived—despite Goethe. Nietzsche's mistrust is sooner the exception than the rule.[27] Another philosopher of his generation, Gottlob Frege, wrote that "only in the system does science achieve perfection. The system can never be dispensed with. Only through the system can one attain complete clarity and order."[28] The survival of the systematic ideal in the twentieth century, despite a seeming awareness of its unstable foundations, can be seen in the notion of "open systems," which, while feigning openness and mutability, actually lead to a more all-encompassing closure. In describing various attempts to redefine "system" in such a way as to account for its inherent problems, Manfred Zahn arrives at the following generalization: "System is understood not only as the idea of the goal, but also as the procedure appropriate to achieving the goal and as that on which the goal is based" ("System," 1461). The notion of system thus continues to inform both the foundation and the goal, as well as the process of discourse.

The divergence of the essay from systematic discourse, as we have seen, has been the topic of numerous studies of the genre. Lukács implies such divergence, but also believes that someday the un-systematic essay will be eclipsed by some "grand aesthetic system." Adorno, on the other hand, grants the essay a position that is not subordinate to systematic discourse and sees its opposition to system as one of its main determining characteristics— "The essay . . . draws the fullest consequences from the critique of the system" (157; 16). Adorno's description is useful and has been borne out by a reading of the rhetorical strategies of "The Collector" and "Simple Imitation of Nature, Manner, Style." And as we have seen, Goethe's textual performance points, as Adorno's performance of the writing he discusses seems to point,[29] beyond a simply oppositional relationship between essay and system.

In his comments on Spinoza in *Poetry and Truth* Goethe goes beyond a critical attitude toward systematic discourse to question the very possibility of such discourse on the basis of an insight into the nature of language. In this regard he anticipates Nietzsche's and Mauthner's doubts by a century.[30] Lavater presents a similar view: "We by no means either want to, or can, provide a systematic whole" (*Physiognomical Fragments*, I, 18). Given the discussion of Spinoza in the autobiography, we could then assume that what would have caught Goethe's eye in this line is not the word "want," but rather "can."

The question then remains: What *can* we write? The answer, perhaps: Essays. But rather than simply state this, Goethe *does* it. In "The Collector and His Circle" we find an essay that thematizes its own genre, not by simply criticizing or opposing systems, but by showing the *impossibility* of systematic discourse. In that it deconstructs the system in which it culminates, the essay constitutes a fundamental questioning of the grounds of the system's possibility. Furthermore, in that that system thematizes itself *as such* by employing in its syntheses qualities essential to all systems ("truth" and "completion"), the questioning of this system's possibility constitutes a questioning of systems and systematic discourse in general. The essay does not, then, set itself off against another form of discourse; it does not occupy a position simply vis-à-vis systematic discourse. This would allow such discourse to survive as a viable *alternative*. By undermining the notion of systematic closure—with its attendant completion, coherence, consistency, and certainty—the essay reveals a characteristic of *all* writing.

Genre of Genres

Before proceeding, in Part Two, with a discussion of the dialogic orientation of the essay, I would like to suggest another way in which we might think of Goethe's essayistic writing, his subversion of systematic discourse. In an article entitled "Deconstruction and Circumvention," Richard Rorty takes issue with Jonathan Culler's view of deconstruction as a method of reading texts that must operate on the basis of "a distinction between literature and philosophy."[31] Rorty acknowledges that this is one way in which deconstruction has been understood and used, but concentrates on another understanding of the term that has to do not with a *method* of reading, but with Derrida's philosophical project in general:

> Taken this way, breaking down the distinction between philosophy and literature is *essential* to deconstruction. Derrida's initiative in philosophy continues along a line laid down by Friedrich Nietzsche and Martin Heidegger. He rejects, however, Heidegger's distinctions between "thinkers" and "poets" and between the few thinkers and the many scribblers. So Derrida rejects the sort of philosophical professionalism which Nietzsche despised and which Heidegger recovered. This does indeed lead Derrida in the direction of "a general, undifferentiated textuality." In his work, the philosophy-literature distinc-

tion is, at most, part of a ladder which we can let go of once we have climbed up it.[32]

In that Goethe's essayistic writing makes an implied statement about all writing, in that it questions the very possibility of philosophical (in a Kantian sense), systematic discourse, we can see his essayistic writing as analogous to the Derridean boundary-breaking, as a subversion of the traditional distinction between the "metaphorical" (and thus open-ended, non-archeological, non-teleological) text and the supposedly "literal" (and thus truth-seeking, teleological, closed, systematic) philosophical text. In other words the essay, in Goethe's *usage,* comes to be the text of textuality, a genre of genres.

In one of his texts on the natural sciences, Goethe discusses explicitly and performs implicitly this breaking of boundaries. "The Experiment as Mediator between Object and Subject" ["Der Versuch als Vermittler von Objekt und Subjekt"], written after "Simple Imitation of Nature, Manner, Style" and before "The Collector and His Circle," bears a significant relationship to these texts on art and aesthetics. The text begins by discussing the necessity of mediation, of breaking boundaries between subject and object—a requirement that forms the basis of "style" in the essays on art—and calls attention to the pitfalls (also suffered by the "imitators" and "characterists") of attempting to give exclusive validity to the object:

> A far more difficult task arises when people's thirst for knowledge kindles in them a desire to view nature's objects in their own right and in relation to one another. On the one hand they lose the yardstick which came to their aid when they looked at things from the human standpoint, i.e., in relation to themselves. They are now supposed to renounce absolutely this yardstick of pleasure and displeasure, attraction and repulsion, use and detriment; as neutral and, as it were, god-like beings they are supposed to seek out and examine what is, not what pleases. (XII, 11*)

[Ein weit schwereres Tagewerk übernehmen diejenigen, deren lebhafter Trieb nach Kenntnis die Gegenstände der Natur an sich selbst und in ihren Verhältnissen untereinander zu beobachten strebt: denn sie vermissen bald den Maßstab, der ihnen zu Hülfe kam, wenn sie als Menschen die Dinge in bezug auf sich betrachteten. Es fehlt ihnen der Maßstab des Gefallens und Mißfallens, des Anziehens und Abstoßens, des Nutzens und Schadens; diesem sollen sie ganz entsagen, sie sollen als gleichgültige und gleichsam göttliche Wesen suchen und untersuchen, was ist, und nicht, was behagt. (XVI, 844)]

By describing such "exclusionists" as would-be gods, the text simultaneously questions the very possibility of absolute subject-object separation—a questioning implied in the system of "The Collector" and crucial to that text's self-deconstruction.

Like "The Collector," "The Experiment as Mediator" associates an advocacy of observation against a priori theorizing with a critique of systems. We learn that there is "nothing . . . more dangerous than the desire to prove some proposition directly through experiments" (XII, 14*) ["nichts gefährlicher . . . als irgendeinen Satz unmittelbar durch Versuche bestätigen zu wollen" (XVI, 849)] and that this approach is, at the least, disingenuous and, at its worst, bound to fail: "The other method, which tries to prove assertions by using isolated experiments as if they were arguments, often reaches its judgments furtively or even lets them remain in doubt" (XII, 17*) ["Bei der andern Methode aber, wo wir irgend etwas, das wir behaupten, durch isolierte Versuche gleichsam als durch Argumente beweisen wollen, wird das Urteil öfters nur erschlichen, wenn es nicht gar in Zweifel stehen bleibt" (XVI, 854)]. The danger of this method is that it gives undesirable scope to our systematic tendency "to unite everything with tremendous force" (XII, 14*) ["alles . . . mit einer ungeheuren Gewalt zu verbinden" (XVI, 850)]. In a passage reminiscent of Mauthner's description of systems as products of human desire, Goethe both describes the genesis of systems and questions their validity:

Man takes pleasure in a thing only insofar as he has an idea of it. The thing must fit his way of thinking, and no matter how exalted his way of thinking, no matter how refined, it usually remains *just an attempt to bring many objects into an intelligible relationship which, strictly speaking, they do not have.* Thus the tendency to hypotheses, theories, terminologies, and systems, which we cannot disapprove of, since they spring by necessity from the organization of our being. (XII, 14*; my emphasis)[33]

[Der Mensch erfreut sich nur einer Sache, insofern er sich dieselbe vorstellt; sie muß in seine Sinnesart passen, und er mag seine Vorstellungsart noch so hoch über die gemeine heben, noch so sehr reinigen, so bleibt sie doch gewöhnlich *nur ein Versuch, viele Gegenstände in ein gewisses faßliches Verhältnis zu bringen, das sie, streng genommen, untereinander nicht haben;* daher die Neigung zu Hypothesen, zu Theorien, Terminologien und Systemen, die wir nicht mißbilligen können, weil sie aus der Organisation unsers Wesens notwendig entspringen. (XVI, 849–50; my emphasis)]

Goethe finishes his general discussion of the importance of "experience" (and thus the necessity of repeated experiments) with an implied questioning of the possibility of systems when he claims the impossibility of completion or closure: he reminds us to remind ourselves "that no one is able to bring anything to a close" (XII, 16*) ["daß kein Mensch Fähigkeiten genug habe, in irgendeiner Sache abzuschließen" (XVI, 852)]. Paradoxically, the text then goes on to present what seems to be a systematic ideal by positing mathematics as the prime example of how to approach experimentation:

From the mathematician we must learn the meticulous care required to connect things in unbroken succession, or rather, to derive things step by step. Even where we make use of no calculation, we must always work as though we had to satisfy the strictest of geometricians. (XII, 16*)

[Diese Bedächtlichkeit, nur das Nächste ans Nächste zu reihen oder vielmehr das Nächste aus dem Nächsten zu folgern, haben wir von den Mathematikern zu lernen, und selbst da, wo wir uns keiner Rechnung bedienen, müssen wir immer so zu Werke gehen, als wenn wir dem strengsten Geometer Rechenschaft zu geben schuldig wären. (XVI, 852)]

This approach yields what Goethe calls "experiences of the higher sort" (XII, 16*) ["Erfahrungen der höhern Art" (XVI, 852)]. The systematic quality of these "higher experiences" lies in what the researcher can do with them: "These . . . may be expressed in concise axioms and set side by side, and as more of them emerge they may be ordered and related in such a way that, like mathematical axioms, they will remain unshakable either singly or as a whole" (XII, 17*) ["Diese lassen sich durch kurze und faßliche Sätze aussprechen, nebeneinander stellen, und wie sie nach und nach ausgebildet worden, können sie geordnet und in ein solches Verhältnis gebracht werden, daß sie so gut als mathematische Sätze entweder einzeln oder zusammengenommen unerschütterlich stehen" (XVI, 853)]. Here, it seems, we are confronted with systematic order, certitude, and absolute logical consistency—"Nothing here is arbitrary" (XII, 17) ["Hier findet keine Willkür statt" (XVI, 854)].

The text does not, however, end with this advocacy of systems that its beginning would have seemed to preclude. The systematic gesture of constructing those "experiences of the higher sort" is relativized by being reduced to one aspect or phase of scientific investigation and by the disparaging way in which Goethe describes how that construction must be achieved: "We cannot exercise enough care, diligence, strictness, even pedantry in carrying out that first task" (XII, 17*) ["Jene erste Arbeit kann nicht sorgfältig, emsig, streng, ja pedantisch genug vorgenommen werden" (XVI, 854)]. The text then goes on to stress the importance of not allowing those higher experiences, which take the form of mathematical theorems, to come together and create a system: "But these materials must be ordered and shown in sequence, not arranged in some hypothetical way nor made to serve the dictates of some system" (XII, 17) ["Aber diese Materialien müssen in Reihen geordnet und niedergelegt sein, nicht auf eine hypothetische Weise zusammengestellt, nicht zu einer systematischen Form verwendet" (XVI, 854)]. Goethe refers to this "series" as a "collection" ["Sammlung"] that allows for infinite addition and thus precludes closure (XII, 17*; XVI, 854). With the introduction of the system-subverting *collection*, a textual progression similar to, though more easily discerned than that in "The Collector" emerges: a movement from anti-systematic intention to the apparent formation of a system and then on to the subversion of that system.

"The Experiment as Mediator between Object and Subject" not only has as its *topic* the subversion of boundaries (between subject and object), it also, in its *performance*, subverts boundaries—between fields of investigation and their discourses. Because the same concerns—the subject/object boundary itself, the importance of observation, the concomitant danger of a priori theorizing, the problem of systems—inform our understanding and investigation in both science and art, the barrier between these areas of inquiry begins to dissolve. Moreover, in that the textual strategies (the treatment of systems) of the discourses on these seemingly disparate topics bear a fundamental resemblance, the boundary between scientific and aesthetic discourse is weakened. Indeed, what we approach with the expectation of reading scientific discourse turns out to be an essay. "The Experiment as Mediator" is essayistic by virtue of its questioning of the grounds of the system's possibility and by virtue of its own subversion of the system it constructs; the text is thus self-deconstructive in its function as scientific discourse, at least insofar as that discourse traditionally implies and raises the expectation of the systematic.

In its title, the text provides an image of this subversion of boundaries between types of discourse. The "Experiment" ["Versuch"] does not only mediate, that is dissolve, the separation of subject and object; the word "Versuch" itself is a breaker of boundaries. Goethe uses the German term for the Latin "experimentum," but a term that is at the same time a common translation of the French "essai."[34] "Versuch" thus refers both to the explicit, scientific topic of the text that follows and to that text itself, to its implied performance of essayistic writing—that writing which functions, *generally*, as an (inter-)textual "mediator." The boundary that is broken in this word game is that between literal and metaphoric—between the explicit (literal) reference to "experiment" and the implicit (metaphorical) reference to "essay."[35]

In that "The Experiment/Essay as Mediator" undermines the distinction between types of writing, we might also see this essay as an argument for generic impurity. Since genre is a systematic concept—one that emerges from the act of delineation, the construction of boundaries—and inasmuch as the essay, this essay on "The Essay as Mediator" being a particularly potent example, is writing that *de*-lineates, that subverts boundaries in its *de*-construction of systematic discourse, essayistic writing could be understood as the deconstruction of genre. In the terms of Derrida's "The Law of Genre," the essay would once again emerge as the/a genre of genre(s), insofar as it describes the "law of the law of genre," the "law of impurity" that Derrida locates at the foundation of or prior to the generic purity and self-identity that constitutes the law of genre.[36]

Part Two

TALKING PENS

Dialogue and the DisClosure of Community

Since we are a conversation and hear from one another . . .

[Seit ein Gespräch wir sind und hören voneinander . . .]
                                        —Hölderlin, "Celebration of Peace"

And if in the end you have achieved this, and have come to feel thoroughly convinced that only what bears fruit is true—consider the conduct of the majority, leave them to arrange things as they please, and join the smallest crowd.

[Und war es endlich dir gelungen,
Und bist du vom Gefühl durchdrungen:
Was fruchtbar ist, allein ist wahr—
Du prüfst das allgemeine Walten,
Es wird nach seiner Weise schalten,
Geselle dich zur kleinsten Schar.]
                                        —Goethe, "Legacy" (I, 515)

The Law of the Text

By pointing to its own generic status (or non-status) as a genre of genres, "The Collector" is deconstructive in the broadest sense: it breaks what we might call its own law, the law of genre. This "criminal" act should not surprise us, for such law-breaking occurs throughout the text. In the middle of the first letter we discover the reason for the correspondence that comprises the essay:

> The sample essays for the journal you intend to publish have strengthened my hopes and my support and interest, and I would be glad to contribute in any way I can. Theory has never been my forte, but I would certainly be happy to share with you my experiences, which you may use as you see fit. To prove the sincerity of my intentions I will begin immediately and do what you requested: I am going to write down the history of my collection little by little. (III, 122*)

> [Sie haben für die Schrift, die Sie herauszugeben gedenken, durch diese Probestücke meine Hoffnungen und meine stille Teilnahme verstärkt, und gern will ich auch auf irgendeine Weise, deren ich mich fähig fühle, zu Ihren Absichten mit beitragen. Theorie ist nie meine Sache gewesen, was Sie von meinen Erfahrungen brauchen können, steht von Herzen zu Diensten. Und um hiervon einen Beweis zu geben, fange ich sogleich an, Ihren

Wunsch zu erfüllen. Ich werde Ihnen nach und nach die
Geschichte meiner Sammlung aufzeichnen. (XIII, 260)]

With these words the collector formulates the law of the text—
the avoidance of theory and the concentration on a historical
account and perspective. However, he has barely finished writing that law before he begins to break it. Although he promised
to start "immediately" with the history of his collection, he goes
off on a tangent the moment he begins, and the remainder of the
first letter contains nothing of that history. At the end of the
letter he then reprimands himself for this deviation from his
course—"And now I am approaching the end of my letter without having carried out my intention. I prattled instead of telling
my story" (III, 123*; XIII, 262). Furthermore, the history of the
collection that was to constitute the correspondence, "little by
little," is completed within the second and third letters; the
remaining five letters address different and more general questions about art and its appreciation.

The collector's deviation in the first letter, what he calls prat-
tle, is an excursus into just what he had promised not to discuss:
theory. Theory—theoretical meditations on the reception of
art—fills most of the second half of the letter. The paragraph
immediately following his formulation of the law of the text
introduces a theory of the effects of both personal and cultural
history on the appreciation and accumulation of works of art:

> To be sure, an art lover's character and preferences are
> important in determining how his love of art and his love
> of collecting—two inclinations often found together—
> will develop, but in my opinion he is just as much influ-
> enced by the age into which he is born, by the conditions
> under which he lives, by contemporary artists and art
> dealers, by the foreign countries he has visited first and
> by nations to which he has some personal relationship.
> (III, 122)

> [Freilich kommt es viel auf den Charakter, auf die
> Neigung eines Liebhabers an, wohin die Liebe zum
> Gebildeten, wohin der Sammlungsgeist, zwei Neigungen,

die sich oft im Menschen finden, ihre Richtung nehmen sollen, und ebensoviel, möchte ich behaupten, hängt der Liebhaber von der Zeit ab, in die er kommt, von den Umständen, unter denen er sich befindet, von gleichzeitigen Künstlern und Kunsthändlern, von den Ländern, die er zuerst besucht, von den Nationen, mit denen er in irgendeinem Verhältnis steht. (XIII, 261)]

Then, after he has quickly run through the history of his collection in the second and third letters, the collector allows theoretical considerations to govern the rest of the correspondence: his classification of the types of art lovers, the debate with the characterist, and the further refinement of the classification that culminates in the philosopher's system. Even in the midst of his historical narration, the collector falls again and again into theoretical reflections; for example, when describing his father's love of portrait painting, he theorizes about the advantages and disadvantages of this genre as well as about its relationship to art collecting (III, 124–25; XIII, 264). And whereas the collector criticizes himself at the end of the first letter for a lapse into theory and later ironizes his classifications by referring to them as "curious" (III, 137; XIII, 284–85), what he has produced *is* still theory. "The Collector" thus transgresses the law it has formulated for itself.

The text does not then descend immediately into lawlessness. Theory itself, especially as it appears here in the form of classification and system, carries with it the quality of law. Because of this particular result of the collector's infraction, the transgression of the initial law of the text leads paradoxically to the establishment of a new law, the law of a system of aesthetics. This unstated but implied law rules the remainder of the text, but, as we have seen, only in its explicit statement. Examination of the rhetorical and discursive strategies of "The Collector" enables us to gain access to the transgression of that new law, to the subversion of the essay's apparently systematic discourse.

We might describe that subversion of the system as an undermining of the authority of a unified, totalized, "centralized," closed text. However, that undermining can also be seen to have begun at a much earlier point in the text and to have facilitated or at least reflected the transgression of the law of the text all along. We can locate this feature of the text in the growing attenuation of the authority of the collector's *voice*, an attenuation that begins already in the second letter. The critique of the system in "The Collector" both implies and operates by means of non-closure. In that this rupture occurs at the end of the essay—in its culmination—the text breaches its own closure; it then calls attention to this open-endedness in Julie's invitation to ongoing debate. The text thus forces our attention to its own process, its own strategies, its self-deconstruction; once it has lost its center, its teleological orientation, all that is left is that process. The essay's treatment of systems, its processuality, and its self-reflexivity come together. The undermining of the authoritative voice of the collector occurs in what I consider the most important aspect of the essay's process or textual strategy, and in what will be the topic of this second part of my study: *dialogue*.

Collecting Voices

The collector himself makes the first move toward undermining the univocality of the text, toward opening "his" text to a dialogue of voices. He does this, however, at a point where he does not yet seem quite ready to relinquish his authority. Near the end of the second letter he discusses the obsession that overcame his brother-in-law after the death of his sister, and is then overcome by his own melancholy ruminations—to the point where he feels he can no longer continue to write. Because he is unwilling to end the letter on a sad note, he asks Julie to close the letter: "But I do not want to end this letter on such a melancholy note. I'll hand my pen to Julie, who will tell you . . ." (III, 128) ["Und doch soll dieser Brief mit einem so traurigen Schlusse nicht in Ihre Hand kommen, ich gebe meiner Julie die Feder, um Ihnen zu sagen—" (XIII, 269)]. The ellipsis at the end of this remark indicates that he expects Julie to write exactly as he would have liked to have been able to write, to be an extension of his voice. But she does not meet these expectations. She begins her postscript with an explanation of why it is impossible for her to do as her uncle wishes:

> My uncle has just handed me his pen with instructions to tell you with a pretty turn of phrase that he remains "humbly yours." He still sticks to the formalities of those good old times when it was considered one's duty to take one's leave at the end of a letter with a graceful bow. We are no longer taught to do that, and such a formal curtsy does not seem natural or affectionate enough. (III, 128)

> [Mein Oheim gibt mir die Feder, um Ihnen mit einer artigen Wendung zu sagen wie sehr er Ihnen ergeben sei. Er bleibt noch immer der Gewohnheit jener guten alten Zeit getreu, wo man es für Pflicht hielt am Ende eines Briefes von einem Freund mit einer zierlichen Verbeugung zu scheiden. Uns andern ist das nun schon nicht gelehrt worden; ein solcher Knicks scheint uns nicht natürlich, nicht herzlich genug. (XIII, 270)]

In other words, Julie is very much aware that she has a voice and she plans on using this opportunity to exercise it.

Julie herself then brings up the notion of authority in connection with the voice of her uncle *and* reflects on her inability, her unwillingness to abide by that authority. She speaks of the "task" he has set for her, but then corrects herself and chooses the more accurate word, "command": "Well then, how should I carry out the task, the command, of my uncle, as befits an obedient niece?" (III, 128*) ["Wie machen wir's nun um den Auftrag, den Befehl meines Onkels, wie es einer gehorsamen Nichte geziemt, zu erfüllen?" (XIII, 270)]. She asks the rhetorical question, "Isn't there any pretty turn of phrase I can think of?" (III, 128*) ["Will mir denn gar keine artige Wendung einfallen?" (XIII, 270)], and then indicates that such a closing remark, which would complete her task, is not sufficient. She justifies her deviation from the uncle's command by pointing out that he did not see fit to show her all of his letter, indeed that he *forbade* her (again, the language of law, of authority) to read

the last page. This lack of trust in her, this unpleasant "legislation," gives her license not to feel bound to completing the letter
as her uncle would have, license to say what she wants, and this
is precisely what she does.

The emergence of her voice takes the form of a challenge to
her uncle's opinions about the young philosopher friend:

> Anyway, he allowed me to read the beginning of his let-
> ter, and I think he slandered our good philosopher! I
> don't think it is kind or proper of my uncle to criticize so
> severely a young man who loves and admires both him
> and you so sincerely, only because he is so steadfast in his
> pursuit of the educational goals he considers appropriate
> for himself. (III, 128*)

> [Genug er hat mir erlaubt den Anfang seines Briefes zu
> lesen, und da finde ich, daß er unsern guten Philosophen
> bei Ihnen anschwärzen will. Es ist nicht artig noch billig
> vom Oheim einen jungen Mann, der ihn und Sie wahr-
> haft liebt und verehrt, darum so strenge zu tadeln, weil er
> so ernsthaft auf einem Wege verharrt, auf dem er sich
> nun einmal zu bilden glaubt. (XIII, 270)]

Julie even goes so far as to criticize the collector for being "one-
sided" and for not being willing "to be fair to everyone" (III,
128) ["jedem sein Recht widerfahren lassen" (XIII, 270)]. However, it is not only vis-à-vis her uncle that Julie attempts to define
her own voice, but also vis-à-vis the correspondents, the editors
of the *Propyläen*. Since she apparently knows that they do not
think highly of the kind of art that interests her, she senses
ridicule in the engravings they have sent her as a gift. In order to
defend herself, she employs the rhetorical device of feigned self-
ridicule: "Poor Julie can't help it that strange and imaginative
things fascinate her, that she is fond of pictures with fantastic
subjects, and that she enjoys these weaving, fleeting dreams
fixed on paper!" (III, 129) ["Was kann die arme Julie dafür, daß
etwas Seltsames, Geistreiches sie aufreizt, daß sie gern etwas
Wunderbares vorgestellt sieht und daß diese durcheinander

ziehenden und beweglichen Träume, auf dem Papier fixiert, ihr Unterhaltung geben!" (XIII, 271)]. This first new voice in the text, although originally intended to be nothing more than a continuation of the collector's voice, has already succeeded to a great extent in challenging the authority of that first voice.

Julie does not then forbid her uncle to read her postscript and thus does not, as he had done, make a claim to authority. He begins the next letter with an attempt to reestablish his authority: "In her postscript to my last letter, Julie spoke in defense of our philosopher. Unfortunately, her uncle cannot as yet do the same" (III, 129) ["Julie hat in ihrer letzten Nachschrift dem Philosophen das Wort geredet, leider stimmt der Oheim noch nicht mit ein" (XIII, 272)]. He evidently feels challenged, for he does not leave his difference of opinion at this simple statement, but rather presents a long argument about why he thinks she is wrong. This insistence on his own authority diminishes, however, in the course of his letter. The last part of his historical narration deals mainly with his education and development as an art collector. More specifically, it deals with the important role "contradiction" played in that education and with the significant effects of having viewed the collections of *others*. It is as a result of *this* discussion, I would suggest, that by the end of the letter he is prepared to give up his authority altogether, to abandon the further expression of his ideas, *to stop writing:* "But enough about myself, for now and evermore. May all my egoism satisfy itself in my collection!" (III, 132*) ["Für diesmal und für immer genug von mir selbst. Möge sich mein ganzer Egoism innerhalb meiner Sammlung befriedigen!" (XIII, 277)]. He does not carry out this plan. The editors draw him back into the dialogue by sending him essays from their journal, and he finds it impossible to ignore them, especially since they recall for him the productive discussions he and his correspondents have had in the past.

In the fifth letter, the last time we hear directly from the collector, he takes a further step toward un-privileging his own voice and attributing equal validity to the voice of others. The characterist visits him in order to see the collection; the extreme divergence in their views on art leads to an intense, sometimes heated argument. The collector at first conveys this argument in his letter by reporting what his opponent said. However, this reportage gives way to a supposedly direct transcription of their debate in the form of a dramatic dialogue. And this despite the fact that it is written afterwards and the difference was not resolved. By choosing this form of writing, the collector reveals his willingness to allow others equal rights of expression, no matter how threatening the other's position may be to his own. He no longer finds it necessary, as he had after letting Julie write for him the first time, to subordinate other voices. He has developed a dialogic attitude.

The next two letters are written by the philosopher and by Julie, respectively. They serve to dialogize the essay further both by reproducing debate in the form of dramatic dialogue and, more generally, by varying the writing voices of the text. Any sense of superior authority in the collector's voice has disappeared by now; that voice returns, but only as one among others in a debate or in reports of what was said.

Julie writes the final letter. But we would also be justified in saying that she does *not* write it. Her remarks after describing the first of the artistic biases, imitation, explain this paradox:

> (N.B. Don't be misled and imagine that I thought all this up by myself just because you see my handwriting! At first I wanted to underline what I copied verbatim from the notes I have. But that would have required too much underlining. You will best be able to tell where I am simply reporting; indeed, you will find again your own words from your last letter.) (III, 154*)

> [(Notabene! Daß Sie ja nicht irre werden und, weil Sie meine Hand sehen, glauben, daß das alles aus meinem Köpfchen komme. Ich wollte erst unterstreichen was ich buchstäblich aus den Papieren nehme die ich vor mir liegen habe; doch dann wäre zu viel unterstrichen worden. Sie werden am besten sehen wo ich nur referiere, ja Sie finden die eignen Worte Ihres letzten Briefes wieder.) (XIII, 312)]

For the most part, we *are* able to tell where she is simply reporting, since she often indicates whose idea it is that we are currently reading. But not always. Without "underlining" or quotation marks or some other cue to the presence of another voice, we cannot be certain whether the philosopher, the collector, Julie, or Caroline is responsible for the words on the page. This is especially the case with Caroline, whose voice we never read, even though we are told that she takes part in the discussions. Thus Julie's voice, given her warning and the fact that she is conveying the results of what we know was a communal effort, loses the aspect of authority, the fiercely independent quality it seemed to have when we first read it. What emerges, then, is a multivocal dialogue in which the very idea of one's "own," independent voice is compromised. Moreover, this dialogue of voices involves the reader. Julie remarks that her readers, the editors, will find in her letter the words of their own letter. Since we have not had access to that letter, or to any of their responses, we are unable to recognize their voice in the text. With the introduction of this extreme indeterminacy, the sense, the possibility, of any single authoritative voice is lost. The text thus not only reproduces dialogue and reflects on the value of dialogue; it *becomes* dialogue.

In my preface we already encountered, in Goethe's discussion of Möser's essays, the notion of a dialogue of voices (*Poetry and Truth*, IV, 438–39; X, 653). In "The Collector and His Circle" we get a sense of the extent to which he put such a dialogue into practice in his own writing, a sense of how deeply embedded in the structure, the process, of the text the undermining of a voice of authority is, and how that subversion operates by way of an increasingly *dialogic* attitude and awareness.

Playing with Plato

In another of his *Propyläen* essays, Goethe brings together more explicitly the dialogic and the circumvention, even subversion, of law. "On Truth and Probability in Works of Art" ["Über

Wahrheit und Wahrscheinlichkeit der Kunstwerke"] in its outward form is the most obviously dialogic of Goethe's essays.
Not only does it carry the subtitle, "A Conversation," but whenever Goethe referred to the essay, he used this designation. In the
"Announcement of the *Propylaea*" we read: "This question [of
truth and probability] is addressed in an amusing conversation"
["Diese Frage (ist) in einem heitern Gespräche ausgeführt"
(XIII, 195)]. And in a letter to Schiller of 24 May 1798 he
writes: "I am also sending the conversation I recently mentioned" ["Zugleich erhalten Sie das Gespräch, von dem ich
neulich sagte" (XX, 586)].

But "Truth and Probability" is not just any kind of dialogue.
Its fictional situation and its rhetorical strategy reveal its quality
as a specific type of dialogue steeped in tradition. The situation
is an argument between a spectator and the representative of an
artist who has offended the spectator by painting a background
scene for a theater that portrays an audience watching the performance on stage. The representative is placed in what seems a
position intellectually superior to that of the spectator, and the
course of their discussion consists in his gradually leading the
spectator out of his aesthetic naïveté into "enlightened" awareness. For example, he asks the spectator, whose complaint arose
out of a conviction that everything he sees in the theater should
appear "true and real": "What would you say if I raise the
objection that all theatrical performances by no means appear
true to you, that they have rather only an appearance of the
true?" (III, 74*) ["Was werden Sie sagen, wenn ich Ihnen
einwende, daß Ihnen alle theatralische Darstellungen keineswegs wahr scheinen, daß sie vielmehr nur einen Schein des
Wahren haben?" (XIII, 176)]. The spectator at first objects to
this word game, but eventually accepts the point. Having gained
this ground, the representative is then able to carry his argument
further and argue his opponent into relinquishing even his dimin-
ished ground:

> But when the good people up there on the stage meet and
> greet each other singing, sing the letters they receive,
> expound their love, their hate and all their passions in

song, fight singing and die singing, can you say that the whole performance or even just a part of it appears true? Or indeed even has an appearance of the true? (III, 75*)

[Wenn aber die guten Leute da droben singend sich begegnen und bekomplimentieren, Billets absingen, die sie erhalten, ihre Liebe, ihren Haß, alle ihre Leidenschaften singend darlegen, sich singend herumschlagen, und singend verscheiden, können Sie sagen, daß die ganze Vorstellung, oder auch nur ein Teil derselben, wahr scheine? ja ich darf sagen auch nur einen Schein des Wahren habe? (XIII, 176–77)]

Faced with such argumentation, the spectator is at a loss to defend his position and can only acquiesce.

This purposeful questioning is augmented by a more powerful, if less appealing, rhetorical strategy—the use of examples analogous to the opponent's position, but designed to shock the opponent out of his position by making it impossible for him to continue insisting on it without appearing foolish. Thus the representative uses two examples—that of the sparrow that mistook the cherries in a painting for real cherries and that of the monkey who ate all of the insects out of a naturalist's engravings—in order to show that only the most uncultured of art lovers would want a work of art to be a fully accurate representation of the real world. Finally, the spectator himself comments on the dialogic strategy being employed against him; at a moment of confusion, the representative asks, "Would you allow me to ask a few questions at this point?" ["Wollen Sie mir erlauben auf dem Punkt, wo wir stehen, einige Fragen zu tun?"], to which the spectator replies, "Since you have questioned me into this confusion, it is your duty to question me out of it again as well" ["Es ist Ihre Pflicht, da Sie mich in diese Verwirrung hineingefragt haben, mich auch wieder herauszufragen"] (III, 75*; XIII, 177). Given this rhetorical structure we can conclude that what "Truth and Probability" presents us with is a *Platonic* dialogue.[1]

Goethe introduces the issue of law into his text with his designation of the artist's representative. He does not call him a "representative" and does not, for example, have the director or the artist himself defend the painting. Rather, it is "The Artist's Advocate" ["Der Anwalt des Künstlers"] who takes on the task of defending the stage set; and in the use of the word "advocate" there is at the very least the strong suggestion of "lawyer" and "law." It should strike us as odd that Goethe would have an advocate, not an artist or critic, debating on the relationship between art and nature. This oddity is explained, however, by the fact that it is in a general sense a *legal* problem that is at issue in the essay. And the legal problem under consideration is the problem of law *in general,* insofar as questions of *truth* and *probability* are at issue. Moreover, these issues are related to the Platonic tradition in thought evoked by the essay's form as well as to the problem of system and systematic discourse. In "Pragmatism, Relativism, and Irrationalism" Richard Rorty relates the Platonic search for truth to the problem of method, which he describes in terms that point toward the problem of legislation: the insistence on method "is the myth that rationality consists in being constrained by rule."[2] The issue of truth ties that of law into questions of the system, both in a very specific sense—that of the functioning of a *legal system,* which depends on the discovery of "the truth"—and in a general sense, in that all systematic discourse has truth as its implied goal.

Already in the connections among law, truth, system, and Platonic tradition we should become suspicious of Goethe's composition of an apparently Platonic dialogue. When we examine how the essay treats the law (truth), we discover that in this dialogue truth, the notion of truth, is not served, but rather subverted. This subversion receives special emphasis in the text's basic irony. It is the artist's representative who performs the subversive act. That is, the lawyer breaks the law—the law of truth and by extension the law of the text. When discussing the rhetorical strategy of this essay, I already outlined how the advocate educates the spectator *away* from the belief that works of art must "appear to be true" by first substituting for that notion the idea that they only have an "appearance of the true" and then showing how this as well is not the case. The only sense of truth in art that the advocate allows to survive is the possibility of "an inner truth which results from the consistency of a work of art" (III, 76*) ["eine innere Wahrheit, die aus der Konsequenz eines Kunstwerks entspringt" (XIII, 178)]. After the spectator has agreed with him, we discover his reason for positing such an inner truth: "Shouldn't it follow then that the truth of art and the truth of nature are two completely different things, and that the artist by no means should or may strive to make his work appear as a work of nature?" (III, 76*) ["Sollte nun nicht daraus folgen, daß das Kunstwahre und das Natur-wahre völlig verschieden sei, und daß der Künstler keineswegs streben sollte, noch dürfe, daß sein Werk eigentlich als ein Naturwerk erscheine?" (XIII, 178)]. By eliminating the possibil-ity of correspondence between a work of art and a work of nature, the advocate has succeeded in subverting what Rorty, in the essay cited above, refers to as the Platonic myth of "truth as accuracy of representation" (164). In other words, he uses truth in order to move away from the notion of truth (as accurate representation).

Near the end of the text the advocate discusses why it was possible for the spectator to perceive a "consummate work of art" as a work of nature, and by so doing addresses the *recep-tion* of art:

> Because it corresponds to your better nature, because it is beyond the natural but not outside of nature. A con-summate work of art is a work of the human mind, and in this sense also a work of nature. But because the work of art gathers together objects scattered in nature and incorporates even the most common of them in such a way as to reveal their significance and dignity, it is beyond nature. A work of art has to be compre-hended by a mind harmoniously formed and developed, and such a mind also finds that which is excellent, that which is complete within itself, to be in accordance with its nature. (III, 77–78*)

[Weil es mit Ihrer bessern Natur übereinstimmt, weil es übernatürlich, aber nicht außernatürlich ist. Ein vollkommenes Kunstwerk ist ein Werk des menschliches (*sic*) Geistes, und in diesem Sinne auch ein Werk der Natur. Aber indem die zerstreuten Gegenstände in eins gefaßt, und selbst die gemeinsten in ihrer Bedeutung und Würde aufgenommen werden, so ist es über die Natur. Es will durch einen Geist, der harmonisch entsprungen und gebildet ist, aufgefaßt sein, und dieser findet das Vortreffliche, das in sich Vollendete, auch seiner Natur gemäß. (XIII, 180–81)]

The recipient of art reinscribes the work within the harmony of her*his own mind, which at the same time perceives *itself* as nature, and is thus able to identify nature and art (the connection between nature in general and a person's nature is made here in the language of the text as well—in the rhythmic interchange of the general "nature" ["die Natur"] and the possessively modified "nature"). The only inner truth of the artwork resides, then, in the artwork as it is re-created in the mind of the educated recipient. As a result, we can no longer speak of the inner truth of the work of art *itself*. And the truth of the work for one recipient will differ from its truth for another. The advocate thus makes the point that truth is possible, but only in the individual's complete isolation. This in turn eliminates the possibility of truth in *re-presentation* as well as, paradoxically, in active *reception,* which the advocate himself describes as a process of repeated viewing—"see it again and again" (III, 78) ["es wiederholt anschauen" (XIII, 181)]. The only truth possible in reception would then be the result of a single viewing and of a refusal to see the work again, and would thus imply a denial of the continued existence of the work. Repeated re-viewing would mean entering into a dialogue with the work of art, a dialogue that would open up a play of constantly changing meanings and temporary truths— temporary because they will always be relativized by the difference incurred through repetition. Any concern with *the* truth

of the work of art becomes superfluous. (The connection between this treatment of truth and my discussion of systems in
the context of Goethe's remarks on Spinoza can be made, I
think, with relative ease. Truth is possible in total isolation, in
the self-identity of a unified text or subject, just as the subject
has no difficulty in creating what are, for it alone, coherent
systems. Both truth and systems, however, dis-integrate as soon
as they are tested in an *inter*textual or *inter*subjective environment, or in the confrontation of text and subject—that is, in
the context of reception.)

Goethe's essay itself never returns to the question of the
painted audience that had initiated the dialogue. Having traced
the implications of the advocate's argument, however, we can
now return to that question and attempt to justify to the spectator the painting that had offended him. First of all, we could
say that the painting reminds us, the audience, that we are
watching a play, a work of art, and thus not a representation
of the real world. Beyond this, it reminds us that we are not
the only recipients of the performance, that there are other
interpretations that might call ours into question, and that the
fact of these other interpretations prevents us from determining
the absolute inner truth of the work of art. The painting thus
enacts and forces us to enact the subversion of truth (as accuracy of representation) that the work of art necessarily implies.
Furthermore, the *text* of "Truth and Probability," by omitting
this explanation, its own conclusion, involves us, its recipients,
in a dialogue with the text that attenuates *its* own boundaries,
its autonomy of interpretation.

Goethe's *Propyläen* essays are, as we have seen, generally held
to represent his most thorough development of the idea of the
autonomous work of art. One of the more important consequences of this reading of "Truth and Probability" for German
intellectual history and for a widely accepted view of Weimar
Classicism is the disclosure of Goethe's *questioning* of that idea.
The inner truth to which the essay restricts the truth of the work
of art would seem to attribute absolute autonomy to the work.
But in that the essay then makes that truth dependent on

reception—on that which is "outside" the work, on us, and on that which changes with repetition—it ultimately *subverts* that notion of autonomy.

*   *   *

Goethe employs the form of the Platonic dialogue in order to ironize it and its attendant philosophical tradition. Rorty describes that tradition as follows:

> According to this Platonic myth [that rationality consists in being constrained by rule], the life of reason is not the life of Socratic conversation but an illuminated state of consciousness in which one never needs to ask if one has exhausted the possible descriptions of, or explanations for, the situation. One simply arrives at true beliefs by obeying mechanical procedures.
>
> Traditional, Platonic, epistemologically-centered philosophy is the search for such procedures. It is the search for a way in which one can avoid the need for conversation and deliberation and simply tick off the way things are. ("Pragmatism, Relativism, and Irrationalism," 164)

The analysis in Part One of Goethe's treatment of systematic discourse should explain why he would challenge the tradition. However, the question remains: Why would Goethe attack, in this dialogic essay, the Platonic dialogue itself?

We can attempt to answer that question by turning to Goethe's own explicit discussion of that kind of dialogue in an essay of 1796 (two years prior to "Truth and Probability"), entitled "Plato as Party to a Christian Revelation" ["Plato als Mitgenosse einer christlichen Offenbarung"]. In what is a critique of a new translation of Plato, and in particular a critique of the elevation of "Ion" to the status of a canonical text, we find as well a critique of the Platonic dialogue. In reference to "Ion" we read: "As a matter of fact, in this as in other Platonic dialogues, the incredible stupidity of some characters is emphasized to make Socrates alone appear truly wise" (III, 201) ["Überhaupt fällt in diesem Gespräch, wie in andern Platonischen, die unglaubliche Dummheit einiger Personen auf, damit nur Sokrates von seiner Seite recht weise sein könne" (XIV, 693)]. Earlier, Goethe had mentioned Plato's polemical tendency (III, 200; XIV, 691), and here we see that what such a tendency leads to is one-sidedness in his dialogues, and thus not to dialogues at all, but rather to texts that tend toward monologism. The essay emphasizes the unfairness of this tendency by discussing "the silly question" ["die alberne Frage"] of the "wise" Socrates (III, 201*; XIV, 693). This criticism then leads to consideration of the detrimental effect of that monologism in its failure to address sufficiently the questions it raises; Goethe suggests that a discussion between more equally privileged and able dialogic partners would have produced something more than the discussion we find in "Ion." He thus supplies some details for Rorty's argument that Platonic philosophy looks for a way to "avoid the need for conversation." In terms of my current discussion, that criticism of monologism is especially significant, since the question "Ion" raises but fails to address is at the heart of "Truth and Probability"—the problem of truth in art and truth in nature: "These fictions, these hieroglyphs [e.g., old cameos on which horses without harness are still supposed to be pulling a chariot], which all art requires, are so miserably understood by all of those who want all that is true to be natural and thereby force art out of its sphere" (III, 202*) ["Diese Fiktionen, diese Hieroglyphen, deren jede Kunst bedarf, werden so übel von allen denen verstanden, welche alles Wahre natürlich haben wollen und dadurch die Kunst aus ihrer Sphäre reißen" (XIV, 693)].

Again, "On Truth and Probability in Works of Art" leads the spectator, and the reader, away from the notion of truth. Moreover, it does not replace that lost notion with some other *telos*, but remains open-ended, stopping as almost all of Goethe's essays do with an intimation of or invitation to continuing dialogue.[3] The essay does not portray the more experienced advocate's partner in dialogue as "incredibly stupid." The advocate takes advantage of nearly every opportunity to diminish any impression of his great "wisdom": he emphasizes that anyone can achieve a higher level of aesthetic judgment and that the spectator's misconceptions are understandable, the points he makes important ones that deserve and require consideration. The essay is an anti-Platonic Platonic dialogue, dialogic rather than polemically monologic, law-breaking rather than law-making.

*   *   *

Until now I have concentrated on the interplay of dialogue and authority in two of Goethe's essays, on the way in which dialogic strategies not only *accompany* the transgression of laws, but also, by performing the texts' implicit statement about law and authority, *accentuate* and *reinforce* that transgression. In what follows I will discuss the pervasiveness of Goethe's dialogic awareness, the theoretical environment of dialogue, and the many forms dialogue takes, in order to proceed then to the main business of Part Two: the workings and implications of what I call *public intertextual dialogue.*

Conversations

Ideal Dialogues and the Dialogic Ideal

We have already seen, albeit only briefly, what a prominent place dialogue occupies in Goethe's understanding of art and art criticism. In the "Introduction to the *Propylaea*" he remarks explicitly on "how well conversation serves in communicating ideas" (III, 80) ["welche Vorteile . . . das Gespräch gewährt" (XIII, 138)]. He then expands the notion of dialogue in three steps—first by including correspondence, then short essays, and finally by alluding to the writer's situation with respect to his wider audience as a dialogic relationship. He sums up the form of the *Propyläen* with a further reinforcement of their dialogic foundation: "We are of course referring here especially to the exchange of ideas" (III, 80) ["Daß hier besonders von einem Ideenwechsel . . . die Rede sei . . . versteht sich von selbst" (XIII, 139)]. A dialogic awareness also permeates Goethe's ("scientific") essay on the essay—"The Essay as Mediator between Object and Subject"—where we read that, without dialogue, scientific inquiry would stagnate: "We cannot acknowledge fully enough how necessary communication, assistance, reminders, and contradiction are to keep us on the right path and help us progress" (XII, 13*) ["Wir können . . . nicht genug anerkennen, wie nötig Mitteilung, Beihülfe, Erinnerung und Widerspruch sei, um uns auf dem rechten Wege zu erhalten und vorwärts zu bringen" (XVI, 847).

Beyond the context of his essays, Goethe often discussed dialogue both in its specific manifestations (for example, in relation to drama) and in general terms. At one point in *Poetry and Truth* he brings the specific and general together, in that he describes how the dialogue of *Götz von Berlichingen* arose out of the sway that dialogue in general held over his entire life, even in isolation. This long passage is extraordinary, both in its detailed discussion of the process of dialogue and in its revelation of a thoroughly dialogic orientation:

> Accustomed to spending his time preferably in company, he [Goethe] transformed even solitary thinking into social conversation, and in the following way: namely, when he found himself alone, he would summon up in spirit some person of his acquaintance. He would ask this person to be seated, pace up and down by her*him, stand in front of her*him, and discuss with her*him whatever subject he had in mind. The person would occasionally answer him and indicate, with the customary gestures, her*his agreement or disagreement; and everyone has a particular way of doing this. Then the speaker would continue and expand on whatever seemed to please his guest or qualify and characterize more precisely what the latter disapproved of; he was even finally willing to abandon his thesis. The most curious aspect of this was that he never chose persons of his closer acquaintanceship, but those he saw only rarely, even quite a few who lived in far-off places and with whom he had merely had a passing relationship. But usually they were persons more receptive than giving in nature, open-minded and prepared to be calmly interested in matters within their ken, although sometimes he would also summon contentious spirits to these dialectical exercises. Persons of both sexes, and of every age and station, made themselves available for this and proved agreeable and charming, because the conversation was only about subjects they had thought about and held dear. Yet some of them would have been greatly amazed, had they been able to learn how often they were summoned to this ideal conversation, since they could hardly have come to a real one. (IV, 424*)

[Gewöhnt am liebsten seine Zeit in Gesellschaft zuzu-
bringen, verwandelte er auch das einsame Denken zur
geselligen Unterhaltung, und zwar auf folgende Weise. Er
pflegte nämlich, wenn er sich allein sah, irgendeine Person seiner Bekanntschaft im Geiste zu sich zu rufen. Er
bat sie, nieder zu sitzen, ging an ihr auf und ab, blieb vor
ihr stehen, und verhandelte mit ihr den Gegenstand, der
ihm eben im Sinne lag. Hierauf antwortete sie gelegent-
lich, oder gab durch die gewöhnliche Mimik ihr Zu- oder
Abstimmen zu erkennen; wie denn jeder Mensch hierin
etwas Eignes hat. Sodann fuhr der Sprechende fort,
dasjenige was dem Gaste zu gefallen schien, weiter auszu-
führen, oder was derselbe mißbilligte, zu bedingen, näher
zu bestimmen, und gab auch wohl zuletzt seine These
gefällig auf. Das Wunderlichste war dabei, daß er niemals Personen seiner näheren Bekanntschaft wählte, sondern solche, die er nur selten sah, ja mehrere, die weit in
der Welt entfernt lebten, und mit denen er nur in einem
vorübergehenden Verhältnis gestanden; aber es waren
meist Personen, die, mehr empfänglicher als ausgebender
Natur, mit reinem Sinne einen ruhigen Anteil an Dingen
zu nehmen bereit sind, die in ihrem Gesichtskreise liegen,
ob er sich gleich manchmal zu diesen dialektischen
Übungen widersprechende Geister herbeirief. Hiezu be-
quemten sich nun Personen beiderlei Geschlechts, jedes
Alters und Standes, und erwiesen sich gefällig und anmu-
tig, da man sich nur von Gegenständen unterhielt, die
ihnen deutlich und lieb waren. Höchst wunderbar würde
es jedoch manchen vorgekommen sein, wenn sie hätten
erfahren können, wie oft sie zu dieser ideellen Unterhaltung berufen wurden, da sich manche zu einer wirklichen
wohl schwerlich eingefunden hätten. (X, 630–31)]

For Goethe, then, dialogue is not just a posture one assumes, a
form one applies, a quality of a particular discourse, but a mode
of thought and a way of life.[4]

That "ideal conversation" did not, however, satisfy Goethe's
need for real dialogue. In Book 19 of the autobiography he
brings dialogue into the proximity of the essay genre when he

discusses the acuity of Lavater's intellect; he says that what he enjoyed most about the physiognomist was his conversation, and attributes to it the power to produce greater understanding (V, 581; X, 817). The productive power of dialogue also constitutes the core of Goethe's explanation of how the Storm and Stress movement came into being. He discusses the failure of Klopstock's sale by subscription of his *Republic of Scholars* [*Gelehrtenrepublik*] and the hopes for broader and faster dissemination of literary works dashed by that failure. Within close circles, however, literary communication did not suffer, for the journals and "poetic almanacs" ["Musenalmanache"] had already established and assured such communication (IV, 383–84; X, 567–68). Goethe speaks of his own limitless pleasure in writing at that time, but points out that without a context in which to present his work and find a response to it, the texts already written struck him as dead: "My fondness for them [my productions] would be renewed only when I happily revived them again for myself and others at social gatherings" (IV, 384) ["Nur wenn ich es mir und andern in geselligem Kreise froh wieder vergegenwärtigte, erneute sich die Neigung daran" (X, 569)]. Dialogue saves the text from oblivion. And he sees this same dialogue as having been responsible for the emergence of the new literary era:

> This reciprocal harassment and incitement, which could grow excessive, had a good influence on each of us in his own way. And out of this creative whirl, this desire to live and let live, this give-and-take within a group of unbuttoned youths recklessly following their individual innate characters without any theoretical guidance emerged that famous, much discussed and decried literary epoch. (IV, 384)

> [Dieses wechselseitige, bis zur Ausschweifung gehende Hetzen und Treiben gab jedem nach seiner Art einen fröhlichen Einfluß, und aus diesem Quirlen und Schaffen, aus diesem Leben und Lebenlassen, aus diesem Nehmen und Geben, welches mit freier Brust, ohne irgendeinen theore-

tischen Leitstern, von so viel Jünglingen, nach eines jeden angebornem Charakter, ohne Rücksichten getrieben wurde, entsprang jene berühmte, berufene und verrufene Literaturepoche. (X, 569)]

When discussing a further literary project, Goethe calls our attention once again to the constitutive role of dialogue. He speaks of the "lively exchange of knowledge, opinions, and convictions" ["lebhaften Austausch von Kenntnissen, Meinungen, Überzeugungen"] that had characterized his involvement with the *Frankfurter Gelehrten Anzeigen* (IV, 406; X, 603) and brings this constructive conversation into contact with a fundamentally non-systematic way of thinking that allowed him to discuss various topics in his contributions to the journal "without real philosophical coherence but with sporadic accuracy" (IV, 406) ["ohne eigentlichen philosophischen Zusammenhang, aber sprungweise treffend" (X, 602)]. This connection between the dialogic and the unsystematic receives even greater emphasis, however, in one of Goethe's literary texts.

In the enigmatic "Fairy Tale" with which Goethe's novel *Conversations of German Emigrés* [*Unterhaltungen deutscher Ausgewanderten*] ends, the snake, with her newly acquired glow, enters the cavern in order to satisfy her curiosity and finally see what she had hitherto only been able to feel in this dark, secret place.[5] Just as she peers at the golden king, he begins speaking to her and directs a series of questions at her:

> "Whence comest thou?" "From the clefts where the gold dwells," replied the serpent. "What is more glorious than gold?" asked the king. "Light," answered the serpent. "What is more stimulating than light?" he asked. "Conversation," she answered. (X, 74*)

> [Wo kommst du her?—Aus den Klüften, versetzte die Schlange, in denen das Gold wohnt.—Was ist herrlicher als Gold? fragte der König.—Das Licht, antwortete die Schlange.—Was ist erquicklicher als Licht? fragte jener.— Das Gespräch, antwortete diese. (IX, 374–75)]

As with so many statements and descriptions in this fairy tale, this strange comparison between light and dialogue is never explained, but simply abandoned (the very next line describes how the snake's attention has already been captured by another "splendid image"). Within the context of the narration we can perhaps explain the references of the two terms in isolation from one another. "Light" might refer to the light of the old man's lamp that has the capacity to turn stone into gold, wood into silver, and dead animals into gems; but we might also understand it as a reference to the snake's glow, or to the "will-o'-the-wisps" [*Irrlichter*]. "Conversation," especially since it is the snake who brings it up, is related to the apparent theme of the tale—the sacrifice of the autonomous individual for the sake of the collective (the snake's *Entsagung*). If one accepts this interpretation and reads "light" as a reference to the lamp, then we could say that dialogue, which changes things in society for the better, is seen to be of greater value than light, which changes things, but only material things. Or, if we concentrate on the progression of phenomena that the golden king elicits with his questions and then attempt to explain why one surpasses the other, we could say that the progression is one of increasing enhancement of that which precedes: in other words, light is that *by which* gold is "glorious" and conversation is that *by which* knowledge (i.e., light understood in the Enlightenment sense of *Erkenntnis*) is "stimulating." But in order to explain more exactly why it is specifically "conversation" vis-à-vis "light" that is so important, I would suggest a reading that moves further beyond the bounds of the text. "Conversation" need not be read as an expansion or enhancement of "light," in the sense of a progression, but, given the comparative construction, can also be seen in juxtaposition to "light." In keeping with the evocation of the ages of mankind in the tale (the golden, silver, and bronze kings), we could then read "light" as referring not only to the light of knowledge [*Licht der Erkenntnis*], but specifically to the *age* of the Enlightenment, the age of Wolff, Baumgarten, and Gottsched, the age of *monologic, systematic discourse*. "Conversation" could then be seen to refer to the ages that followed the Enlightenment, not as enhancements, but as fundamental questionings of their predecessor—that is, to Storm and Stress[6] and Classicism, to the questioning of Enlightenment discourse that occurs in the writings of Lessing, Herder, and Goethe.

This enumeration of some of Goethe's many expressions of his commitment to the dialogic gives us cause to return to the passage that summed up his general attitude toward systems—his reaction to Spinoza's philosophy. In Book 16 of *Poetry and Truth,* Goethe describes how he had been drawn back to reading Spinoza by the discomfort a polemical pamphlet against the philosopher had caused him (V, 522; X, 730–31). The remainder of this section of the autobiography then produces the dialogue that ensued between text and reader; Goethe presents Spinoza's ideas in an unpolemical fashion, notes his praise and sometimes disagreement, but also presents counterarguments. He then reflects, as I pointed out in Part One, on the quality of language that makes it impossible "to form concepts that are imperishable" (V, 523) ["solche Begriffe zu bilden, welche unverwüstlich sind" (X, 732)] and impossible, as a result, to create a dependable, thoroughly coherent system. This recognition of the difficulties and indeterminacies of language in the intersubjective realm—he alludes to such a context by mentioning the linguistic situation of dialogue and reading (V, 524; X, 733)—explains his inability to subscribe to Spinoza's system.

In "Philosophy in America Today," where he makes the case for interdisciplinary dialogue, Rorty provides a strikingly similar argument against systematic philosophy, and for "*giv[ing] up* the notions of 'system,' 'method,' and 'science' ": "If there is one thing we have learned about concepts in recent decades it is that to have a concept is to be able to use a word, that to have a mastery of concepts is to be able to use a language, and that languages are created rather than discovered."[7] Neither Rorty nor Goethe treats language as useless or dangerously misleading. Rather, they are saying that we must see that the use of language is one of tentative agreement and disagreement, that the situation of communication and of writing is dialogic. A unidirectional, monologic use of language rests on a misconception about language and must fail to achieve what it pretends or at least hopes to achieve—authority and final, true answers to what *it* deems the most important questions.

Différance(s)

Rorty's introduction of Goethe into his own work is less gradual than my introduction of Rorty into the discussion of Goethe. Indeed, it is rather sudden and unexplained. At the end of his argument in "Deconstruction and Circumvention" for doing away with the distinction between philosophy and literature, he suggests "that we return to the ironic eclecticism of the *Phenomenology of Mind* and the second part of *Faust*" (20). This is the first and only mention of *Faust* in the essay. Near the end of *Philosophy and the Mirror of Nature* we read: "On the periphery of the history of modern philosophy, one finds figures who, without forming a 'tradition,' resemble each other in their distrust of the notion that man's essence is to be a knower of essences. Goethe, Kierkegaard, Santayana, William James, Dewey, the later Wittgenstein, the later Heidegger, are figures of this sort."[8] Rorty thus surprisingly places Goethe not only in what he does, indeed, constitute as a discontinuous tradition, but also at the start of his own study's lineage. Again, this is the only mention of Goethe in the entire, long book. However bewildering these references to Goethe might seem, they are nevertheless appropriate.

In "Philosophy Without Mirrors," the last chapter of *Philosophy and the Mirror of Nature,* Rorty describes in more general terms the opposition he sees between the Cartesian/Kantian tradition in philosophy and the thought of Dewey, Wittgenstein, and Heidegger: "I shall thereby develop a contrast between philosophy which centers in epistemology and the sort of philosophy which takes its point of departure from suspicion about the pretensions of epistemology. This is the contrast between 'systematic' and 'edifying' philosophies" (366). The resemblance between what Rorty calls edifying philosophy and one of the main qualities of essayistic writing—its questioning of the grounds of the system's possibility—begins to develop when he describes what the edifying philosophers attempt to combat: "The mainstream philosophers are the philosophers I shall call 'systematic,' and the peripheral ones are those I shall call 'edifying.' These peripheral, pragmatic philosophers are skeptical primarily *about systematic philosophy*, about the whole project of universal commensuration" (367–68). What these "new" philosophers offer, rather than universal commensuration, is a continuing discussion: "One way of thinking of wisdom as something . . . of which the achievement does not consist in finding the correct vocabulary for representing essence, is to think of it as the practical wisdom necessary to participate in a conversation. . . . [E]difying philosophy aims at continuing a conversation rather than at discovering truth" (372–73).

Rorty's description of a divergent vein in the history of thought is useful in that it calls our attention to the significance of texts that the history of "normal" philosophy would exclude—texts such as Goethe's essays. Goethe's *Propyläen* also bring together the notions of edification and conversation. In the "Introduction," when he discusses the "advantages of dialogue," Goethe specifies what it is advantageous *to*—namely, "a continuous learning process" (III, 80) ["sich fortschreitend auszubilden" (XIII, 138)]. In "The Collector and His Circle" the collector then repeats this conviction that continuing dialogue is essential to the growing understanding of art: "We mustn't fail to make this communication, so that we may soon receive something back from them [the editors] and the snowball may always roll onward and keep growing larger" (III, 149*) ["An dieser Mitteilung muß es nicht fehlen, damit wir auch bald wieder etwas von dort her erhalten und so der Schneeball sich immer fortwälze und vergrößere" (XIII, 303)]. The crucial word here, both for Rorty's concerns and for Goethe's essays, is "always": the dialogue does not take place in order to reach some final answer or truth, but for its own sake and for the sake of a continuing, unending process of edification.

Rorty notes the paradox inherent in speaking of edifying "philosophy" (370). The Western tradition in philosophy would not recognize this philosophy *as philosophy*, precisely because it does not seek to attain "the secure path of a science" (372).

Rorty, in other words, is advocating a different conception of philosophy altogether, one that diverges from the Kantian tradition, that is from philosophy as *Goethe* received it (in his *Propyläen* years) and opposed it implicitly in his essays—most obviously in the collector's critique of his young philosopher friend. This different philosophy produces writing that, like essayistic writing, concerns itself more with process than with results: "The way things are said is more important than the possession of truths" (359). Indeed, it questions the very possibility of such possession. Here we reach the closest affinity between Rorty's concerns and Goethe's deconstruction of systematic discourse. We have seen how essayistic writing does not consider systematic discourse to be an *alternative* and how, in "The Essay as Mediator," Goethe questions the very possibility of the system's logical coherence and thus of systematic commensuration—the "relationship which, strictly speaking, they [the objects] do not have" (XII, 14; XVI, 850). Systematic philosophy thinks of itself as content-oriented; from the point of view of the essay, however, which openly acknowledges and calls attention to its textuality, the system *is* text, but text that is revealed as (self-)deceptive in its attempt to deny its own textuality, to disregard, in its concentration on achieving truth, the effects of rhetorical and discursive strategies—strategies that are always in operation, regardless of whether or not the writer wants them to be. Rorty makes a similar point when he discusses the discursive manipulation or reduction that results from systematic philosophy's content-orientation, its determination to achieve final commensuration. His description of edifying, dialogic philosophy culminates in the suggestion that "edifying philosophers . . . put the very idea of universal commensuration, and of systematic philosophy, in doubt" (387). This suggestion is preceded by a remark on the main tendency of normal philosophy: "The objectionable self-confidence in question is simply the tendency of normal discourse to block the flow of conversation by presenting itself as offering the canonical vocabulary for discussion of a given topic—and, more particularly, the tendency of normal epistemologically centered philosophy to block the road by putting itself forward as the final commensurating vocabulary for all *possible* rational discourse" (386–87). This brings us back from the more general opposition of systematic discourse and anti-systematic, conversational writing to our more immediate concern: the opposition of *dialogue* and *monologue*.

*　*　*

Thus far in Part Two, I have been using "monologic" as a "natural" analogue to "systematic" and have been treating its opposition to "dialogic" as a matter of course. If we believed the most prominent theorist of dialogue, however, that opposition would not even be an issue. In "Discourse in the Novel" Mikhail Bakhtin treats dialogue as a quality of *all* language and *all* discourse.[9] He asserts that "the dialogic orientation of discourse is a phenomenon that is, of course, a property of *any* discourse. It is the natural orientation of any living discourse" (279). He criticizes "linguistics and the philosophy of discourse" for having ignored this pervasiveness: "The internal dialogism of the word (which occurs in a monologic utterance as well as in a rejoinder), the dialogism that penetrates its entire structure, all its semantic and expressive layers, is almost entirely ignored" (279). Bakhtin would have an end to all talk of monologue and his most prominent critical biographer, Tzvetan Todorov, takes him at his word.[10] Todorov devotes all of half of a page to the issue of monologue, only to dismiss it with a few short quotations and uncritical commentaries: "Bakhtin uses 'dialogic' and 'dialogism' in a very broad sense that makes even the monologue dialogical" (63) and "the opposition of the dialogic and the monologic gives way to an internal cleavage of the dialogic, which assumes different forms" (64).

Bakhtin's investigations into the nature of dialogue have been crucial to our understanding of dialogue. Because of him, we think about dialogue in more than the quotidian sense, in more than simply its most concrete manifestation—the form of dramatic dialogue, where we find a name followed by a colon and the "direct" speech of the named person. We now discuss implied dialogues, dialogue as an aspect of language, and dialogue as embedded in the fabric of texts.

What restricts the usefulness of Bakhtin's theory, however, are the limitations he places on himself. Even though he says that dialogue is the nature of all discourse, he concentrates almost exclusively on the novel. His first "definition" of the dialogic reveals this concentration: "Authorial speech, the speeches of narrators, inserted genres, the speech of characters are merely those fundamental compositional unities with whose help heteroglossia [*raznorečie*] can enter the novel; each of them permits a multiplicity of social voices and a wide variety of their links and interrelationships (always more or less dialogized)" (263). He then justifies his concentration with a dubious notion of the "unity" of language in other genres, that is, with a claim that contradicts his point about the "internal dialogism of the word": "But—we repeat—in the majority of poetic genres, the unity of the language system and the unity (and uniqueness) of the poet's individuality as reflected in his language and speech, which is directly realized in this unity, are indispensable prerequisites of poetic style. The novel, however, not only does not require these conditions but (as we have said) even makes of the internal stratification of language, of its social heteroglossia and the variety of individual voices in it, the prerequisite for authentic novelistic prose" (264).[11] By restricting the dialogic to the dialogue of voices within *a* text, *a* novel (I will return to the question of intertextuality later), Bakhtin limits his discussion to a particular group of dialogue's textual manifestations. Furthermore, by retaining the notion of "individual voices" he undercuts his own assertion of the internal dialogism of the word, which otherwise would imply a *plenitude* of non-self-identical, non-distinguishable voices within *every* voice, *every* word. Finally, although he exhibits a concern for the dialogic quality of all discourse, his insistence and concentration on the implicit dialogism of every word fails to take into account other qualities of writing that might attempt to challenge that dialogism.

As Bakhtin says, monologue, strictly speaking, is not possible. And deconstruction, as we have seen in Goethe's and Rorty's texts, questions the grounds of the system's possibility. But both system and monologue do survive, not as such, but in their *adjectival* form, as *attributes* of thought and discourse. This is the form that must concern us if our main concern is with qualities of writing. Even if, by definition, there can be no absolute monologue or system, there can be and are texts that in their discursive strategies and rhetorical gestures reveal *systematic* and *monologic* tendencies.

Monologue remains an important issue not only for the general reasons just outlined, but also because it was an issue for Goethe, whose notion of philosophy had been informed not only by Kant, but also by the more crudely systematic and monologic philosophy of Wolff and his followers.[12] In his discussion of the lively conversation that arose out of his involvement with the *Frankfurter Gelehrten Anzeigen,* Goethe explicitly opposes the usefulness of dialogue to the uselessness of monologue: "At that time I was not yet clearly aware of the fact that it was very easy for me to learn things from books and conversations, but not from a coherent professorial lecture" (IV, 406–7*) ["Ich war mir damals noch nicht deutlich bewußt, daß ich wohl aus Büchern und im Gespräch, nicht aber durch den zusammenhängenden Kathedervortrag etwas lernen konnte" (X, 603)]. In *Campaign in France 1792 [Kampagne in Frankreich 1792]* he describes how his lectures (*Contributions to Optics [Beiträge zur Optik]*), while they helped him to develop his thoughts in the process of speaking, carried with them an inherently negative quality. Again, he calls attention to the divergence of the monologic and the dialogic: "To be sure, I could proceed in this manner [lecturing] only didactically and dogmatically—I had no talent for true conversation or for dialectics" (V, 712) ["Freilich konnte ich auf diese Weise nur didaktisch und dogmatisch verfahren, eine eigentlich dialektische und konversierende Gabe war mir nicht verliehen" (XII, 374)]. Given Goethe's repeated testament to the significance of dialogue in his literary and intellectual development, we would have to take this self-deprecating remark as a subtle irony, perhaps an example of false modesty.

Goethe's description of the way thoughts develop in the process of giving a lecture calls forth a contrast to another writer and text of his age, a contrast that shows how even the seemingly dialogic can prove to be monologic. Heinrich von Kleist's "On the Gradual Completion of Thoughts While Speaking" ["Über die allmähliche Verfertigung der Gedanken beim Reden"] is a text now much in vogue as a result of its apparently programmatic statement on the advantages of dialogue. On closer examination, however, we would have to see Goethe's remarks in *Campaign in France* as an implied critique of the kind of dialogue Kleist describes. The text begins with what seems to be advocacy of dialogue: "If you want to know something and cannot gain access to it through meditation, then I advise you, my dear, wise friend, to talk about it with the next acquaintance you run into" ["Wenn du etwas wissen willst und es durch Meditation nicht finden kannst, so rate ich dir, mein lieber, sinnreicher Freund, mit dem nächsten Bekannten, der dir aufstößt, darüber zu reden"].[13] As it turns out, however, what he is aiming at is not a dialogue, not an interchange in which one progresses with the help and contribution of an interlocutor, but rather a monologue. We learn that this "next best" acquaintance "need not be a particularly intelligent person" ["braucht nicht eben ein scharfdenkender Kopf zu sein" (III, 319)] and cannot help but be reminded of Goethe's critique of Plato's "fixed" dialogues between the "wise" Socrates and his "incredibly stupid" interlocutors. What Kleist's text advocates is not talking *with* an equally privileged partner, but talking *at* the other: "Such speaking is a veritable thinking aloud" ["Ein solches Reden ist ein wahrhaftes lautes Denken" (III, 322)]. This talking does not aim, as dialogue does in Goethe's "Introduction to the *Propylaea,*" at keeping the process of thought open and thus subsuming any particular result to that ongoing process, which always draws such results into question; rather, it aims at a final resolution ["Auflösung" (III, 319)], at finding an *end* to the thought process that one has begun, and thus at participating in a systematic, archeo-teleological discourse: "While speaking, the mind, driven by the necessity of finding an end to the beginning, develops that confused idea [with which one began] toward complete clarity, and does so to such an extent that, to my amazement, the perception is finished by the time I stop speaking" ["So prägt . . . das Gemüt, während die Rede fortschreitet, in der Notwendigkeit, dem Anfang nun auch ein Ende zu finden, jene verworrene Vorstellung zur völligen Deutlichkeit aus, dergestalt, daß die Erkenntnis, zu meinem

Erstaunen, mit der Periode fertig ist" (III, 319–20)]. This systematic ideal goes hand in hand with the monologic attitude and is
already expressed in the title of the text—in the notion of a
completion [*Verfertigung*] of thoughts. Furthermore, that monologic attitude is reflected in each of the examples cited, all of
which reveal the desire for a hierarchical relationship between
speaker and other or for a relationship in which the speaker gains
power over the other. The speaker in Kleist's text is likened to a
great general (III, 320) and the speaking situation is compared
with Molière speaking to his maid. The other two examples demonstrate an even greater anti-dialogic consciousness: we learn
first of the way in which Mirabeau annihilated his opposition
["Vernichtung seines Gegners" (III, 321)] in order to achieve his
goal, and then, in a summary of one of Lafontaine's fables, of the
use of speech both to destroy the other and to maintain a hierarchy. Rather than open up a dialogic relationship, Kleist would
have one *use* the other as a mirror or sounding board that makes
it possible for the speaking subject to enlighten *itself* ["sich
aufzuklären" (III, 319)] and thereby to achieve the final formulation of an idea, of the self. The contrast to Goethe's "ideal conversation" is extreme; there, given the imaginary situation, the
"speaker" necessarily is in a superior position with regard to the
other and has power over her*him, but also willingly surrenders
this control in the face of the other's objections and for the sake of
having a conversation. The monologic discourse Kleist's text advocates is precisely what Goethe, in *Campaign in France,* calls
"didactic and dogmatic," and the subordination/annihilation of
the other to/by the autonomous speaking subject reveals an extreme agonistic orientation that is foreign to the notion of dialogue that emerges from Goethe's essays and autobiography. The
snake in Goethe's "Fairy Tale" would hardly find this orientation
"stimulating."[14]

Goethe's own private manifesto of dialogism, his description
in *Poetry and Truth* of his ideal conversations, is at the same
time explicitly a description of his tendency to avoid monologue, to *transform* monologue into dialogue—"the author's
peculiar habit of recasting even soliloquy as dialogue" (IV, 424)
["eine Eigenheit des Verfassers, die sogar das Selbstgespräch

zum Zwiegespräch umbildete" (X, 630)]. What is more, the discussion of the dialogue that emerges from that subversion of monologue describes more than just the workings of dialogue. Because it is a dialogue created by and within the self, it simultaneously describes the implications of dialogue for the self. Goethe's "ideal conversation" relinquishes the autonomous authority of the individual subject by virtue of the subject's willingness, when challenged by others, to change or abandon ideas. The subject relinquishes its self-identity and presence by making other subjects part of itself *and,* conversely, by making itself a function of those other, non-present subjects.[15]

The collector of Goethe's essay thematizes this dis-integration of the self-identical subject when he speaks of the "void" (III, 121) ["Lücke und Leere" (XIII, 259)] left by the departure of the editors. We might at first see this as a fairly typical expression of sadness at a friend's absence, but coming as it does in an essay that deals with philosophical issues, it has broader implications—implications for the relationship of dialogue and subjectivity. Without the other—without dialogue—the self is not complete, there is no unified subject. And since achieving such "unity" would require the presence of the other, there can be no such thing as a self-identical, unified subject.

Inasmuch as the system is the province of such an individual subject and inasmuch as the deconstruction of the system thus goes hand in hand with the deconstruction of that subject, we have come full circle. We have two sets of mutually implicit terms (on the one hand—the anti-systematic, dialogic, and intersubjective [the essayistic]; on the other—system, monologue, and subject [the philosophical/scientific treatise]), where the former group undermines the latter by implicitly questioning the grounds of its possibility.

＊　＊　＊

The term *différance* describes more precisely how the subversion of system, self-identical subject, and monologue work together. Indeed, it was already at work in the subversion of the system in "The Collector and His Circle." Différance first of all can be seen as another way of formulating my definition of the term "style" as a "double-edged" word that both articulates and breaks apart the system. In *The Critical Difference* Barbara Johnson describes the term as a "designation for what both subverts and produces the illusion of presence, identity, and consciousness."[16] But the relationship between "style" in Goethe's essay and différance is, I think, even closer than this. In his essay "Differance" Derrida begins his discussion of the term by pointing to its double signification: "The verb 'to differ' [*différer*] seems to differ from itself. On the one hand, it indicates difference as distinction, inequality, or discernibility; on the other, it expresses the interposition of delay, the interval of a *spacing* and *temporalizing* that puts off until 'later' what is presently denied, the possible that is presently impossible."[17] He later expands on these general significations. On the temporal: " 'To differ' in this sense is to temporalize, to resort, consciously or unconsciously, to the temporal and temporalizing mediation of a detour that suspends the accomplishment or fulfillment of 'desire' or 'will,' or carries desire or will out in a way that annuls or tempers their effect" (136). Here we are reminded of the "Introduction to the *Propylaea*," of the sense of constant deferral that prescribes the entire essayistic project—both in the explicit emphasis on the introductory nature of the journal's essays and in the title itself ("Introduction to the Introductions"). We are also reminded of the deferring effect of "style" in "The Collector," of its function as intertextual bait. In our desire to complete the system of "The Collector" we take a detour through another text, "Simple Imitation of Nature, Manner, Style." That detour both postpones the fulfillment of our desire and ultimately, in initiating an infinite regress, thwarts that fulfillment—we are never able to determine what style is and complete the system. And in that the postponement leads us to another text, "this temporalizing is also a temporalizing and spacing" (136); that is, "style" introduces différance in both the temporal and spatial sense.

"The other sense of 'to differ' [*différer*] is the most common and most identifiable, the sense of not being identical, of being other, of being discernible, etc." (136). "Style," as it is used in the system, also differs from itself. It is used as a concept among others that describes a *what,* but perhaps more accurately and in divergence from those other concepts, describes a *how.* In other words, the question we should ask is perhaps not What is style? but How is style? In this one word, then, Goethe combines the various constituents of différance—temporal differing, spatial differing, and self-differing. At what purports to be the center of the system we find the play of différance.

"The Collector" and the *Propyläen* project are not the only instance of différance in Goethe's work. We can see it at work, for example, in the deconstruction of the self-identical subject implied by the description of his "ideal conversation." In reviewing that description of a non-self-identical, non-present subject, it would be difficult to deny a close affinity to another of Derrida's formulations of différance: "Differance is what makes the movement of signification possible only if each element that is said to be 'present,' appearing on the stage of presence, is related to something other than itself. . . . In order for it to be, an interval must separate it from what it is not; but the interval that constitutes it in the present must also, and by the same token, divide the present in itself, thus dividing, along with the present, everything that can be conceived on its basis, that is, every being—in particular, for our metaphysical language, the substance or subject" (142–43). Another crucial passage in the autobiography problematizes the constitution of the subject in a manner that is also strongly reminiscent of différance. In the discussion of Spinoza in Book 16—that is, in the context of some of Goethe's most important remarks on language, systems, and dialogue—we read: "And so, unconsciously, we are always recreating ourselves our whole life long . . . only to exclaim at last that all is vanity" (V, 523*) ["Und so stellen wir uns unbewußt unser ganzes Leben immer wieder her . . . um zuletzt auszurufen, daß alles eitel sei" (X, 732)]. While Goethe does not greet this as a happy state of affairs, he portrays the constitution of the subject as an always incompleted process, as a constant postponement that never leads to the final fulfillment of our desire for a self-identical subject. Just as I have "produced" something I might call "myself," I already discard the product ["entsagen"] and strive for something else ["nach etwas Neuem greifen"] (V, 523*; X, 732). The subject is never finally constituted.

The terms introduced in the last several pages also describe the undermining of the voice of authority in "The Collector" and "Truth and Probability" discussed earlier. The "subversion of the authoritative voice" that we witness in the dialogism of Goethe's essays is another way of talking about the deconstruction of the autonomous subject. Texts like "The Collector" enact the inevitability of dialogue and hence illustrate the hypocrisy of system, which in its attendant claim to truth would deny that inevitability. Différance is at work here as well. Indeed, it is indispensable, since recognizing the inevitability of dialogue also implies recognizing the impossibility of a single authoritative voice, of an autonomous, self-identical subject, of a unitary language.[18] The constant postponement of final decisions that dialogue engenders, its open-endedness through deferral, undermines the illusion of presence. Perhaps it is dialogue's dis-closure of the subject *as* différance that Hölderlin also means when he writes the words—"Since we are a conversation" ["Seit ein Gespräch wir sind"].

Collecting Voices₂

In "The Collector and His Circle" we find a particularly potent example of how dialogically saturated Goethe's essays are.[19] Besides the dialogism discussed at the beginning of Part Two and implied in Julie's prophecy of continued dialogue at the end of the eighth letter, "The Collector" is dialogic in a number of other ways as well. The classifications and categorizations that lead to the final system themselves arise out of dialogue (which, in turn, constitutes a further ironization of the system). And the essay as a whole represents several different dialogues. Most obviously, it is a dialogue between the collector, Julie, and the philosopher on the one hand and the editors of the *Propyläen* on the other (Goethe explicitly draws the connection between dialogue and correspondence in *Poetry and Truth* [IV, 424; X, 631]). However, it is also a dialogue between that first group and *us* as readers. The editors' letters are never reproduced; we are therefore implicitly forced into the position of the respondents and must try to supply the missing part of the dialogue by gleaning from the letters we read what the editors might have written. *We* thus "write," however inexactly, the missing letters.[20] Furthermore, the letters we read imply another, broader dialogue between the collector and his circle and the literary public, in that these letters are to be published in the editors' journal. Indeed, they are then published, and herein lies one of the text's great self-reflective moments. In that the editors' journal is the *Propyläen*—that is, *Goethe's* journal—and in that the letters are actually published there (as we read them), the essay constitutes a highly ironic public dialogue *between Goethe and himself.* Again Goethe has transformed a monologue into a dialogue, but this time it does not remain only a private "ideal conversation"; rather, it becomes a text and thus a "real" and public dialogue. We might then read the passage in the autobiography where Goethe compares correspondences specifically with that ideal dialogue—"It is clear enough how closely related to correspondence such a thought-conversation is" (IV, 424*) ["Wie nahe ein solches Gespräch im Geiste mit dem Briefwechsel verwandt sei, ist klar genug" (X, 631)]—not just as a general reflection on dialogues, but as a direct though obscure reference to "The Collector."

Goethe's essay not only directly represents various dialogues and implies others. It also, as mentioned before, openly discusses dialogue and its advantages. At one point, however, the collector comments on the significance of dialogue in a way that points beyond the specific help he elsewhere says it affords in intellectual endeavors. Just after expressing his intention to stop writing and find another way to subsume his "egoism," he signs off with the following proclamation: "Let communication and receptivity be the password" (III, 132*) ["Mitteilung und Empfänglichkeit sei übrigens das Losungswort" (XIII, 277)]. He conflates "communication" and "receptivity" into one concept by using the singular verb and equating the two terms with one "word"; the result is a definition of dialogue. The emphasis on bi-directionality is crucial, for "communication" by itself, without "receptivity," would be a unidirectional, univocal communication equivalent to monologue. In the early stages of the essay, this is the state in which we find the philosopher—insistent on his newfound philosophical passion, unreceptive to the collector's ideas on art, and thus unable to participate in the dialogue. Only by opening up, by becoming receptive to the ideas of others (and thus implicitly relinquishing the notion of autonomous ideas), can he then join in what is for him, for the collector, for Julie, for the editors, and for us an "edifying" dialogue. But there is more to the collector's remark than this. By designating dialogue as "the password" or secret key, he simultaneously alludes to dialogue's power to carry us over thresholds and to cross boundaries, boundaries between texts and between subjects. In other words, he alludes to the access dialogue provides to that which is desired or desirable. What follows will move in the direction of that desideratum, a desire foreign to the discourse of hierarchy and power outlined in Kleist's text on the completion of thoughts—namely, *community*.

Into the World

In describing the multifarious dialogism of "The Collector and His Circle" I omitted one of that essay's most important dialogic aspects. The first lines of the collector's first letter introduce the notion of a *dialogue of texts:*

> Many thanks for your letter and the enclosed manuscripts which arrived so soon after you left. The two days you spent with us were most enjoyable, yet much too short, and I felt keenly the void caused by your departure. But your letter and the manuscripts lifted my spirits, and I felt almost as happy as when you were here. (III, 121–22*)

> [Wenn Ihr Abschied, nach den zwei vergnügten nur zu schnell verfloßnen Tagen, mich eine große Lücke und Leere fühlen ließ, so hat Ihr Brief, den ich so bald erhielt, so haben die beigefügten Manuskripte mich wieder in eine behagliche Stimmung versetzt, derjenigen ähnlich, die ich in Ihrer Gegenwart empfand. (XIII, 259)]

Thus it is not only correspondence that constitutes dialogue, but also the exchange of texts. The collector then "responds" to the manuscripts he has received with the text of the history of his collection. This dialogue of texts is continued both between the collector and the editors, and within his circle. Julie's "completion" of the second letter, which her uncle reads and responds to, is a textual response to the text of the uncle's own letter; since she and the collector do not first discuss that difference of opinion, her text is itself part of a dialogue and not simply a report of a spoken interchange. When, at the end of the third letter, the collector has decided to stop writing, it is the editors' conveyance of both letters and printed texts that draws him back into dialogue. And later, after the philosopher has become an active member in the discussion of art, the group refines the classification of artists and art lovers not only through conversation, but also in response to his written text.[21] (Here we can already see how, by creating a dialogue of texts, Goethe's essayistic writing frees dialogue from the traditional hegemony of the spoken word and thus also contributes to the subversion of the speech/writing hierarchy that survived well into our century. But more on this later.)

In the final letter of "The Collector," the dialogue of texts becomes the quality of a "single" text. Julie writes the letter, but, as we are informed, the majority of the text is constituted by the philosopher's text, presented here in quotation without quotation marks, and by the views of the collector and his family. In other words, the supposedly "individual" text is actually a collection of various texts, an internal dialogue of (un)quoted texts. Furthermore, Julie's letter incorporates the text (unknown to us) of the editors' last letter. The inclusion of another text that is not explicitly identified calls our attention to the inherent intertextuality of writing, to the fact that intertexts are woven into the fabric of what we might otherwise deem a "particular" text, that every text occurs in an intertextual space, that every text *is* an intertext.

With the introduction of intertextual dialogue we are once again in Bakhtinian territory. Bakhtin did not use the term "intertextuality"; it was introduced by Julia Kristeva in her discussion of his work:

> By introducing the *status of the word* as a minimal structural unit, Bakhtin situates the text within history and society, which are then seen as texts read by the writer, and into which he inserts himself by rewriting them. . . . The word's status is . . . defined *horizontally* (the word

in the text belongs to both writing subject and addressee) as well as *vertically* (the word in the text is oriented towards an anterior or synchronic literary corpus).

The addressee, however, is included within a book's discursive universe only as discourse itself. He thus fuses with this other discourse, this other book, in relation to which the writer has written his own text. Hence horizontal axis (subject-addressee) and vertical axis (text-context) coincide, bringing to light an important fact: each word (text) is an intersection of words (texts) where at least one other word (text) can be read. In Bakhtin's work, these two axes, which he calls *dialogue* and *ambivalence,* are not clearly distinguished. Yet, what appears as a lack of rigour is in fact an insight first introduced into literary theory by Bakhtin: any text is constructed as a mosaic of quotations; any text is the absorption and transformation of another. The notion of *intertextuality* replaces that of intersubjectivity, and poetic language is read as at least *double.*[22]

Despite the systematizing tendency of this reading of Bakhtin, the problematic reduction of the temporality of textual dialogue exclusively to either an anterior or synchronic relation, and the equally problematic subsumption of the intersubjective (which is not *eliminated* by the intertextual, but goes hand in hand with it), Kristeva's discussion of the status of the *word* in Bakhtin as also a question of *texts* has been essential to our understanding of the quality of dialogue as *writing.* In "Discourse in the Novel" we can see the justification for Kristeva's term especially clearly when Bakhtin criticizes traditional "stylistics" for having ignored dialogue:

> A literary work has been conceived by stylistics as if it were a hermetic and self-sufficient whole, one whose elements constitute a closed system presuming nothing beyond themselves, no other utterances. . . . From the point of view of stylistics, the artistic work as a whole— whatever that whole might be—is a self-sufficient and closed authorial monologue, one that presumes only pas-

sive listeners beyond its own boundaries. Should we imagine the work as a rejoinder in a given dialogue, whose
style is determined by its interrelationships with other
rejoinders in the same dialogue (in the totality of the
conversation)—then traditional stylistics does not offer
an adequate means for approaching such a dialogized
style. (273–74)

Todorov echoes Kristeva in making the intertextuality implied in
Bakhtin's theory explicit: "No utterance is devoid of the intertextual dimension. . . . In the later writings, Bakhtin will particularly insist on another patent fact: whatever the object of speech,
this object, in one way or another, has always already been said,
and it is impossible to avoid encountering the discourse previously held upon this object" (62). Bakhtin's implied description
and Kristeva's theoretical adduction of intertextuality, along
with Todorov's explication, are useful up to a point. They recognize a state of affairs—the "patent fact," as Todorov calls it—but
this determination that intertextuality is the condition of all texts
has limited usefulness for the actual analysis of texts.

As in the case of the inherently dialogic, non-monologic quality of all writing, Bakhtin's and Kristeva's recognition of the
necessary intertextuality of all texts has historical importance
for literary criticism and theory. If we remain with this recognition of "the way it is," however, there would be no particular
significance in discussing the intertextually dialogic quality of
Goethe's essays, or of any specific texts. We could simply decide, in accord with Bakhtin, that every piece of expository
writing, from Kant's critiques to many of the articles in contemporary scholarly journals, is necessarily a "rejoinder in a given
dialogue" and leave it at that. But then we would also be ignor-
ing the systematic, monologic tendencies of those texts, that is,
the exclusionary qualities of their discursive and rhetorical
strategies, their implicit attempt to *deny* the "patent fact."

It is my assertion that certain eighteenth-century German
writers—in particular Lessing, Herder, and Goethe—worked
out and participated in a form of writing that actively *acknowledges*, in its performance, the necessity of intertextuality in the

Kristevan sense, writing that calls attention to the fact that every text is an intertext, that every text occupies a non-autonomous textual space and spans a time not uniquely identifiable as the present, and that as a result we cannot, strictly speaking, think in terms of "a particular" text. To make this point, however, it is necessary to enter into the paradox of discussing texts *individually,* as if they could be individual "responses" to other individual texts—the paradox of treating intertextuality as if it were not just "the way it is," but as something that can be *done* (i.e., a matter of textual strategy); otherwise, it would not be possible to examine *how* and *to what extent* Goethe's essays acknowledge that which would constitute a theoretical "discovery" a century and a half later. The discussion of Goethe's (and Lessing's, and Herder's) "participation" in intertextual dialogue, in that it takes the form, explicitly or implicitly, of saying what a particular writer does, also gives rise to the paradox of positing an identifiable, unique individual as the performer of that which implicitly denies the very possibility of such an autonomous writing subject. However, once we see in detail how the intertextuality of the essays operates, we will be in a better position to address the implications of what we read in the texts for the producers of those texts.

Examining the intertextual dialogism of Goethe's essays also provides access to another crucial generic issue: the question of *reading* in general and of the place of the reader in the essay. And insofar as the dialogue occurs on the *public* level, intertextual dialogue—which implies both a mingling, a community, of texts and the subversion of isolated, unique subjectivity—will be seen to have implications for the *social* aspect of the essay, for the place essayistic writing assumes in Goethe's notion of community.

Laocoön Goes Public

Lessing's *Laocoön* provided Goethe with an epoch-making and emulable example not only of the implicit deconstruction of systematic discourse, but also of public intertextual dialogue. We also find throughout Lessing's work an overriding concern with dialogue as a means of intellectual inquiry, as a mode of thought, as a quality of texts. In a draft for "Ernst and Falk: Conversations for Freemasons" ["Ernst und Falk: Gespräche für Freimäurer"] Lessing interprets Freemasonry on the basis of an etymological analysis of the word: "What is called Free Masonry in English should be called Massony, and what we have translated as *Maurerei* should have been translated by the old word Massony, which is as German as it is English" ["Was im Englischen Free Masonry heißt, sollte Massony heißen, und was wir durch Maurerei übersetzt haben, hätten wir durch das alte, aber eben so deutsche als englische Wort Massoney übersetzen müssen" (VIII, 536)].²³ This etymology is incorrect, but still significant because it allows Lessing to determine the constitutive moment of Freemasonry as *dialogue:* "The word Massony, according to its origin, means something like dinner party. . . . Our forebears were most social at table; that is where they talked things over, where they plotted communal undertakings" ["Das Wort Massoney heißt, seinem Ursprunge nach, so viel als Tischgesellschaft. . . . Am Tische waren unsre Ureltern am gesellschaftlichsten, da überlegten sie mit einander, da machten sie gemeinschaftliche Anschläge" (VIII, 537)].

Laocoön is also not the only text in which Lessing brings together dialogic structure and the critique of systems. "A Counter-Riposte" ["Eine Duplik"] has acquired its fame as a result of the passage that states a preference for the unending, always unfulfilled search for truth over the possession of truth (VIII, 33).²⁴ This critique of systematic endeavor is reflected in the structure of the text, which is divided into sections called "Contradictions" (which, incidentally, provide a strong contrast to the systematized tables of "antinomies" in Kant's critiques). The use of "contradictions" already implies a dialogic approach to the topic, an approach that is made explicit in the invention of a conversation on biblical problems. The form of dramatic dialogue is then employed to initiate yet another dialogue—a dialogue between text and reader: in the third "Contradiction" Lessing forces the reader into a dialogic involvement with the text by inserting a conversation in which the counterpart is designated as "You," that is, *as the reader* (VIII, 55–60).

In an earlier text, Lessing directly criticizes systems and systematic intentions. "Pope, a Metaphysician!" ["Pope ein Metaphysiker!"] attacks the prize topic to which it is a response by questioning whether the statement, *"Everything is good"* [*"Alles ist gut"*],[25] can be the summary of Pope's system of thought: "If I could, therefore, believe that whoever conceived of the topic absolutely insisted on finding a system in the words, *Everything is good*, then I might justifiably ask whether he is taking the word system in the strict sense that it should actually have" ["Wenn ich also glauben könnte, der Konzipient der Akademischen Aufgabe habe schlechterdings in den Worten *Alles ist gut* ein System zu finden verlangt; so würde ich billig fragen, ob er auch das Wort System in der strengen Bedeutung nehme, die es eigentlich haben soll?" (III, 634)]. The text then questions the very possibility of Pope having formulated a system "in a poem" (III, 635) and formulates its own project on this basis: "This was hard to accept—Nonetheless I tried in every possible way to convince myself that it is so. And in the end the following thoughts held sway, which I would like to call a PRELIMINARY INVESTIGATION *Of whether a poet, as a poet, can have a system*" ["Dieses wollte mir schwer ein—Gleichwohl suchte ich mich auf alle Art davon zu überzeugen. Und endlich behielten folgende Gedanken Platz, die ich eine VORLÄUFIGE UNTERSUCHUNG, *Ob ein Dichter, als ein Dichter, ein System haben könne?* nennen will" (III, 635–36)]. Woven into the subtext of this quotation is an indication of the text's foundation in dialogue. The word "I," insofar as we would normally take it as a reflection of an autonomous subject/author, is a lie. The text was written by both Lessing and Mendelssohn, but uses only, and often, the first person singular, never the plural. As we receive it, then, the text is a dialogue of voices that we cannot separate and identify. "Pope, a Metaphysician!" thus implicitly thematizes the notion that a "single," a "particular" text is not the product of an "individual" author. Here there is already a connection to Goethe, who wrote "On Epic and Dramatic Poetry" ["Über epische und dramatische Dichtung"] together with Schiller. Goethe and Schiller make no attempt to reduce this dialogue of voices, which also uses the first person singular, to two individual, identifiable voices. Editors, despite attempts to attribute the text or parts of it to one or the other writer, have not solved this "problem." Indeed, the essay appears in critical editions of the works of both Goethe *and* Schiller, and always as "by" Goethe and Schiller.

What I have just discussed are only a few of the many instances in Lessing's work where his anti-systematic use of dialogue becomes apparent. *Laocoön*, however, is his most dialogically permeated text.

What was to become an overt dialogue with the 1766 publication of *Laocoön* grew out of a covert dialogue that can be traced in detail. Lessing made his drafts for the various stages of his argument available to his friends Mendelssohn and Nicolai, who then provided him with their commentary. Mendelssohn's was by far the more extensive, and Lessing's reception of his comments then appeared in the final version.

Lessing rejected some of Mendelssohn's suggestions and accepted others. Regarding the spatial perception of bodies, Mendelssohn says: "Thus we look at (1) the parts singly, (2) their combination, (3) the whole. Our senses perform this with such an astonishing speed that we believe we perform all of these operations at the same time" ["So betrachten wir 1) die Teile einzeln, 2) ihre Verbindung, 3) das Ganze. Unsere Sinne verrichten dieses mit einer so erstaunlichen Geschwindigkeit, daß wir alle diese Operationen zu gleicher Zeit zu verrichten glauben" (VI, 566)].[26] In Lessing's final version there then appears an astonishingly close "paraphrase" of Mendelssohn's explanation: "We first look at its parts singly, then the combination of parts, and finally the whole. Our senses perform these various operations with such astonishing rapidity that they seem to us to be but one single operation" (85–86*) ["Erst betrachten wir die Teile desselben einzeln, hierauf die Verbindung dieser Teile, und endlich das Ganze. Unsere Sinne verrichten diese verschiedene Operationen mit einer so erstaunlichen Schnelligkeit, daß sie uns nur eine einzige zu sein bedünken" (VI, 110)]. In contrast to this total assimilation is the determined disregard of Mendelssohn's objection to his use of the word "action" in the place of "movement" (discussed in Part One). In other instances Lessing took a middle road, maintaining his previous point, but also taking Mendelssohn's criticism into account. For example, we read in the draft that *"Harmless ugliness* is *ridiculous.* . . . *Harmful ugliness* is *terrible* and, accordingly, *sublime"* [*"Unschädliche Häßlichkeit* ist *lächerlich.* . . . *Schädliche Häßlichkeit* ist *schrecklich,* folglich *erhaben"* (VI, 571)], to which Mendelssohn objected, among other things, that "not all that is terrible produces the feeling of sublimity" ["nicht alles Schreckliche erregt die Empfindung der Erhabenheit" (VI, 571)]. In the final version Lessing retains his differentiation between the types of ugliness, as well as his assertion that it is of greater use in poetry than in painting, but he eliminates his emphasis on the aspect of sublimity (chapter 24).

Thus, before even considering Lessing's "response" to Winckelmann in the published essay, we can see how *Laocoön* had its genesis in a dialogue of texts. The fact that Lessing did not consider it necessary to acknowledge publicly the contributions of his friends indicates that he took the constitutive function of dialogue in his writing as a matter of course. Not only does he not name the source of many of his points, but even his quotations are presented without quotation marks. In other words, we can trace in *Laocoön* an example of what Roland Barthes, in the Kristevan aftermath, describes as an untraceable "intertextual in which every text is held": "The citations which go to make up a text are anonymous, untraceable, and yet *already read:* they are quotations without inverted commas."[27]

Along with Barthes we can say that the text of *Laocoön,* like any text, is bound to be made up of innumerable untraceable citations; whatever sources we might trace will never exhaust its network of intertexts and whatever sources we might find can never claim to be absolute origins, for these sources themselves have sources, which in turn have sources, and so forth, *ad infinitum.* But texts, like *Laocoön,* where we *can* trace some of the hidden citations, are especially important because they take us beyond the recognition of the necessary existence of a network of intertexts to show *how* such intertextuality works, *how* sup-

posedly autonomous texts—"areas where monologism appears
to be the Law" (Barthes, 160)—are actually dialogues. Such
texts *thematize* "the text" as a "multi-dimensional space in
which a variety of writings, none of them original, blend and
clash."[28]

As a published text *Laocoön* represents, in its response to
Winckelmann, the inauguration of a public intertextual dialogue.
In his *Thoughts on the Imitation of Greek Works* Winckelmann
had discussed art solely from the perspective of painting and
sculpture.[29] He took no trouble to distinguish those arts from
poetry; indeed, he went so far as to speak of poets who paint with
their words (24) and of painters who draw their inspiration from
models that can be "poetically" executed in their art (39). It was
this tendency to leave the arts essentially undifferentiated, and
more specifically his critique of Virgil's description of Laocoön
(20), that elicited Lessing's response (7–8; VI, 12–13). And it
was Winckelmann's positing of the Laocoön group as a "consummate rule of art" ["vollkommene Regel der Kunst" (4)] that dictated Lessing's concentration when replying.

In the process of addressing such topics from Winckelmann's
study as beauty, allegory, the notion of painting invisible things,
and the didactic purpose of art, Lessing reinscribes those concepts in the context of his own (ostensible) theoretical concern of
differentiating poetry and painting. He tries not to polemicize
against Winckelmann or to reject the latter's views outright, but
that reinscription leads to a reevaluation of the concepts contrary
to Winckelmann's statements at nearly every point. Winckelmann subordinates beauty in Greek art to what he calls the
"distinguishing feature of the Greek masterpieces" ["Kenn-
zeichen der griechischen Meisterstücke"]—"a noble simplicity
and a quiet grandeur" ["eine edle Einfalt, und eine stille Größe"]
(20). Lessing shows that those qualities in the Laocoön group are
merely the result of the artist's choice of the most "pregnant
moment," that there is no scream as in Virgil *because* the work is
a statue and must avoid that peak of the implied action; Lessing
then posits beauty as the highest ideal of Greek art. To Winckelmann's assertion that painters could learn a great deal from
poetic allegory (37), Lessing, for whom "allegory" is a pejora-

tive, counters that poetry is not allegorical in its portrayal of personified "Abstracta" and that only the fine arts, because they do not use words, can be allegorical (60; VI, 80). Near the end of his study Winckelmann describes painting's "greatest fortune" as "the presentation of invisible, past and future things" ["die Vorstellung unsichtbarer, vergangener und zukünftiger Dinge"] (38); in chapter 12 of *Laocoön* we then read Lessing's refutation of this point: "Homer treats of two kinds of beings and actions, visible and invisible. This distinction cannot be made in painting, where everything is visible and visible in but one way" (66) ["Homer bearbeitet eine doppelte Gattung von Wesen und Handlungen; sichtbare und unsichtbare. Diesen Unterschied kann die Malerei nicht angeben: bei ihr ist alles sichtbar; und auf einerlei Art sichtbar" (VI, 89)]. Finally, whereas Winckelmann subscribes to Horace's dictum that art should both educate and give pleasure (39), Lessing insists that the single goal of art is pleasure (14; VI, 19). Lessing's discussions throughout his text repeatedly, though not always explicitly or with quotations, refer back to Winckelmann's text and thus assume a dialogic attitude toward that text.

Lessing's dialogic attitude is not simply the result of the topics he chooses to discuss. It is embedded in the structure of *Laocoön*. The fiction outlined in Part One that Lessing creates about the composition of his text has implications for the dialogic quality of the essay as well as for its stance toward systematic discourse. That Lessing did not just read Winckelmann's study and then sit down and write *Laocoön*, but rather added the framework of a response to his predecessor only in the final draft; that he did not write down his thoughts according to the developing order of his ideas; that his chapters did not emerge by chance and according to the sequence of his readings; that he announces that he will not discuss certain points because the publication of Winckelmann's *History* will clear them up, when that work had actually already been in print for several years; and that he then later discusses issues from *Thoughts on the Imitation of Greek Works* in the posture of just having read and responding to the *History*—all of these components of the grand fiction indicate that what Lessing apparently did was consider the *process* of responding to Winckelmann and then incorporate that process into his essay. The structure and process of *Laocoön* reveal *the staging of a dialogue with Winckelmann's text*.

Winckelmann did not respond to Lessing's dialogic overtures, but Herder did—in the first of his *Critical Forests* [*Kritische Wälder*]. With this response the Laocoön debate becomes a public written dialogue. In his *Treatise on the Origin of Language* [*Abhandlung über den Ursprung der Sprache*], Herder had stated his view of dialogue not as *a* mode of thought but as *the* mode of thought:

> I cannot think the first human thought, I cannot align the first reflective argument without dialoguing in my soul or without striving to dialogue. The first human thought is hence in its very essence a preparation for the possibility of dialoguing with others! The first characteristic mark I register is a characteristic word for me and a word of communication for others!
>
> [Ich kann nicht den ersten Menschlichen Gedanken denken, nicht das Erste besonnene Urtheil reihen, ohne daß ich in meiner Seele dialogire, oder zu dialogiren strebe; der erste Menschliche Gedanke bereitet also seinem Wesen nach, mit Andern dialogiren zu können! Das erste Merkmal, was ich erfaße, ist Merkwort für mich, und Mittheilungswort für Andre!][30]

Herder had also already had some practice at participating in public dialogue with Lessing. His *On Recent German Literature* [*Über die neuere Deutsche Litteratur*] of 1766–67 carries the subtitle, *A Supplement to the Letters on the Most Recent Literature* [*Eine Beilage zu den Briefen, die neueste Literatur betreffend*], Lessing's periodical publication of the years 1759–65. In that collection he excerpts, comments on, and criticizes parts of Lessing's *Letters on Literature* to produce what Klaus Berghahn calls the "continuation of a conversation on literature."[31]

In the first chapter of the "First Grove" ["Erstes Wäldchen"]

Herder comments on the value of Lessing's dialogic attitude in *Laocoön* when he says, "His book is an entertaining dialogue for our mind" ["Sein Buch (ist) ein unterhaltender Dialog für unsern Geist" (III, 12)]. He also reveals his understanding of the significance in Lessing's text of the process of thought vis-à-vis the presentation of the results of thought: "Lessing's style is the style of a poet, i.e., not of a writer who has done something, but of a writer who is doing something" ["Lessings Schreibart ist der Styl eines Poeten, d.i. eines Schriftstellers, nicht der gemacht hat, sondern der da machet" (III, 12)]; what matters here is not whether the text *actually* reflects the process of its writer's thought, but that the writing itself has the quality of process, that the notion of process is inscribed in the text's "style."

Herder then proceeds to write his own text in much the same way by staging a dialogue with Lessing and Winckelmann in which he acts as both moderator and contributor. He sees value in the work of both L. and W. and attempts to juggle acceptance and rejection of Lessing's points in such a way to save Winckelmann from the obscurity into which Lessing's essay threatens to cast him. That he sees his studies as entering into a broader dialogue with the *texts* of his time is revealed by the subtitle of the *Critical Forests: Observations Concerning the Science and Art of the Beautiful, According to Recent Writings* [*Betrachtungen, die Wissenschaft und Kunst des Schönen betreffend, nach Maasgabe neuerer Schriften* (III, 1)].

As a dialogic partner Herder addresses himself to nearly all of the arguments raised in *Laocoön* and brings in his own arguments to reach different conclusions concerning the divergence of poetry and painting. Where Lessing had employed the distinction of space and time, for example, Herder introduces the "work"/"energy" ["Werk"/"Energie"] distinction (chapters 16–19). Although Herder assumes the attitude of "saving" Winckelmann, the advances he makes in the discussion of artistic production actually result more from the dialogue he enters into with Lessing. One of Herder's main contributions in the first "Grove" is a further development of the delimitation of the arts that had caused Lessing's objection to Winckelmann. Lessing portrays poetry and painting as two types of imitation—that of objects and that of successive actions. Herder, however, sees the two arts as altogether different processes; he describes painting as activity directed at an object and poetry as activity in and of itself—that is, in poetry activity is the end in itself. Furthermore, this definition of poetry recalls Herder's concern with the process of writing and, more specifically, his description of the character of Lessing's, "the poet's," essay as a whole. Thus Lessing's text has *become* a part of Herder's text, the textual strategy of *Laocoön* has been transformed into the theoretical subject matter of the "First Grove."

Herder's dialogic posturing becomes most apparent in his parodistic quotations of key phrases from Lessing's text. When reacting to Winckelmann's discussion of the Laocoön group and Sophocles' *Philoctetes*, Lessing specifies his objection by saying, "But as to the reasons on which Mr. Winckelmann bases this wisdom . . . I venture to be of a different opinion" (8*) ["Nur in dem Grunde, welchen Herr Winckelmann dieser Weisheit gibt . . . wage ich es, anderer Meinung zu sein" (VI, 13)]. In Herder's discussion of Lessing's argument about Homer's depiction of invisible objects we then read, *without* "inverted commas": "I am satisfied with the difference Mr. L. names, but the reason he gives for the difference is not the same as mine" ["Mit dem Unterschiede, den Hr. L. angiebt, bin ich zufrieden; nur der Grund des Unterschieds, den er angiebt, ist nicht der meine" (III, 105)]. In his preface Lessing defends his project as follows: "Although my reasoning may not be so compelling as Baumgarten's, my examples will at least smack more of the source" (5) ["Wenn mein Raisonnement nicht so bündig ist, als das Baumgartensche, so werden doch meine Beispiele mehr nach der Quelle schmecken" (VI, 11)]. Herder justifies his own endeavor by quoting this remark, with quotation marks, but he effectively subverts those marks by altering the sense of the citation significantly: " 'Although my reasoning may not be so compelling as Lessing's, my critical discussions will perhaps smack more of the source' " [" 'Wenn mein Raisonnement nicht so bündig ist, als das Leßingsche, so werden vielleicht meine kritischen Erörterungen mehr nach der Quelle schmecken' " (III, 185–86). (In that Herder places additional emphasis on his tentative attitude toward what he writes, we might say that he "out-essays" Lessing.) Finally, Herder states, again without quotation marks, that his "Critical Forests . . . were written as chance dictated and more through the sequence of my reading than through any systematic development of general principles" ["meine Kritischen Wälder . . . sind zufälliger Weise entstanden, und mehr durch die Folge meiner Lectüre, als durch die Methodische Entwicklung allgemeiner Grundsätze angewachsen" (III, 187)]. Except for replacing the preposition "in keeping with" [*nach*] with "through" [*durch*], this is a direct quotation. Moreover, in that it is the quotation of a claim that had been crucial for Lessing's dialogic structuring of *Laocoön*, it reveals the great extent to which Lessing's dialogic "style" informs Herder's critical writing. Herder evidently recognized and accepted the challenge to carry on the public dialogue Lessing initiated in *Laocoön*.[32]

Lessing responded to Herder's response, but not at length. In "How the Ancients Portrayed Death" ["Wie die Alten den Tod gebildet"] (to which Herder also responded) he speaks favorably of the *Critical Forests* and differentiates his attitude toward Herder, "whom I have to thank for more important reminders" ["dem ich wichtigere Erinnerungen zu danken habe" (VI, 422)], from his current polemic against Klotz. By only briefly praising Herder in the context of the study's diatribe and not mentioning him by name, Lessing implies that a proper response, a dialogic response, would have to take place in a framework other than that of polemic, where Lessing does not take his opposition seriously or treat it fairly. (We can distinguish here between Lessing's *contentious,* but nevertheless dialogic, response to Winckelmann—whose points he discusses and challenges while at the same time recognizing their importance for the genesis of his "own" text—and the *polemic* against Klotz, which, like the discourse of hierarchy and power Kleist describes, aims at the defeat of the "interlocutor," at the obliteration of the opponent. Klotz had attacked only a minor point from a footnote to *Laocoön,* but Lessing took this as an opportunity to make a full-scale attack on Klotz.)

Lessing's response to Herder, we might expect, would have come in the second or third part of *Laocoön,* which he planned, but never wrote. However, the Winckelmann-Lessing-Herder dialogue did not die in 1769. It hibernated for three decades and then, in the middle of the 1790s, went back to press. The scene was no longer Berlin, but Weimar.

Snakebites, Screams, and the Quotation of Textual Strategy

There is extensive evidence of Goethe's active reception of *Laocoön* in the late 1760s, as well as of his, relatively silent, involvement in the Winckelmann-Lessing-Herder public dialogue. The most often cited proof that he read Lessing's text soon after it appeared comes in Book 8 of *Poetry and Truth:*

> We enthusiastically welcomed that beam of light directed down on us from the gloomy clouds by a most excellent thinker. One has to be a young man to visualize what an effect Lessing's *Laocoön* had on us, this work that swept us away from the regions of meager contemplation and onto the open terrain of thought. . . . The full consequence of this brilliant thought was illuminated for us as though by a flash of lightning. We cast off all previous critical instructions and judgments like a worn-out coat. (IV, 238)

> [Jener Lichtstrahl (war uns) höchst willkommen, den der vortrefflichste Denker durch düstre Wolken auf uns herableitete. Man muß Jüngling sein, um sich zu vergegenwärtigen, welche Wirkung Lessings Laokoon auf uns ausübte, indem dieses Werk uns aus der Region eines kümmerlichen Anschauens in die freien Gefilde des Gedankens hinriß. . . . Wie vor einem Blitz erleuchteten sich uns alle Folgen dieses herrlichen Gedankens, alle bisherige anleitende und urteilende Kritik ward, wie ein abgetragener Rock, weggeworfen. (X, 348)]

Thus the enthusiastic response of a seventeen-year-old student in Leipzig. Within just a few years what had been fully accepted as a revelatory insight, a critical epiphany, began to undergo a more critical reception.

In February 1769, after having read Herder's "First Grove," Goethe wrote a letter to Oeser that, while it does not see Lessing's point as having been undermined by Herder, does reveal a nascent desire to criticize Lessing that is as yet held in check by admiration for his critical powers, inhibition in the face of his great stature, and some fear of the kind of polemics he employed against Klotz:

> Lessing! Lessing! If he weren't Lessing, I would say something. I'd rather not write against him; he is a conqueror, and he'll be a merciless lumberjack when he comes across Mr. Herder's grove. He is a phenomenal intellect and such phenomena are quite rare in Germany. No one is forced to believe everything he says, just don't refute him.
>
> [Lessing! Lessing! wenn er nicht Lessing wäre, ich möchte was sagen. Schreiben mag ich nicht wider ihn, er ist ein Eroberer und wird in Herrn Herders Wäldchen garstig Holz machen, wenn er drüber kommt. Er ist ein Phänomen von Geist, und im Grunde sind diese Erscheinungen in Teutschland selten. Wer ihm nicht alles glauben will, der ist nicht gezwungen, nur widerlegt ihn nicht. (XVIII, 124–25)]

Within three quarters of a year Goethe overcame his inhibition. In a letter of 30 November 1769 he describes to Langer the "ecstasy" he experienced when viewing a copy of the Laocoön group in Mannheim and then indicates that he has his own ideas about the statue that lead to an illumination of the Lessing-Herder dialogue: "I've made some remarks about the Laocoön which illuminate that famous dispute among great men" ["Jai fait des remarques sur le Laocoon qui donnent bien de lumiere a cette fameuse dispute, dont les combattans sont de bien grands hommes" (XVIII, 127)].[33] Moreover, those remarks result in an insight into the shortcomings of his predecessors: "But, as we see every day, genius is never universal and being a good poet does not make one an architect; the same is true with Lessing, Herder, and Klotz. In order to talk about the fine arts one has to be more than a critic and has to be able to do more than form pretty hypotheses" ["Mais comme nous voyons touts les jours, que jamais genie n'est universel, et que bon poete n'est pas d'abord architecte, c'est de meme de Lessing, de Herder, de Klotz. Pour parler des beaux arts il faut plus que d'etre critique et que de scavoir former de belles hypotheses" (XVIII, 127–28)]. Whereas in 1766 he accepted without reservation Lessing's differentiation between the arts (if we can assume that the autobiography gives an accurate account), he now implies that neither Lessing nor Herder was even qualified to make that distinction.

Finally, in his diary of the following year we find a direct attack on Lessing's central assertion in *Laocoön,* on the notion, which Goethe supposedly praised so highly in 1766, that the sole purpose and highest goal of Greek art was the portrayal and creation of *beauty.* In the "Ephemerides," his diary for the years 1770–71, Goethe enters a quotation from Lessing's text (on the portrayal of the Furies) that he then discusses in terms of the theoretical issue of beauty in art, concluding that "one has to seek the excellence of the ancients in something other than the creation of beauty" ["dass man die Fürtrefflichkeit der Alten in etwas anders als der Bildung der Schönheit zu suchen hat" (IV, 966)].

We thus have evidence not only of Goethe's reading of Herder and repeated reading of *Laocoön,* but also of his increasing critical involvement in the debate. And his involvement was not restricted to the reception of Lessing's and Herder's texts; in the diaries he notes Reynolds's opening of the London Academy and praises him for supporting one of Winckelmann's main points: "He especially insists . . . on the feeling of Ideal quiet grandeur. He is right" ["Er dringt besonders . . . auf das Gefühl der Idealischen stillen Grösse. Er hat recht" (IV, 973)]. What is more, the letter to Langer reveals his intention of joining in that public dialogue, "that famous dispute": "I've written to Oeser in order to communicate to him my discoveries. I will try to organize them this winter so that I can put the finishing touches on them and give this small work all possible elegance" ["J'ai ecrit a Oeser, pour lui communiquer mes decouvertes, je tacherai de les mettre en bon ordre cet hyver, pour pouvoir y toucher de la derniere main, et pour donner a ce petit ouvrage toutte elegance possible" (XVIII, 128)]. We would have to assume that this study is what he then refers to in the "Ephemerides" when he says he has treated elsewhere the problem of beauty and ugliness in Greek art.

Goethe's public contribution to the Laocoön debate did not materialize, at least not until many years later. However, just a few years after he revealed his plan to Langer, he entered into what resembles a textual dialogue with Lessing. His drama *Clavigo* forms a link between his novel, *The Sorrows of Young Werther* [*Die Leiden des jungen Werthers*], and Lessing's *Emilia Galotti*. Through allusion on the thematic level—the inner conflict between duty and desire, necessity and freedom—*Clavigo* provides an explanation for Werther's reading of Lessing's play just before he commits suicide. Moreover, *Clavigo* is a dialogic text that rather conspicuously betrays its intertextuality and its relationship to *Emilia Galotti*. Large parts of the text are direct quotation from Beaumarchais's report (the source of the plot), and we also find what approach direct citations, without inverted commas, from Lessing's text. In discussing Appiani's imminent marriage to Emilia, Marinelli claims, "A girl . . . was able to lure him into her trap—with a little deception, but with a resplendent show of virtue and feeling and wit" ["Ein Mädchen . . . hat ihn in ihre Schlinge zu ziehen gewußt, —mit ein wenig Larve: aber mit vielem Prunke von Tugend und Gefühl und Witz" (II, 137)]. Carlos criticizes Marie with a similar argument: "In all classes there are good children who occupy themselves with plans and prospects for getting hold of you. This one makes use of her beauty, that one counts on her wealth, her station, her wit, her relatives" ["Unter allen Ständen giebts gute Kinder, die sich mit Planen und Aussichten beschäftigen, dich habhaft zu werden. Die eine bringt ihre Schönheit in Anschlag,

die ihren Reichtum, ihren Stand, ihren Witz, ihre Verwandte"
(IV, 784)]. When Marinelli and Carlos ask for permission to
arrange the affairs of their friends as they see fit, their requests
are not only similar, but nearly identical: Marinelli—"Are you
willing to give me free rein, Prince? Are you willing to sanction
anything I do?" ["Wollen Sie mir freie Hand lassen, Prinz?
Wollen Sie alles genehmigen, was ich tue?" (II, 141)]; Carlos—
"And so you give me free rein; you needn't do or write anything" ["Und somit läßt du mir freye Hand; du brauchst nichts
zu thun, nichts zu schreiben" (IV, 793)].[34] Goethe thus maintains his involvement in Lessing's texts; in his allusions to and
"quotations" of Lessing he performs a dialogic incorporation of
the predecessor text similar, in some respects, to Herder's response to *Laocoön*.

✻   ✻   ✻

Goethe returned to Laocoön and *Laocoön* in 1797. In a letter of
5 July he writes to Schiller that he will take up the project he
believes he once completed—the essay announced in the letter
to Langer—and write a new piece on the topic: "On this occasion I have recalled an essay I wrote a number of years ago, and
since I could not find it, I have assembled the material that is still
present to me according to my (and I trust our) current conviction" ["Ich habe bei dieser Gelegenheit mich eines Aufsatzes
erinnert, den ich vor mehrern Jahren schrieb, und habe, da ich
ihn nicht finden konnte, das Material, dessen ich noch wohl
eingedenk bin, nach meiner (und ich darf wohl sagen unserer)
jetzigen Überzeugung zusammengestellt" (XX, 374)]. The "occasion" to which he refers is a study entitled "Laokoon" written
by the Berlin art historian Aloys Hirt and published later that
year in Schiller's *The Horae* [*Die Horen*].[35] In his study, Hirt
rejects both Winckelmann's and Lessing's positions; in the place
of Winckelmann's "noble simplicity and quiet grandeur" and
Lessing's emphasis on beauty, he attempts to erect a new law for
Greek art:

> Assuming that we were to go along with Lessing and see
> beauty as the first principle of the ancients, it would be

impossible to hold this view in the narrow sense he seems to demand. And the opinion of Winckelmann, who locates this first principle in a noble simplicity and quiet grandeur, is just as untenable. . . . The main principle of ancient art was a completely different one.

In all works of the ancients, without exception . . . we find individuality of meaning—characteristic.

[Gesezt: wir nähmen mit Leßing die Schönheit, als das Grundgesez an, nach welchem die Alten arbeiteten; so können wir dieß unmöglich in dem beschränkten Verstande gelten lassen, wie es dieser Kunstrichter zu verlangen scheint: Eben so wenig kann die Meinung Winkelmann's gelten, der dieß Grundgesez bei den Alten in eine stille Grösse, und edle Einfalt sezet. . . . Das Hauptprincip der alten Kunst (war) ein ganz anderes.

In allen Werken der Alten ohne Ausnahme . . . zeiget sich Individuellheit der Bedeutung—Karakteristik. (11–12)]

For Hirt, "the characteristic," which in turn requires "truth" (23–24), is the sole determining aspect of ancient art, its central principle, and its goal. Schiller, in the mistaken belief that he was in full agreement with Goethe, welcomed Hirt's analysis and his emphasis on truth enthusiastically: "It's about time someone dared to take the concept and even the word 'beauty,' to which all those false concepts are inseparably linked, out of circulation, and, as is only proper, to replace it with 'truth' in its most complete sense" ["Möchte es doch einmal einer wagen, den Begriff und selbst das Wort Schönheit, an welches einmal alle jene falsche Begriffe unzertrennlich geknüpft sind, aus dem Umlauf zu bringen und, wie billig, die Wahrheit in ihrem vollständigsten Sinn an seine Stelle setzen" (XX, 375; to Goethe, 7 July 1797)]. Thus Goethe misled himself in thinking that his response to Hirt would accord to Schiller's convictions, for his own reception of Hirt had been lukewarm: "And so, in the essay on Laocoön I am enclosing, he is right in many respects, but still on the whole he comes up too short. . . . At the same time, his insistence on the characteristic and the emotive is fairly good" ["So hat er in dem Aufsatz über Laokoon, den ich hier beilege, gar vielfach recht, und doch fällt er im ganzen zu kurz. . . . Indessen ist es recht gut, wie er aufs Charakteristische und Pathetische . . . dringt" (XX, 373–74; to Schiller, 5 July 1797)]. Although he considers Hirt's exposition of the characteristic an important contribution (XX, 377; to Schiller, 8 July 1797), he nevertheless accuses him of extreme bias: "But it often happens that he posits what are, if not false, then at least limited and one-sided premises as general ones" ["Er kommt aber oft in den Fall, daß er, wo nicht falsche, doch beschränkte und einseitige Prämissen als allgemeine voraussetzt" (XX, 373; to Schiller, 5 July 1797)].

Goethe's own essay—"On Laocoön"—can then be seen almost as a point by point attack on Hirt.[36] He discusses "the characteristic" as one among many of the qualities of a great work of art, and throughout his analysis makes statements that directly contradict Hirt's claims. He says that the father and his sons had been attacked in their sleep by the snakes, which Hirt denies. Whereas Hirt claims that the elder son screams to his father for help, Goethe interprets his position as one of only marginal involvement in the scene, since he is as yet hardly in the power of the snake and has a chance of escaping. Hirt asserts that both the father and the younger son have been bitten by the snakes, but Goethe insists that the younger son has not yet been bitten—"It does *not* bite" (III, 18) ["Keineswegs aber beißt sie" (XIII, 166)]. These are just a few examples of Goethe's opposition to Hirt's interpretation.[37] Perhaps the most significant point of specific disagreement concerns the question that was also central to Winckelmann's and Lessing's studies— namely, the reason why the father does not scream (and consequently the question of which moment in an action the artist chooses to portray). Both Hirt and Goethe assert that he does not scream because it is physically impossible, but their explanations of this impossibility diverge. Hirt believes that the snake's poison is taking effect and that the father, close to death, can *no longer* scream. Goethe, however, claims that he *is being* bitten (that is, that no effect of poison can be visible [III, 20; XIII,

169]) and that the contortions and tension of his body make the scream impossible. Thus Hirt would locate the most advantageous phase of an action as the "denouement," while Goethe designates "the highest moment for representation" (III, 16*) ["den höchsten darzustellenden Moment" (XIII, 163)] as the artistically most profitable.

Goethe published his essay in the *Propyläen,* that is, in the context of an essayistic project that had its foundation in dialogue. The journal as a whole, as well as individual essays such as "The Collector" and "On Laocoön," grew out of a dialogue between Goethe, Schiller, and Meyer, and out of a broader dialogue on the concept of beauty; the genesis of "The Collector" even resembles that of Lessing's *Laocoön* in that Goethe sent sections of it to Schiller for criticism and suggestions.[38] In "On Laocoön," however, Goethe's "response" to Hirt sooner resembles a sub-textual polemic than an attempt to enter into a dialogue. On the other hand, although Goethe apparently sensed the need to dismiss Hirt's theses, he did find Hirt's attempt to be valuable precisely in terms of such a dialogue. What Hirt's study had done, regardless of its questionable argument, was to set the stage for a revival of the Winckelmann-Lessing-Herder dialogue that would give Goethe an opportunity to make up for his failure to continue the dialogue in the 1770s. This is also how Goethe viewed the situation; in his letter to Schiller we read: "The Hirt essay is a good preparation for it [for Goethe's reformulation of twenty-five-year-old ideas—P.B.], since he has provided the most recent instigation" ["Der Hirtsche Aufsatz ist eine gute Vorbereitung dazu, da er die neuste Veranlassung gegeben hat" (XX, 374; to Schiller, 5 July 1797)]. This much of Goethe's intent Schiller did understand, for in his answer to that letter he says, "I would very much like to have the Hirt essay in the Horae. Once the path is open, you and Meyer would be able to take up the thread that much more easily and would also find the public better prepared" ["Den Hirtschen Aufsatz hätte ich recht gern in den Horen. Sie und Meyer würden dann, wenn der Weg einmal offen ist, den Faden um so bequemer aufnehmen können und das Publikum auch schon mehr vorbereitet finden" (XX, 375; to Goethe, 7 July 1797)]. By responding to Hirt, even

in a polemical fashion, Goethe was able not only to continue the
critical dialogue of *Die Horen,* to create a dialogic relationship
between his and Schiller's journals, but also to hold up finally
his end of the dialogue with Lessing, to carry out on a public
level what he had long since done in private.[39] What we read in
"On Laocoön" is a variety of texts that blend and clash in a way
characteristic of what Barthes calls the intertextual nature of
writing, and in the way Lessing's text had blended and clashed
with Winckelmann's, and Herder's with Lessing's.

The place of Winckelmann's *Thoughts on the Imitation of
Greek Works* in Goethe's essay is less significant than that of
Laocoön. Nevertheless, there are echoes of some major points.
At the beginning of his study Winckelmann asserts that "Laocoön was to the artists in ancient Rome precisely what it is to
us . . . a consummate rule of art" ["Laokoon war den Künstlern
im alten Rom ebendas, was er uns ist . . . eine vollkommene
Regel der Kunst" (4)], and likewise in the first pages of "On
Laocoön" we read that the group fulfills all "conditions we
demand of a great work of art" ["Bedingungen, welche wir von
einem hohen Kunstwerke fordern"] and "that we can derive all
of them from this particular work alone" ["daß man sie aus
derselben allein entwickeln könne"] (III, 16*; XIII, 163). Wohlleben reads in Goethe's description of the statue as a "tragic
idyll" (III, 17; XIII, 166) an allusion to the central oxymoron of
Winckelmann's text—the postulation of "noble simplicity" and
"quiet grandeur" as the essence of Greek art (Wohlleben, 94).
(We might also see in this notion of a tragic idyll, as well as in
the use of the concept "grace" [*Anmut*], an allusion to Schiller's
aesthetic treatises.) In connection with one of Winckelmann's
assertions, we find an example of how Goethe's text both blends
and clashes with the earlier writing it absorbs. Winckelmann
claims that Laocoön "does not raise the terrible scream of which
Virgil sings: The opening of the mouth does not permit it. . . .
Laocoön suffers, but he suffers like Sophocles' Philoctetes" ["Er
erhebet kein schreckliches Geschrei, wie Vergil von seinem
Laokoon singet: Die Öffnung des Mundes gestattet es nicht. . . .
Laokoon leidet, aber er leidet wie des Sophokles Philoktet"
(20)]. Like Winckelmann, Goethe would have us believe that

Laocoön does not scream because all of the movements of his body, which determine "the facial expression" (III, 20) ["die Züge des Angesichts" (XIII, 168)], prevent it.[40] But Goethe diverges from Winckelmann, even attacks him, on the issue of comparison to literary texts: "We are doing a great injustice to Virgil and poetry in general if we compare, even for a moment, the most self-contained of all sculptural masterpieces with the episodic treatment the subject receives in the *Aeneid*" (III, 23) ["Man ist höchst ungerecht gegen Virgilen und die Dichtkunst, wenn man das geschlossenste Meisterwerk der Bildhauerarbeit mit der episodischen Behandlung in der Äneis auch nur einen Augenblick vergleicht" (XIII, 174)]. With this disagreement we are already in the realm of allusion to Lessing's text, which begins with a critique of that same passage in Winckelmann.

In the "Ephemerides" Goethe's main objection to *Laocoön* had concerned Lessing's emphasis on beauty as the goal of Greek art. Hirt rejected Lessing's view altogether. In his attempt to counteract the effect of Hirt's bias, Goethe then rehabilitates the significance of beauty. He at first avoids reinstating the concept to its full previous stature by treating it as one among several characteristics of "great works of art" and by limiting the role it plays to a spiritual one: "Furthermore, the object is subject to the law of spiritual beauty, which results from the proper measure to which the person trained in the portrayal or creation of the beautiful knows how to subject everything, even extremes" (III, 16*) ["Ferner ist er (der Gegenstand) dem Gesetz der geistigen Schönheit unterworfen, die durch das Maß entsteht, welchem der zur Darstellung oder Hervorbringung des Schönen gebildete Mensch alles, sogar die Extreme zu unterwerfen weiß" (XIII, 163)]. He follows this rather circular definition with a circular "proof" that the statue is beautiful: "The beauty of the work is obvious to anyone who perceives with what proper measure the extreme physical and mental suffering is presented" (III, 16*) ["Daß man das Werk schön nennen müsse, wird wohl niemand bezweifeln, welcher das Maß erkennt, womit das Extrem eines physischen und geistigen Leidens hier dargestellt ist" (XIII, 163)]. What we then read is a subversion of the limitation he has just made: "Every work of art must be identifiable as such; this is only possible if it exhibits what we call sensual beauty, or grace" (III, 16*) ["Jedes Kunstwerk muß sich als ein solches anzeigen, und das kann es allein durch das, was wir sinnliche Schönheit oder Anmut nennen" (XIII, 164)]. Here he is already approaching Lessing in granting beauty all-encompassing ("spiritual" *and* "sensual") importance. He later undermines the aspect of "spiritual beauty" by eliminating from his description of the statue what had been the definition of such beauty—measure [*Maß*]: "His [Laocoön's] companions in suffering are two boys who are disproportionately small compared to him" (III, 21) ["Mit ihm leiden zwei Knaben, die, selbst dem Maße nach, gegen ihn klein gehalten sind" (XIII, 170)]. What we are left with, then, is "sensual beauty"—in other words, Lessing's position. Goethe enters into an implied dialogue with Lessing and ends up agreeing with him; their texts clash, but finally come together.

On another crucial point, Goethe's and Lessing's texts seem to do just the opposite—first converge, then diverge. Both place great emphasis on the "moment" of an action chosen by the artist. Goethe says that the artist must find "the highest moment for representation," and we immediately think of Lessing's argument, central to his explanation of why Laocoön does not scream, that the sculptor or painter must portray the most "pregnant moment." Goethe's further assertions—that the work of art must show "a fleeting moment" (III, 18) ["ein vorübergehender Moment" (XIII, 166)] and that "the most highly emotive expression which art can achieve is to be found in the transition from one condition to another" (III, 20*) ["der höchste pathetische Ausdruck, den sie darstellen kann, schwebt auf dem Übergange eines Zustandes in den andern" (XIII, 169)]—support that sense of fundamental similarity. However, he then subtly modifies his description of that moment in a way that contradicts Lessing: "If we now visualize the action from the very beginning, we recognize that it has reached its highest point" (III, 22*) ["Denken wir nun die Handlung vom Anfang herauf und erkennen, daß sie gegenwärtig auf dem höchsten Punkt steht" (XIII, 172)]. It is no longer the highest moment of representation ["den höchsten *darzustellenden* Moment"], but the height of the entire *action,* and this is precisely what Lessing avoids in speaking of the most *pregnant* moment: "The artist must maintain proper measure in the expression and never present an action at its highest point" (19*) ["Der Künstler (müsse) in dem Ausdrucke Maß halten, und ihn nie aus dem höchsten Punkte der Handlung nehmen" (VI, 25)]; "The more we add in our imagination, the more we must think we see. In the full course of an emotion, no point is less suitable for this than the highest" (19*) ["Je mehr wir darzu denken, desto mehr müssen wir zu sehen glauben. In dem ganzen Verfolge eines Affekts ist aber kein Augenblick der diesen Vorteil weniger hat, als die höchste Staffel desselben" (VI, 26)]. According to Lessing, if the statue depicted the height of the action, then Laocoön would be depicted as screaming, which in turn would prevent the artist's achievement of beauty. In one sense, however, the two texts reconverge. The "Announcement of the *Propylaea*" does not describe the contents of "On Laocoön" as much as it supplements, rewrites the essay. In this dialogue of Goethe with himself, he returns to Lessing's view, more explicitly than anywhere in the essay, when he says that the artist "can only present a single moment in an isolated work, and should choose the most pregnant one possible" ["in einem isolierten Werke nur einen einzigen Moment darstellen kann, . . . denselben so prägnant als möglich zu nehmen hat" (XIII, 192)].

In the "Announcement" Goethe praises Winckelmann and Lessing in general—"two men who have never been honored enough"—and Lessing specifically for having worked toward the strict theoretical separation of poetry and painting: "He initiated the strict separation of the procedure of the poet from that of the artist" ["Er (begann) das Verfahren des Poeten von dem Verfahren des bildenden Künstlers scharf zu sondern" (XIII, 191)]. In "On Laocoön" he then uses the statue as a demonstration of that separation: "Laocoön lends only his name to the sculpture, since the artists have stripped him of his priesthood, his Trojan nationality, and of all poetic and mythological attributes. He is not the Laocoön as portrayed in the story" (III, 17*) ["So ist auch bei dieser Gruppe Laokoon ein bloßer Name; von seiner Priesterschaft, von seinem trojanisch-nationellen, von allem poetischen und mythologischen Beiwesen haben ihn die Künstler entkleidet; er ist nichts von allem wozu ihn die Fabel macht" (XIII, 165)]. Goethe's essay ostensibly carries on the process Lessing was said to have begun, but in its most salient allusion to Lessing it undermines this project.

Near the end of the essay, Goethe introduces the terms "fear, terror, and pity" ["Furcht, Schrecken und Mitleiden"] in defense of his claim that Laocoön is a complete, closed work of art. The use of these concepts has been understood as a reflection of Goethe's and Schiller's correspondence on Aristotle's *Poetics* in the spring of 1797.[41] But given the context—a discussion of Laocoön and the limits of art—and the fact that Goethe elsewhere employs the criterion of the proper relationship of "cause" and "effect" (III, 20; XIII, 168), the introduction of those terms would have to be seen primarily as an allusion to Lessing, specifically to the *Hamburg Dramaturgy* [*Hamburgische Dramaturgie*]. Goethe then uses Lessing's terms in the service of Lessing's project of differentiating the arts: "As soon as the fine arts, which always work for the moment, choose an emotive subject, they will select the one that evokes terror, whereas poetry stays with those that evoke fear and pity" (III, 22*) ["Die bildende Kunst, die immer für den Moment arbeitet, wird, sobald sie einen pathetischen Gegenstand wählt, denjenigen ergreifen der Schrecken erweckt, dahingegen Poesie sich an solche hält, die Furcht und Mitleiden erregen" (XIII, 172)]. In addition to the subversive irony of using the terms of *poetics* in order to prove the divergence of the fine arts from poetry, Goethe even undermines the distinction he makes *in those terms* by asserting that Laocoön, that exemplary work of art free of all poetic "attributes," represents and excites *all three* of those sensations: "All three reactions are represented as well as evoked by this work. . . . The father's suffering evokes terror. . . . [The Laocoön group] evokes pity for the younger son and fear for the older" (III, 22*) ["Alle drei werden durch dieses Kunstwerk dargestellt und erregt. . . . Das Leiden des Vaters (erregt) Schrecken. . . . (Die Gruppe) erregt Mitleiden für den Zustand des jüngeren Sohns, und Furcht für den ältern" (XIII, 172–73)]. Goethe still insists that the statue is "a spiritual as well as a sensual totality" (III, 22*) ["sowohl ein geistiges als ein sinnliches Ganze" (XIII, 173)], but the reader must view this as an ironic statement, since the work's closure *as* a work of "bildende Kunst" has just been undermined. After having broken the law of his text by rendering Laocoön a *poetic* "text," Goethe exits with an ironic question that leaves the issue of differentiation, and his text, open: "In any event, it is highly debatable whether this occurrence is a poetic subject at all" (III, 23*) ["Es ist noch eine große Frage, ob die Begebenheit an sich ein poetischer Gegenstand sei" (XIII, 174)].

The undermining of the poetry/painting distinction began before the introduction of the terms fear, terror, and pity, and it undergoes further subversion after the "end" of the text. Just after asserting that in its portrayal of the highest moment of an action Laocoön is devoid of all poetic enhancement, Goethe begins to discuss the preceding and following moments which we infer from examining the moment portrayed. He describes how the snakes crept up on the sleeping family, tied them up, and why one of them then bites the father; later he describes the possible results of the moment we see (III, 22; XIII, 172). At one point he even indicates that the preceding moment is actually *part* of the statue, part of that highest moment: "The fettered feet and wrestling arms indicate the situation or action immediately preceding" (III, 18) ["(Der Überrest der vorhergehenden Situation oder Handlung zeigt) sich nun noch in den Füßen, die gefesselt, und in den Armen, die ringend sind" (XIII, 168)]. Thus Goethe not only supplies the statue's implied *narration,* and by so doing poeticizes the work, but also treats the work itself as presenting the narration, the stages of an *action.*[42] Goethe thus shows, by extension, that *Lessing's* argument had already implied the inclusion of such elements of narration in the statue, since without that narration no "highest" or "pregnant" moment could be shown in the first place. In Lessing's argument, then, the statue's portrayal of a particular moment, and thus its fundamental difference from poetry, is subverted by its, the statue's, latent narration, much as Lessing's *text,* which has as its express goal the fundamental differentiation of the arts and which makes the explicit assertion that the statue does not narrate, is subverted by its own latent argument/narration, which implies that the statue does narrate after all. In undermining the ostensible goal of Lessing's text, "On Laocoön" continues Lessing's actual project—the subversion of the strict differentiation of the arts disclosed both by this narration and by his play with systematic structures.

As a result of its inclusion of the three essential sensations, Goethe concludes that Laocoön is a model of the "complete" work of art. He has adduced the work's system and recognized the closure that system implies. But in the essay's supplement he undermines that system. Whereas in the essay he states that the father excites terror, the younger son pity, and the older son fear, in the "Announcement" we read: "This, we are convinced, is the main point: the father is being wounded at that very moment, the youngest son is entangled and frightened in the extreme, the oldest could perhaps still save himself. The first terrifies us, the second tortures us with fear, and the third consoles us with hope" ["Dieses ist nach unserer Überzeugung die Hauptansicht: der Vater wird im Augenblicke verwundet, der jüngste Sohn ist aufs äußerste verstrickt und geängstigt, der älteste könnte sich vielleicht noch retten. Das erste erschreckt uns, das zweite quält uns mit Furcht, und das dritte tröstet uns durch Hoffnung" (XIII, 193)]. The element of pity has disappeared and to the figure who previously was held to cause pity Goethe now attributes the arousal of fear. Furthermore, the context of this subversive alteration supports the opposition to systems it reveals. Goethe begins his announcement of "On Laocoön" as follows: "Laocoön, a short essay in the first number, is written with the purpose in mind of calling attention, more precisely than has hitherto been the case, to the intention of the artists who produced this work" ["Laokoon, ein kleiner Aufsatz Stück eins, ist in der Absicht geschrieben, um auf die Intention der Künstler, die dieses Werk verfertigten, genauer als es bisher geschehen, aufmerksam zu machen" (XIII, 192)]. By the end of the next paragraph, however, he has undermined the possibility of even being aware of the artist's intention, much less making it clear to anyone else: "One can certainly say that no observer of later generations can ever read out of a work of art what the

artist put into it" ["Man kann wohl sagen, daß keine beobach-
tende Nachwelt jemals aus dem Kunstwerke heraus forschen
kann, was der Künstler hineingelegt hat" (XIII, 192)]. In the
subversion of intentionality and the concomitant concentration
on reception also lies the subversion of the autonomous subject,
insofar as the subject ceases to be the first authority in our
understanding of the work of art. The work of art is not foremost an expression of an individual subject; such expression is
perhaps one aspect of the work, but an aspect that we cannot
perceive. This movement away from the authority of the individual subject occurs not only in the "Announcement," but also
implicitly in the reduction of the characteristic (which Hirt also
describes as "Individuality" [12]) to only one of the many qualities of the work (XIII, 162), and in "The Collector," where
Goethe again criticizes Hirt in the person of the characterist and
describes "the characteristic" as a dangerous bias.

By "continuing" "On Laocoön" beyond the boundaries of
the text and in a way that further subverts its apparent system,
Goethe breaches the closure of his text. It is in connection with
the *notion* of closure that the intertextuality of Goethe's essay
emerges most forcefully. Goethe, like Lessing, plays with systems—avoids them, then sets them up, then tears them down.
This strategy characterizes Goethe's essay "as a whole," but he
also gives us a more immediately recognizable example of it in
the first two pages. In the second paragraph he advocates, as in
other texts, the temporal priority of observation over theory—
"derive the general from a specific case" ["das Allgemeine aus
einem . . . besonderen Fall entwickeln"]—but then immediately breaks this "law": "Therefore, [!] let me begin with something general" (III, 15*) ["Deswegen sei hier auch etwas Allgemeines vorausgeschickt" (XIII, 162)]. What we then read is a
list of qualities requisite to a great work of art. Already in this
list, however, the theory begins to crumble, since we are told
that the object must be *either* "At Rest or in Motion" ["*In
Ruhe oder Bewegung*"] and are thus faced with an extreme
indeterminacy unacceptable in what are supposedly hard and
fast principles. Goethe closes the list by making fun of the very
gesture he has just made (in what can then also be seen as a

parody of Hirt's positing of one-sided premises as general
rules)—the systematic gesture of setting a priori postulates and
subsequently accommodating the object of study to them:
"Having named in advance all of the conditions we demand of
a great work of art, I can now say much in few words when I
claim that the Laocoön group fulfills them all. . . . The reader
will spare me the effort of the proof" (III, 16*) ["Nachdem ich
die Bedingungen, welche wir von einem hohen Kunstwerke
fordern, zum voraus angegeben habe, so kann ich mit wenigen
Worten viel sagen, wenn ich behaupte, daß unsre Gruppe sie
alle erfüllt. . . . Man wird mir den Beweis erlassen" (XIII,
163)]. Having thus moved in and out of a priori theorizing, the
essay then goes on to do what it set out to do: it observes the
object and from this observation derives some general principles (the incorporation of fear, terror, and pity). In so doing, of
course, it sabotages other principles, principles as central as
that of the separation of the arts.

"On Laocoön" begins with an implicit critique of systematic
discourse by questioning the grounds of a system's possibility.
In that "a genuine work of art . . . always remains infinite to
our understanding" ["ein echtes Kunstwerk bleibt . . . für
unsern Verstand immer unendlich"], there can never be any
complete understanding, anything even approaching absolute
knowledge—"yet we cannot comprehend it totally" (III, 15*)
["es kann aber nicht eigentlich erkannt . . . werden" (XIII,
162)]. And the system is thwarted in its attempt to formulate
the essence, the center, of the object ["sein Wesen"], since the
"expression" of that essence is deemed impossible. What Goethe offers in place of systematic knowledge is the "effect" of
the work—the relationship between the object and its recipient. Several pages later, however, he implicitly denies that element of reception by saying that the primary and favored objects of sculpture are those which have no relationship to that
which is outside them: "[They] are completely self-contained"
(III, 17) ["Sie ruhen auf und in sich" (XIII, 165)]. This postulation of an ideal of closure, this systematic gesture, is made
explicit when Goethe says that it is of great advantage for a
work of art "to be independent, to be closed" (III, 17*)

["wenn es selbständig, wenn es geschlossen ist" (XIII, 164)]. However, that closure is then abrogated when Goethe transforms Laocoön from the representation of a single moment into the representation of an action, a narration, and thus posits traces of a before and an after as inscribed in the statue. The temporal boundary to the past is blurred by the statue's inclusion of traces of the previous moment; the breaking of the temporal boundary to the future lies in the hope that supposedly remains for the older son's escape.

Goethe re-closes the work when he claims that, because the older son is both a participant in and an observer of the action, that is, because the work includes an image of its own reception, it is "closed off" (III, 21*) ["abgeschlossen" (XIII, 171)]. This statement has been taken to be Goethe's most forceful assertion of the autonomy of the work of art.[43] I would suggest that it is just the opposite—an implicit repeal of that supposed autonomy. At the beginning of the essay Goethe says that all we can know about a work of art is how it "has an effect" ["wirkt"], how we receive it, and shortly before his interpretation of the older son as a recipient, he says that the effect of the work lies in us, not in the work itself (III, 20; XIII, 169). Furthermore, the repeated emphasis on the moment the statue portrays implies our own interpretive addition to what we see; we can only recognize that the work shows the highest moment of the action, that it represents "the transition from one condition to another," by *ourselves* supplying the previous and the possible following moments. The inclusion of the image of reception within the work breaks the boundaries of the work, its closure, by presenting an image of what is "outside" the work: *us*. Thus the spatial boundaries become porous: what is inside is also outside and what is outside is also inside. Thus also the systematic claim of closure is subverted.

Like *Laocoön,* and later "The Collector," Goethe's first *Propyläen* essay proceeds from ostensible anti-systematic intention to the presentation of a system and on to the sub-textual subversion of the system. It thereby enters into dialogue not only with the content of Lessing's text—the aesthetic issues—but also with its *structure.* Whereas Herder had quoted key phrases from *Laocoön,* phrases crucial to its staging of a public dialogue, Goethe joins in that dialogue by "quoting" the strategies and gestures, the *process* of *Laocoön.* "On Laocoön" is both on (about) the statue Laocoön and on (forms a palimpsest with) the text *Laocoön.*

*   *   *

By arguing that the statue includes an image of its own reception, Goethe introduces the notion of self-reflexivity into his discussion. Here we can see how self-reflection, which in its involvement of the recipient also implies dialogue, might seem to indicate closure, but actually breaches closure. It thus renders the text open-ended—whether the "text" of the narrative Laocoön statue or the text of Goethe's essays, which reflect on their own process. Self-reflection creates an other that is outside as well as inside and thus engenders a tension that attenuates the boundaries of the apparently self-contained text or self and thereby opens it.

The introduction of the image of reception into the Laocoön group also introduces différance. The deferring and differing occur in the dis-integration of the statue's temporal and spatial boundaries, in the attenuation through narration of the "presented" moment's presence, and in the inner division of each of the three figures, all of whom, Goethe insists, express a "two-fold action" (III, 21) ["doppelte Handlung" (XIII, 171)]. Most of all, the description of the eldest son as being at once observer, witness, and participant constitutes an *image* of différance, in that it thematizes the notion of non-self-identity.

In more general terms, the essay "as a whole," in its converging, diverging, and reconverging, its blending and clashing with its intertexts, reflects and promotes the play of différance. Indeed, différance seems to be the main feature of public intertextual dialogue itself. The intertextual involvement results in self-differing by means of repetition, in spatial deferral—to different texts—and in temporal deferral, in that the text breaks itself open to earlier texts and also reopens those earlier texts, which in turn leads to an after-the-fact postponement of the fulfillment of the earlier text's goals, its desire. (Goethe's interpretation of the statue, his notion that it contains traces of previous and following moments, reflects this textual temporalization.) And insofar as such dialogue takes place in public, in published texts, and thereby involves an indeterminable and uncontrollable field of recipients, of future texts, that will or may join in the debate, the differing and deferring are infinitely magnified and multiplied. We might then think of public intertextual dialogue as a "discourse of différance."

Writing the (Inter-)Text of Dialogue

In the next number of the *Propyläen* Goethe included an essay that produces, within the "bounds" of a single text, a model of this "différant" writing. "Diderot's Essay on Painting" is an image of public dialogue that not only explicitly discusses the subversion of systematic discourse in dialogue, but also performs it. The "Translator's Confession" ["Geständnis des Übersetzers"] that precedes the treatment of Diderot's text introduces both that subversion and that performance. It begins with a description of the writer's unwillingness and inability to compose a systematic, monologic treatise:

> How is it that, despite being strongly urged to do so, one still makes the decision to write a coherent treatise or to draft a lecture on familiar material with such great hesitation? One has carefully thought everything over, has recalled the material and ordered it just as well as one could, has withdrawn oneself from all diversions, one takes the quill in hand, and still one hesitates to begin.
>
> [Woher kommt es wohl, daß man, obgleich dringend aufgefordert, sich doch so ungern entschließt, über eine Materie, die uns geläufig ist, eine zusammenhangende Abhandlung zu schreiben? eine Vorlesung zu entwerfen? Man hat alles wohl überlegt, den Stoff sich vergegenwärtiget, ihn so gut man nur konnte geordnet, man hat

sich aus allen Zerstreuungen zurückgezogen, man nimmt
die Feder in die Hand, und noch zaudert man anzu-
fangen. (XIII, 201)]

We then learn of the intellectual invigoration provided by a
conversation on the same topic, but also that this dialogue does
not then make it easier to write the treatise; indeed, the
dialogue—the play of agreement, disagreement, contradiction,
modification, inconclusiveness—makes the treatise impossible
and reminds us that dialogue, not monologue, is or should be
the way of the world, the nature of intellectual endeavor: "But
conversation does not aid in the writing of the treatise or the
lecture. . . . One recalls with pleasure the peculiar turns of the
dialogue . . . and any one-sided lecture . . . seems sad and stiff.
Perhaps the reason [for that reluctance] is that the human being
is not a didactic being. We find delight only in effect and
counter-effect!" ["Aber (durch Gespräch) wird die Abhandlung,
die Vorlesung nicht gefördert. . . . Man erinnert sich mit Vergnügen der sonderbaren Wendungen des Dialogs . . . und jeder
einseitige Vortrag . . . kommt uns traurig und steif vor. Daher
mag es kommen: Der Mensch ist kein lehrendes . . . Wesen. Nur
in Wirkung und Gegenwirkung erfreuen wir uns!" (XIII, 202)].
   Instead of writing his planned treatise on art, Goethe picks up
Diderot's essay on painting and, in reading it, enters into a dialogue with the text that he also describes in terms of dialogue:

> I converse with it [Diderot's essay] once again; I repri-
> mand it when it strays from what I consider the right
> path; I am happy when we come together again; I get
> worked up over its paradoxes; I take delight in the liveli-
> ness of its overviews; its presentation enraptures me; the
> argument becomes intense; and I of course have the last
> word, since I am dealing with a departed opponent.
>
> [Ich unterhalte mich mit ihm aufs neue, ich tadle ihn,
> wenn er sich von dem Wege entfernt, den ich für den
> rechten halte, ich freue mich, wenn wir wieder zusam-
> mentreffen, ich eifre über seine Paradoxe, ich ergötze

mich an der Lebhaftigkeit seiner Überblicke, sein Vortrag reißt mich hin, der Streit wird heftig, und ich behalte freilich das letzte Wort, da ich mit einem abgeschiednen Gegner zu tun habe. (XIII, 202–3)]

What is seen as so attractive about Diderot's text is its use of anti-systematic rhetoric—"rhetorical-sophistic boldness" ["rhetorisch-sophistischer Kühnheit"]—not in order to erect a new system, "a new edifice of art" ["ein neues Kunstgebäude"], but to tear down the old one, to cause a "revolution" (XIII, 203). The "translator" then realizes that in entering into a dialogue with Diderot he is also taking arms against those who in his own time continue to hinder that revolution. He sees his translation and commentary as a reinvigoration of Diderot's text and consequently a means of propagating the revolutionary, anti-systematic dialogue, and as itself a dialogue—"this conversation [the entire text of the essay], which is carried out on the border between the realms of the dead and living" ["dieses Gespräch, das auf der Grenze zwischen dem Reiche der Toten und Lebendigen geführt wird" (XIII, 203)]. The "Confession" describes the stages of movement away from the plan to write a treatise. It is first a movement away from writing, but then, after conversation and dialogue with a text while reading, back to writing, but to an essentially different kind of writing—to a dialogue of texts that is carried out in the hope of encouraging further dialogue.[44]

Although Goethe assumes the attitude of pointing out and clearing up Diderot's "sophisms," it is also this sophistry that, as we saw in the "Confession," attracts him so strongly to the essay on painting. In other words, Goethe, who repeatedly refers to Diderot (even affectionately) as a sophist, is fascinated by his misleading, spurious argumentation and his subversion of logic—that is, by the anti-systematic quality of his writing. At one point he translates a passage in which Diderot expresses distaste for logic: " 'It's just the same in literature: a hundred cold logicians against one great orator; ten great orators against one excellent poet' " [" 'Ebenso verhält sich's in der Literatur, hundert kalte Logiker gegen Einen großen Redner, zehn große

Redner gegen Einen fürtrefflichen Poeten' " (XIII, 229)]. Goethe criticizes this remark as a "falsely employed example" taken from the "verbal arts" but used to make a point about the fine arts. By thus limiting his correction, however, he implicitly allows the critique of logic itself to stand.

The opposition to systematic discourse becomes more direct in Goethe's support of Diderot's attack on "demi-connoisseurs" ["Halbkenner"]. Diderot says that they often fail to recognize great works of art, to which Goethe responds that the term "demi-connoisseur" itself is too kind for such philistines, whose greatest shortcoming is that they hold their understanding of art to be *complete*. True artists and art lovers, on the other hand, know that such understanding can never be completed, that the understanding of art is an open-ended, constant process (XIII, 232). This sense of necessary incompletion in comprehension carries over into Goethe's view of his own text, which he hopes might form, instead, a stage in an incomplete dialogue on art: "Perhaps the remarks I add will make possible a certain survey of what has been accomplished and of what remains to be accomplished" ["Indem ich . . . meine Anmerkungen hinzufüge, so mag eine gewisse Übersicht desjenigen, was geleistet ist, und desjenigen, was zu leisten übrig bleibt, möglich werden" (XIII, 228)]. So Goethe introduces the second half of his project—the translation of Diderot's chapter on color. The first half had ended on a similar note, with a similar fusion of the notion of ongoing dialogue and divergence from the goal of systematic completion: "Thank you for having induced us to argue, to chat, to get worked up, and to cool down again. The greatest effect of intellect is to call forth intellect" ["Habe Dank, daß du uns veranlaßtest zu streiten, zu schwätzen, uns zu ereifern, und wieder kühl zu werden. Die höchste Wirkung des Geistes ist, den Geist hervorzurufen" (XIII, 227)]. Given Goethe's introduction of his translation project in the "Confession," we might then take this remark as a statement that the greatest effect of a *text* is to call forth another text, not to answer questions, resolve paradoxes, and thus eliminate the need for further texts.

What Goethe *says* about dialogue and the subversion of systems he also *does*. In that his dialogue with Diderot occurs on the boundary between the realms of the living and the dead, that boundary—between past and present writers, between "their" past and present texts—dissolves. Furthermore, he mitigates any sense of closure Diderot's text might convey by translating only two of its seven chapters. He sabotages whatever unity there might be to Diderot's text by inserting commentary and, more specifically, by undermining the order of the text in what is ostensibly its translation: "I have therefore separated his sections and put them together under certain headings and in a different order" ["Ich habe daher seine Perioden getrennt und sie unter gewisse Rubriken, in eine andre Ordnung, zusammengestellt" (XIII, 228)]. Translations generally make at least implicit claims to providing us with an "authentic" and thorough representation of the "original"; to rendering not only all of that text's ideas, but also its argument, its order; to making the writing of the "original" writer directly accessible at the cost of the translator's own writing subject. Goethe, however, "renders" Diderot's text in an order and with supplemental chapter headings that suit his own interests and thus the purpose of his *dialogue* with the predecessor text. This last gesture is paradoxical, in that Goethe reorders the text in the name of rendering it more comprehensible (more systematic?); but, then again, he has already justified such paradox in his own writing by claiming that Diderot's "paradoxicalness" has made him "paradoxical" as well (XIII, 226).

The free play of paradox, without a concomitant attempt to resolve it, itself reflects Goethe's divergence from systematic intentions. Insofar as paradox in Goethe's text is portrayed as having been determined by the predecessor text, it claims to produce an adequate reading of that text; this "adequacy through paradox" itself, however, is another paradox that subverts the very notion of adequacy. The reflection or repetition of paradox is also a sign of the dialogic relationship with Diderot into which Goethe has entered. Here, as well as when he declares that his text will be repetitive because Diderot's text is repetitive (XIII, 213), Goethe "explicates" the sort of quotation of textual strategy that he had performed in "On Laocoön." And at the beginning of the "translation" he draws our attention to his text's status as dialogue by "quoting" Herder's manner of quoting Lessing. Following his translation of the opening lines of Diderot's first chapter—" 'Nature does nothing incorrect. Every form, whether beautiful or ugly, has its cause, and among all existing beings there is not one that is not as it should be' " [" 'Die Natur macht nichts Inkorrektes. Jede Gestalt, sie mag schön oder häßlich sein, hat ihre Ursache, und unter allen existierenden Wesen ist keins, das nicht wäre, wie es sein soll' "]—we read Goethe's quotation: "Nature does nothing inconsistent; every form, be it beautiful or ugly, has its cause by which it is determined, and among all the organic natures that we know of there is not one that is not as it can be" ["Die Natur macht nichts Inkonsequentes, jede Gestalt, sie sei schön oder häßlich, hat ihre Ursache, von der sie bestimmt wird, und unter allen organischen Naturen, die wir kennen, ist keine, die nicht wäre, wie sie sein kann"] (XIII, 204). By bringing the intertextuality of his own text to the surface, by so obviously carrying on, in public, a dialogue with another text that allows him to develop certain points and encourage further debate, Goethe both performs and thematizes the public intertextual dialogue in which his essays otherwise participate implicitly.

*   *   *

The play of paradox in Goethe's essay calls our attention to the play of différance as well. In that it is a translation, it "presents" a text that has been rendered different from itself. And Goethe's own text, as a whole, differs from itself, since it is neither *only* Goethe's text nor *only* Diderot's text. Especially in its reorganization of the second chapter of the essay on painting and its introduction of headings that were not used in the predecessor text, "Diderot's Essay on Painting" ceases to be what it purports to be—"simply" a translation with interspersed commentary. However, it *remains* a translation in another sense, insofar as it quotes, or translates, textual strategy.

Goethe's essay is *différant*, however, in more than just the sense of non-self-identity. The "presenting" of Diderot's text simultaneously subverts the presence of the "original" text. It reinscribes the text in a public dialogue non-contemporary to

Diderot's writing and thus also temporalizes it by submitting it to a detour, through Goethe's text, that postpones its—the earlier text's—effect, that suspends the fulfillment of its desire (the revolution Diderot advocated). The text's non-self-identity and the reinscription that results in temporal tensions reveal how différance functions as an internal structural factor. However, the essay also *reflects* explicitly on this non-presence through temporal deferral. This reflection on past and future texts constitutes a historical representation of that (inevitable) internal tension. Différance describes a situation in which "each element that is said to be 'present,' appearing on the stage of presence, is related to something other than itself but retains the mark of a past element and already lets itself be hollowed out by the mark of its relation to a future element" ("Differance," 142). By using the ideas of "past," "present," and "future" in a more literal sense than Derrida uses them, we can gain access to the historical representation in "Diderot's Essay"—to the replication in history of the temporal tensions that already inform the text *as* text:

"Diderot's Essay" appears on the stage of presence—the publication of the *Propyläen* in 1799—but it retains the mark of past elements. Specifically, by taking up Diderot's attack on mannerism, by questioning his advocacy of the accurate imitation of nature, and by bringing the criterion of style into the debate, the essay continues the discussion of "Simple Imitation of Nature, Manner, Style." Furthermore, by concentrating on the problem, raised by Diderot's text, of the relationship between art and nature and on the implications of this relationship for the question of the truth of a work of art, Goethe's text carries the mark of "On Truth and Probability in Works of Art." All of these questions point toward a future text—"The Collector and His Circle"—where they will then undergo more extensive and detailed discussion. We might also say that the essay points to both future and past texts, in that it, like Goethe's other essays, reveals the strategy that I have called the subversion of authoritarian, systematic discourse.

But "Diderot's Essay" is also much more explicitly hollowed out by the mark of its relation to another future text. Near the beginning of the second part of the text, Goethe bemoans the lack of a useful theory of colors:

> But in order to convince oneself of the sad state of affairs in our textbooks with regard to this category [coloring], one can, for example, look at the article on coloring in Sulzer's general theory of the fine arts with the eyes of an artist who wants to learn something, to find instructions, to follow a hint! Where in that work is there even the slightest trace of theory?

> [Wie traurig es aber mit dieser Rubrik (Kolorit) in unsern Lehrbüchern aussehe, kann man sich überzeugen, wenn man zum Beispiel den Artikel Kolorit in Sulzers allgemeiner Theorie der schönen Künste mit den Augen eines Künstlers betrachtet, der etwas lernen, eine Anleitung finden, einem Fingerzeig folgen will! Wo ist da nur eine theoretische Spur? (XIII, 230)]

Goethe is not able, or at least not prepared, to provide that theory in the "present" text, but in the section on the harmony of colors he indicates that a future text will fill the gap left by this essay: "We now come to an important point [the harmony of colors], about which we already said a few things above. This point cannot be presented and discussed in detail here, but rather only in the course of the entire theory of color" ["Wir kommen nunmehr an einen wichtigen Punkt, über den wir oben schon einiges geäußert, der aber nicht hier, sondern in der Folge der ganzen Farbenlehre nur vorgetragen und erörtert werden kann" (XIII, 238)]. "Diderot's Essay" undermines its presence by postponing the fulfillment of desire to a (possible/probable) later text—Goethe's *Theory of Color* [*Farbenlehre*]. We can then say that Goethe's essay is non-present as a result of the rupture of its temporal boundaries to both the past and the future.

Finally, the publication of the essay itself constitutes a symbol of its temporal and spatial deferral, as well as of its difference from itself: the text did not appear in its entirety all at once, but was divided over two issues of the journal—"Volume One, Number Two and Volume Two, Number One."

Traces

The "mark" of which Derrida writes is what he calls a "trace" ("Differance," 142). The différance introduced by the trace is a quality of *writing* and is what *speech* purports to avoid by claiming presence for itself. This differentiation of writing from speech provides access to the reasons for Goethe's implicit advocacy of a specifically inter*text*ual dialogue and his preference for such written interchange over spoken conversation.[45] If Goethe's main concern had simply been dialogue in general, then he could have simply discussed the advantages of conversation and left it at that. Instead, in his essays he repeatedly carries out an extraordinarily complex establishment of dialogue between texts—complex in that he not only declares his preference, but also performs what he advocates through an elaborate web of quotation and allusion. The question is *Why?*

The immediate presence of signs in speech carries over to the speaker, who in speaking experiences her*himself as present by *hearing* her*himself: "It is implied in the very structure of speech that the speaker *hears himself:* both that he perceives the sensible form of the phonemes and that he understands his own expressive intention."[46] This hearing oneself while speaking and understanding one's own intention, the telos of the utterance, approximates what Goethe describes in *Poetry and Truth* when he recalls his oral presentation of a story: "From my father I had inherited a certain didactic loquacity, from my mother the gift of depicting brightly and forcefully everything produced and comprehended by the imagination: of freshening up familiar fairy tales, of inventing and narrating new ones, indeed of *inventing as I went along*" (IV, 330; my emphasis) ["Mir war von meinem Vater eine gewisse lehrhafte Redseligkeit angeerbt; von meiner Mutter die Gabe, alles was die Einbildungskraft hervorbringen, fassen kann, heiter und kräftig darzustellen, bekannte Märchen aufzufrischen, andere zu erfinden und zu erzählen, *ja im Erzählen zu erfinden*" (X, 489; my emphasis)]. In *Campaign in France,* his account of his lectures on optics reveals an almost identical view of the nature of speech: "I never presented a lecture without learning something myself as a result; usually I acquired new insights while I was speaking, and in fact the flow of speech itself was the surest medium of invention for me" (V, 712) ["Ich hielt niemals einen Vortrag ohne daß ich dabei gewonnen hätte; gewöhnlich gingen mir unterm Sprechen neue Lichter auf, und ich erfand im Fluß der Rede am gewissesten" (XII, 374)]. Whereas the passage from the autobiography occurs in the context of a defense of speech against writing, the similar passage in *Campaign* is followed by a critique of that speech as necessarily didactic, dogmatic, and un-dialogic—in other words, an expression of the self-identical, self-present subject.

Writing, on the other hand, does not have the quality of presence. It does not claim self-identity, but rather always refers to something outside itself, to something before and after itself.[47] Goethe recognizes this temporal deferral when he says that "what is written has the advantage that it lasts and can await the time when it will have an effect" ["das Geschriebene (hat) den Vorteil, daß es dauert und die Zeit abwarten kann, wo ihm zu wirken gegönnt ist" (IX, 616)]. And he explicitly opposes this temporal deferral to the presence of speech: "What one expresses orally has to be dedicated to the present, to the moment; what one writes, one dedicates to the distance, to the future" ["Was man mündlich ausspricht, muß der Gegenwart, dem Augenblick gewidmet sein; was man schreibt, widme man der Ferne, der Folge" (IX, 616)]. Speech thus lacks *effect,* and it is effect that concerns Goethe most—whether in terms of the reception of art as discussed in "Diderot's Essay" or in terms of ongoing debate as discussed in "The Collector," "Truth and Probability," and any number of other texts. By *writing* dialogue he is able to avoid the presence of speech and its necessary death ("*A voice without differance, a voice without writing, is at once absolutely alive and absolutely dead*" ["Speech and Phenomena," 102]).

We find indications of Goethe's sense of the necessity of

writing throughout his work. One might say that, given the incredible volume of his writing over the course of his long life, we could hardly expect otherwise. But it is still significant—for our understanding of the way in which he articulates the breach of both temporal and spatial closure and thus for our understanding of Goethe the essayist—that he repeatedly calls our attention to the privilege writing enjoys. He does so not only in the (perhaps obscure) instances cited immediately above, but also in his essays—for example, in the constant transformation/transcription of conversation into writing in "The Collector." He does so as well in "Diderot's Essay," when the translator, in his confession, wishes that his conversation could have been written down and thus not lost (XIII, 202).

In the "Introduction to the *Propylaea*" we read what might be considered Goethe's most important statement on the (fortunate) divergence of writing from the presence of speech. He calls spoken conversation "transitory" and laments the subsequent loss of the process of thought it had presented. Written conversation, on the other hand, allows us to preserve that process and use it later; on the basis of this writing we can then both look *back* to what has been achieved and look *forward* to further progress (XIII, 138–39).[48] Thus writing for Goethe results in a play of différance, a play of traces both backward and forward (unlike the exclusively backward—"anterior"—or synchronic relation that Kristeva reads in Bakhtin's dialogism). Intertextual dialogue both implies and performs such a play of traces. Insofar as the dialogue occurs in public it thematizes the subversion of self-identical interiority by conveying the sense of being "outside," "in the world." And the going-forth "into the world" is also primordially implied in the movement of temporalization.[49]

* * *

The more aspects of Goethe's essayistic writing we address—its treatment of systematic discourse, its dialogism, its open-endedness, its self-reflexivity, its intertextuality—the more we are able to see not only the correlativity of these aspects, but also the sometimes extraordinary degree to which the work and vocabu-

lary of poststructuralism, in particular that of Derrida, enable us
to understand with greater theoretical precision and to formulate with greater economy both the way the essays work and
what is at stake in them. This should not, of course, imply that
Goethe is a direct prefiguration of Derrida, since without the
latter it would be impossible to recognize the full implications of
the former's strategies. And when we carry out a detailed interpretation of the essays and their strategies, we are reminded of a
fundamental difference between Goethe's texts and most texts
of contemporary literary and philosophical theory: Goethe's
"theories" reside in the performance of his essays and in the
irony that inhabits both their structures and the space between
those structures and the texts' explicit statements.[50]

    In the current discussion of the non-presence of writing, a
specific difference arises, since the emergence into the world that I
attributed to intertextual dialogue, and thus to writing, is actually part of Derrida's discussion of *speech*. Whereas Derrida
deconstructs speech as presence by showing that it is not as present as it purports to be (chapter 6 of "Speech and Phenomena"),
Goethe straightforwardly posits speech as presence and as a result moves away from it and toward writing. In other words,
Goethe's essays represent an implicit opposition to speech (which
would efface the trace and institute a system of presence), but not
a deconstruction of speech. The difference evident here can be
attenuated, but in order to do so, we would have to travel deep
into the jungle of Goethe's posthumous works. There we do find
an aphorism that constitutes a more fundamental critique of
speech as presence. He at first appears to promote speech—"One
should only argue orally about the most important matters of
feeling as well as reason, of experience as well as reflection"
["Über die wichtigsten Angelegenheiten des Gefühls wie der
Vernunft, der Erfahrung wie des Nachdenkens soll man nur
mündlich verhandeln" (IX, 616)]. The next sentence, however,
undermines the presence of speech by saying that the spoken
word dies if it is not followed by another and thus dialogized:
"The spoken word is immediately dead if it is not kept alive by
another that follows it and that befits the listener" ["Das
ausgesprochene Wort ist sogleich tot, wenn es nicht durch ein

folgendes, dem Hörer gemäßes am Leben erhalten wird"] (IX, 616). Without différance, we could say—that is, without the temporal deferral inherent in dialogue—the spoken word is dead. Since, in order to survive, it *must* be followed by another spoken word, and presumably another and another, *ad infinitum*, we get a sense of the necessity that speech *chase* itself. The spoken word is always hollowed out by the mark of a future utterance, indeed does not have any existence to speak of without that future utterance, just as the future word carries the trace of its predecessor and must be in accordance with ("gemäß") the previous speaker and her*his word. The spoken word thus exists only in an *intertextual* space, that is, the space of writing, the space of dialogue, the space of différance. In that its presence is thus subverted, the spoken word ceases to *be* speech in the traditional sense.

In the World

Multiple Readings

The advocacy of written dialogue that we find in the "Introduction to the *Propylaea*" is a two-sided coin. It not only describes how writing results in delay, temporalization, and a play of traces, but also implies the advantages of writing for reception. The reception of speech is temporally limited, it dies out with that speech. With writing, on the other hand, the possibility of an infinite process of *rereading* emerges.

The provocation of active reception, the call to endless rereading, is a quality of essayistic writing in general. Hugo Friedrich recognized this aspect of Montaigne's essays when he called Montaigne "a classic example of an author who has to be reread, because he fills the background of what is said with unsaid or half-said possibilities."[51] The necessity of rereading results from the essay's anti-systematic formulation; its incompletion, its refusal to resolve the problems it raises, its lack of concern for saying everything that might be said on a topic, its subversion of logical discourse, the extent of its operation on the subtextual level—all of these tendencies challenge the recipient and force her*him to reread.

Essays, despite their often rambling quality or perhaps precisely because of it, are "difficult" to read. This difficulty forms one of their rhetorical gestures, is part of their textual strategy. In "The Collector and His Circle" Goethe subtly calls our attention to this quality by inserting a "flaw," an annoying if relatively minor example of incomprehensibility. At the beginning of the essay we assume that the collector is writing to one person; even if "your departure" ["Ihr Abschied"] does not necessarily refer to a single person, "your letter" ["Ihr Brief"] does seem to limit the addressee. Near the end of the letter, however, he confuses us by addressing his correspondent as "gentlemen" ["meine Herren"] (XIII, 261). Our confusion only grows when Julie then writes of her appreciation (regardless of the implied ridicule) of the gift she has received: "Enough of that! You made me very happy, although I do realize that I have taken on a burden by accepting you as my second uncle" (III, 129) ["Genug, Sie haben mir eine große Freude gemacht, ob ich gleich wohl sehe, daß ich mir eine neue Rute aufgebunden habe, indem ich Sie zu meinem zweiten Oheim annahm" (XIII, 271)]. The singularized correspondent is then pluralized once again when the collector addresses him/them as "gentlemen" ["meine Herren" (XIII, 272)]. In the eighth letter we are again led to believe that there is a single addressee when Julie asserts the intertextuality of the letter: "Indeed, you will find again your own words from your last letter" (III, 154*) ["ja Sie finden die eignen Worte Ihres letzten Briefs wieder" (XIII, 312)].[52] Since we are never given any indication of the editors'('s) separate identities, we cannot simply assume that the instances in which there seems to be a single addressee reflect an answer to one *or* the other. Given the essay's treatment of subjectivity and its intertextuality—the breaking down of boundaries between individuals and between texts—we could say that this uncertainty about the number of correspondents reflects the indistinctness of such boundaries or that the apparently individually authored letters are actually jointly authored texts. But such a conclusion is already a result of repeated rereading of the essay. It is precisely this rereading that Goethe's destabilization and problematization of his essay engenders.

Goethe did not only perform, as in his essays, the provocation of rereading; he also explicitly commented on the importance of this kind of ongoing reception—most notably in his remarks on his novel, *Elective Affinities* [*Die Wahlverwandtschaften*]. In a conversation with Eckermann of 6 May 1827 he noted his preference for the sort of difficult text that he holds his novel to be: "Rather, I am of the opinion that the more incommensurable and incomprehensible a poetic production is, the better it is" ["Vielmehr bin ich der Meinung: je inkommensurabeler und für den Verstand unfaßlicher eine poetische Produktion, desto besser" (XXIV, 636)]. Shortly after completing the novel, Goethe wrote a letter to Cotta expressing his hope that this problematic text would necessitate rereading: "Quite a few things are embedded there that will, I hope, challenge the reader to repeated reflection" ["Es ist manches hineingelegt, das, wie ich hoffe, den Leser zu wiederholter Betrachtung auffordern wird"].[53] Twenty years later he held the same conviction: "There is more in there than anyone could possibly grasp in a single reading" ["Es steckt darin mehr, als irgend jemand bei einmaligem Lesen aufzunehmen imstande wäre" (XXIV, 310)]. At one point, Goethe even explicitly brought together the notion of rereading and his belief in the advantages of that which is written. In a letter to Reinhard of 31 December 1809 he describes how he looks forward to the effect his novel will have in the future, "when reread" ["bei'm Wiederlesen"], and attributes the possibility of that future effect to the fact of the *written* text—"That which is written asserts its rights" ["Das Gedichtete behauptet sein Recht"].[54]

Undevoured Texts

The dialogism of Goethe's essays, in the play of différance it reveals, implies the necessity of rereading. But it also implies more than just this—it implies a certain *way* of rereading. In the "Introduction to the *Propylaea*" the "look back" ["Blick rückwärts"] enabled by written dialogue is described as *simultaneously* that which allows "an indefinite continuation" ["künftiges, unablässiges Fortschreiten"] (III, 80; XIII, 139). In other words, in that we reread the text, we also continue the process of the text. And that process is writing itself.

In *S/Z* Barthes describes this reading that is also writing as "writerly" reading.[55] In order to perform a writerly reading, we must reread, for in this rereading we maintain the plurality and

non-closure of the text, the subversion of any supposed final
signified, and a play of differences—"that play which is the
return of the different" (16). Barthes's goal in promoting the
writerly is "to make the reader no longer a consumer, but a
producer of the text" (4). The reader who acts as a consumer is
the "readerly" reader; s*he does not reread and thus reduces the
text to a commodity: "Rereading, an operation contrary to the
commercial and ideological habits of our society, which would
have us 'throw away' the story once it has been consumed ('de-
voured'), so that we can then move on to another story, buy
another book . . . rereading is here suggested at the outset, for it
alone saves the text from repetition (those who fail to reread are
obliged to read the same story everywhere)" (15–16).[56] Barthes
draws the connection between the writerly, productive, *non*-
consumable text and essayistic writing when, after discussing
how the writerly opposes the stasis and finality of systems, he
states that "the writerly is . . . the essay without the dissertation" (5). This comparison also recalls Adorno's opposition of
the essay to the treatise, of "unsolid" writing to the "solidity" of
systematic discourse, where "solidity" is seen as a desideratum
that has been adopted from "property-relationships" (168; 29).
The solid text, with its logical progression toward a final signified, is a passively consumable commodity. The essay, on the
other hand, challenges us to produce the text actively as we read
it.

*   *   *

The sense of the danger of reading the same text everywhere, and
as a result simply consuming stories, is echoed by the storyteller
in Goethe's *Conversations of German Emigrés*. The baroness
praises the old man for having told a moral story and then requests more such stories from him, but he replies: " 'If this story
meets your approval, then I am indeed delighted, but I am sorry if
you want still more moral tales; for this one is the first and the
last' " (X, 54) [" 'Wenn diese Geschichte Ihren Beifall hat, so ist
es mir zwar sehr angenehm, doch tut mir's leid, wenn Sie noch
mehr moralische Erzählungen wünschen, denn es ist die erste und
letzte' " (IX, 343)]. In his explanation of why it is the "first and

last" moral story, the affinity to Barthes's description of the consumerism inherent in the readerly becomes apparent: " 'This is
not the only moral tale I can tell; but they all resemble one another so closely that one always seems to be telling the same
one' " (X, 54) [" 'Es ist nicht die einzige moralische Geschichte,
die ich erzählen kann, sondern alle gleichen sich dergestalt, daß
man immer nur dieselbe zu erzählen scheint' " (IX, 343)]. By
establishing a final signified—the moral message that is essentially always the same—such stories *and* our reception of them,
insofar as we extract that message, eliminate the play of differences. They are readerly texts; and as long as we desire that final
meaning and attempt to derive it from them, as do the baroness
and Luise, we mirror their readerliness. The storyteller, then, is
attempting to educate his audience away from their readerly comfort. His last attempt—"The Fairy Tale"—is the most extreme. It
is introduced with a paradox—" 'a fairy tale that will remind you
of nothing and of everything' " (X, 70) [" 'ein Märchen, durch
das Sie an nichts und an alles erinnert werden sollen' " (IX, 368)];
it proceeds from paradox to paradox; and it creates a bizarre
symbolic matrix for which it provides no clear references. In
other words, it makes reception difficult at nearly every turn.

*   *   *

Returning to Goethe's essays, we find that they do not simply
necessitate rereading and imply writerly reading by virtue of
their subversion of systematic discourse. Their intertextual dialogism forcefully calls our attention to this quality of reading by
performing the kind of reading that writes the text.

"Diderot's Essay on Painting" is the most obvious in its practice of writerly reading. In that it is a translation, it literally rewrites the text it reads; and the insertion of point-by-point commentary emphasizes the fact that it is a *reading*. Moreover, the
reading forms a second reinscription of Diderot's text, beyond
the translation itself, in that we can see how Goethe assimilates,
modifies, and *restates* the essay on painting—most forcefully in
the reorganization of the chapter on color. Again, as in the case
of public intertextual dialogue, the opening paragraphs of the
translation and commentary—Diderot's " 'Nature does nothing

incorrect . . .' " followed by Goethe's "Nature does nothing inconsistent . . . " (XIII, 204)—constitute an especially palpable
image of the text's writerly approach to its predecessor text.

In one brief essay Goethe openly employs translation for the
purpose of reinscription. "A Second Harvest of Aristotle's *Poetics*" ["Nachlese zu Aristoteles' Poetik"] includes a rereading of
the *Poetics* that translates the text in such a way as to give it a
meaning that can be used in the reader's, Goethe's, argument.[57]
Goethe does not attempt to hide the fact that his reading adds to
and changes the text: "By this translation I believe to have
clarified the passage which has so far been considered obscure"
(III, 198) ["Durch vorstehende Übersetzung glaube ich nun die
bisher dunkel geachtete Stelle ins klare gesetzt zu sehen" (XIV,
710)]. He undermines the closure of the text by implying that its
meaning occurs in its reading, is postponed beyond the temporal
and spatial boundaries of the text. Moreover, if one can alter the
meaning through rereading, through translation, then there can
be any number of (re-)writings of the text and thus never a final
signified.

"On Laocoön," like "Diderot's Essay," performs a multiple
writerly reading, but in a less immediately apparent manner. Its
writing is a rereading of Lessing's *Laocoön* that not only reinscribes issues from Lessing's text such as beauty, the moment
chosen for portrayal in the fine arts, and the relationship of
poetry and painting, but also "quotes" Lessing's textual strategy, his playful treatment of systematic discourse. The participation of Goethe's essay in this written dialogue on Laocoön is
itself a rereading and quotation of Lessing's dialogic, intertextual involvement with Winckelmann and Mendelssohn, and of
Herder's dialogue with Lessing's text. Furthermore, the essay is
a "reading" of the Laocoön *statue* that "rewrites" the statue, in
that it produces an accompanying narration, articulates the action the statue implies, and supplies the reception that Goethe
describes as already implicitly inscribed in the group itself.

In "The Collector" and "Truth and Probability" writerly reading is less a quality of the text than a theoretical topic. In the
eighth letter of "The Collector" we do, however, find an *example* of such reading: Julie's quotational writing is simultaneously

a reading of the "philosopher's" "system" and of the most recent letter from the editor(s) of the *Propyläen*. More importantly, the product of that dialogue itself—the proposal of a combination of biases that would result in "true" art—includes an implied equation of production and reception.[58] At the outset the philosopher is quoted as claiming that his six categories designate "the qualities which, all combined, would describe the true artist as well as the true connoisseur" (III, 154) ["die Eigenschaften, welche, alle zusammen verbunden, den wahren Künstler, sowie den wahren Liebhaber, ausmachen würden" (XIII, 311)], and at the end of the letter the final scheme is introduced with a similar assertion: "If we pair off our one-sided artists and art lovers according to opposing categories . . . there will always emerge, when one combines these opposites, one of the three requirements for the consummate work of art [i.e., artistic truth, beauty, completion]" (III, 159*) ["Wenn unsere einseitigen Künstler und Kunstliebhaber je zwei und zwei einander entgegenstehen . . . so entsteht, indem man diese Gegensätze verbindet, immer eins der drei Erfordernisse des vollkommenen Kunstwerks" (XIII, 319)]. The text's treatment of this system and the impossibility of that combination do not diminish the significance of the attempt to treat "artists" and "art lovers," the creation and the appreciation of art, as subject to the same criteria and the same shortcomings. Throughout the essay, as well as in the last letter, artist and recipient are always mentioned together and never differentiated; production and reception are seen as inseparable, as basically the same activity.

This view of the recipient of art as at the same time its producer is made explicit in "On Truth and Probability in Works of Art," where the equation forms the final argument *against* the possibility of the truth of a work of art. Here Goethe brings together the notions of "rereading" and of the proper reception of art as a "reading" in which the recipient must *become* the producer in order to appreciate the "text": "The true connoisseur . . . feels *that he must rise to the level of the artist* in order to enjoy the work, that he must collect himself from his scattered life, must live with the work of art, *must see it again and again*, and thereby endow himself with a higher existence" (III,

78*; my emphasis) ["Der wahre Liebhaber . . . fühlt, *daß er sich zum Künstler erheben müsse,* um das Werk zu genießen, er fühlt, daß er sich aus seinem zerstreuten Leben sammeln, mit dem Kunstwerke wohnen, *es wiederholt anschauen,* und sich selbst dadurch eine höhere Existenz geben müsse" (XIII, 181; my emphasis)]. Preceding this definition of the ideal recipient is a description of the usual manner of reception that, in its use of the metaphor of consumerism, further demonstrates the remarkably extensive affinity between Goethe's and Barthes's views on reception: "The common art lover . . . treats the work of art like an object that he comes across at the marketplace" (III, 78*) ["Der gemeine Liebhaber . . . behandelt ein Kunstwerk wie einen Gegenstand, den er auf dem Markte antrifft" (XIII, 181)].

What I have been doing in the last pages is also a rewriting—a rereading of my own discussion of dialogue in Goethe's essays that reinterprets that dialogue *as* writerly reading. Intertextual dialogue *is* a reading that rewrites other texts. As such, that dialogue can then be seen to break down the boundaries not only between *texts,* but also between *writer* and *reader.* The reader is always also the writer, and the writer is always also the reader. In the disintegration of this boundary lies a further subversion of systematic discourse, namely a deconstruction of the writer/reader hierarchy established by the authoritative, monologizing voice that subordinates the reader, that constrains her*him to eternal *Unmündigkeit*—an eternal age of minority. It is this escape from subjection that Goethe asserts in "Truth and Probability" when he says that the recipient, who by rereading becomes the producer of what s*he receives, attains "a higher existence."

Supplying the Text

When Barthes discusses writerly reading in terms of a play of differences and portrays its effect as an infinite deferral, thus subversion, of a final signified or meaning, he is also describing the function of différance. Barbara Johnson, in her excellent essay on *S/Z,* makes the connection between these two theoretical positions explicit.[59] But we might also broaden this connection by bringing the Derridean notion of the *supplement*, "another name for differance," into play as well.[60] Introducing the supplement not only enables us to describe more exactly what occurs in writerly reading, it also forces consideration and reevaluation of Goethe's recurrent but elusive concept of "supplying" [*supplieren*].

In chapter 7 of "Speech and Phenomena" we find a definition of the supplement that leaves us somewhat baffled: the structure of the supplement is such that "by delayed reaction, a possibility produces that to which it is said to be added on" (89). The sense of a double function that lurks somewhere in this rather cryptic remark is brought out explicitly in *Of Grammatology*: "The supplement adds itself, it is a surplus, a plenitude enriching another plenitude, the *fullest measure* of presence. It cumulates and accumulates presence. It is thus that art, *technè*, image, representation, convention, etc., come as supplements to nature. . . . But the supplement supplements. It adds only to replace. It intervenes or insinuates itself *in-the-place-of;* if it fills, it is as if one fills a void. If it represents and makes an image, it is by the anterior default of a presence" (144–45). It is in this double sense that we can see the connection to writerly reading. Insofar as it does not attempt simply to formulate an "author's" intention, interpretation necessarily changes its object by incorporating in its reading a constellation of thought and experience non-identical to that of other writers and readers. Such interpretation constitutes writerly, supplementary reading. It *adds* to the received text by supplying the activity of a reader different from the text's "original" writer and *replaces* the text by resulting in writing that is *other than,* but also *of* that text.

Goethe's notion of *supplieren* has been taken to describe supplementarity only in the conventional sense of an addition. Trunz, for example, simply equates the term with "making complete, creating a complementary addition" and offers no further discussion of it.[61] This easy, reductive definition of the concept is especially ironic, since it occurs in a footnote to Goethe's use of the term in a passage that reflects to a remarkable degree Derrida's description of the supplement's way of replacing that to which it adds. In the supplement "*addition* comes to *make up for* a deficiency"; Derrida elaborates on this point by using the example of why writing, in Husserl's phenomenology, must be added to speech: "If indication—for example, writing in the everyday sense—must necessarily be 'added' to speech to complete the constitution of the ideal object [that is, achieve presence—P.B.], if speech must be 'added' to the thought identity of the object, it is because the 'presence' of sense and speech had already from the start fallen short of itself" ("Speech and Phenomena," 87). But the writing that makes up for the deficiency of speech does not, because it is writing, result in the presence that was lacking; the supplement makes up for a deficiency, but in so doing replaces that to which it is added with something *different* and still does not eliminate the deficiency of that which it supplements.

This sense of making up for a deficiency through the supplement is precisely the sense in which Goethe employs the term *supplieren* at the end of the eighth book of *Poetry and Truth*. He writes of how the Elohim decided to intervene after seeing Lucifer's negative effect for creation: "They decided on the latter [intervention], and through their will alone they *supplied* in a moment's time the whole *deficiency* caused by the success of Lucifer's enterprise" (IV, 262*; my emphasis) ["Sie erwählten nun das letztere (eingreifen), und *supplierten* durch ihren bloßen Willen in einem Augenblick den ganzen *Mangel*, den der Erfolg von Luzifers Beginnen an sich trug" (X, 386; my emphasis)]. The deficiency here is not explicitly one of presence, but of "creation." The supplement, however, which Goethe calls "light" and which he says we tend to designate as "creation" (IV, 263) ["was wir mit dem Worte Schöpfung zu bezeichnen pflegen" (X, 387)], does not repair that which was deficient. The new "creation" is also insufficient as such, and so the Elohim supplement it again, this time with "the human being." Humankind, however, finds itself once again "in the same situation as Lucifer" (IV, 263) ["in dem Falle Luzifers" (X, 387)]; it even manifests that deficiency "in all the categories of its existence" and ends up "playing the role of Lucifer." An endless chain of supplements becomes necessary because that to which each successive supplement adds—creation—always already falls short of itself. Goethe concludes his cosmogony by reinscribing "creation" as itself an endless chain of supplements that always move toward the origin, but always also fall away from it: all of creation is nothing and never was anything but "a falling away from and a returning to the original" (IV, 263*) ["ein Abfallen und Zurückkehren zum Ursprünglichen" (X, 387)].

In the "Announcement of the *Propylaea*" Goethe *discusses* supplementarity only in the sense of addition and making complete. He laments the damage that had been done to many works of ancient art and says that we must often supply what is missing: "When contemplating such works, we are often forced to add something to them in our mind, in order, where possible, . . . to re-produce them in their completeness" ["Man (ist) nun oft bei Betrachtung solcher Werke genötigt, etwas hinzuzudenken, um, wo möglich, . . . sie in ihrer Vollkommenheit wieder herzustellen" (XIII, 197)]. But such addition, *Hinzudenken,* results in a *Supplieren* that also replaces the "original" with something different—as, for example, in the narration he supplies to the Laocoön group based on his *Hinzudenken* of the snake's bite. This *Supplieren* does not occur only in "On Laocoön," but also in the "Announcement" itself. As writing supplements speech to make up for its deficiency of presence, but actually further subverts that presence, so the "Announcement" supplements "On Laocoön" in order to complete or solidify its system, but actually further subverts that system—both by contradictorily positing the "pregnant moment" and by altering the manifestation of the fear/terror/pity categorization. In the "Announcement of the *Propylaea*" Goethe performs a writerly reading of his *Propyläen* essay that supplements it in the Derridean sense.

The Community of Writing

What I have been approaching in my discussion of the trace and of writerly reading is an attempt to answer the question: Why the overriding concern with public intertextual dialogue in Goethe's essays? Why would Goethe go to such great lengths to practice essayistic writing *as* dialogue, to acknowledge the fact of intertextuality? Although it is not possible to answer this question with absolute certainty, my provisional answer would be that Goethe complicates his writing, makes it difficult for himself and for us, for the sake of community.

Already in the breaking down of barriers between writers and readers that occurs in the writerly reading of/in Goethe's essays, we can see how intertextual dialogue *implies* community. The dissipation of those barriers brings with it the subversion of both the author and its related phenomenon—the authority of the systematic discourse of closure. Intertextuality—the blending and clashing of a variety of already existing texts within every text *and* the simultaneous inscription of future texts, of the reader's rewriting of the text—renders the text a communal space. Barthes describes this textual space as one "where no language has a hold over any other, where languages circulate" ("From Work to Text," 164), and Bakhtin discusses such a circulation of languages in terms of "social heteroglossia" ("Discourse in the Novel," 264). We can formulate the consequences of this mingling as the opening up of the *text* to other texts, as the circulation of *texts* in a nonhierarchical, open structure that renders every text a community of texts.

"The author is a modern figure, a product of our society insofar as, emerging from the Middle Ages with English empiricism, French rationalism and the personal faith of the Reformation, it discovered the prestige of the individual, of, as it is more nobly put, the 'human person' " ("The Death of the Author," 142–43). In order for the subversion of the author to take place, that which makes the notion of the author possible in the first place—the excessive prestige of the individual—must come under attack and be abandoned. What makes up the community of texts is thus not only the blending and clashing of intertexts past, present, and future, but also the blending and clashing of "individuals," of writers and readers past, present, and future that that textual intermingling implies. Intertextuality and intersubjectivity, the problematics of the text and that of the individual, are mutually implicit. Intersubjectivity, itself another name for or another manifestation of différance, "is inseparable from temporalization taken as the openness of the present upon an outside of itself" ("Speech and Phenomena," 84n.). The subject opens itself up to that which is taken to be outside itself. It relinquishes insistence on its own autonomous individuality in order to mingle with other "subjects" that participate in the same act of relinquishment. These "subjects," like the texts that emanate from them, are intersubjects by virtue of denying the possibility of anything like an inner totality, a self-identity. They thus never finally and completely constitute their subjectivity, but rather always participate in a plurality, a community. This non-constitution of the subject prevents the constitution of the text as unity/identity, just as fundamental textual disunity precludes the establishment, through writing, of an autonomous subject.

Goethe has often been seen as the spokesman of the individual, but his essays force a revision of this view. Both in terms of life in general and specifically in terms of art, Goethe held a view of community as arising out of the individual's willingness to abandon claims to self-identity. In *Poetry and Truth* he describes how the "single" person can only survive if s*he has the courage to lose her*himself in a generality by relinquishing the realization of her*his goals to others:

[A person] urged on to active participation by outward incentives . . . will reach out in all directions, and the wish will stir in him to be effective in a variety of endeavors. But in addition to human limitedness there are so many incidental hindrances that a project begun is left undone or something taken up is laid aside, and one wish after the other dissipates. However, if these wishes issued from a pure heart, appropriate to the needs of the time, then one may well let things lie as they fall, right and left, and can be assured that they will not only be discovered and picked up again, but also that many related matters, not touched on or even thought of, will also come to light. If, during the course of our life, we see others accomplish what we ourselves earlier felt it was our calling to do, but had to abandon along with much else, then we get the beautiful feeling that only humankind all together is the true human being, and that the individual can be glad and happy only when he has the courage to sense himself in the whole. (IV, 287*)

[(Der Mensch wird,) durch äußere Anlässe zu tätiger Teilnahme gedrängt, bald da- bald dorthin greifen, und der Wunsch nach vielen Seiten wirksam zu sein wird in ihm lebendig werden. Nun gesellen sich aber zur menschlichen Beschränktheit noch so viele zufällige Hindernisse, daß hier ein Begonnenes liegen bleibt, dort ein Ergriffenes aus der Hand fällt, und ein Wunsch nach dem andern sich verzettelt. Waren aber diese Wünsche aus einem reinen Herzen entsprungen, dem Bedürfnis der Zeit gemäß, so darf man ruhig rechts und links liegen und fallen lassen und kann versichert sein, daß nicht allein dieses wieder aufgefunden und aufgehoben werden muß, sondern daß auch noch gar manches Verwandte, das man nie berührt, ja woran man nie gedacht hat, zum Vorschein kommen werde. Sehen wir nun während unseres Lebensganges dasjenige von andern geleistet, wozu wir selbst früher einen Beruf fühlten, ihn aber, mit manchem andern, aufgeben mußten, dann tritt das schöne Gefühl ein, daß

die Menschheit zusammen erst der wahre Mensch ist, und
daß der einzelne nur froh und glücklich sein kann, wenn er
den Mut hat, sich im Ganzen zu fühlen. (X, 425)]

If Goethe's portrayal of his "ideal conversation" is his dialogic
manifesto, then this passage can be taken to be his manifesto of
community, of an ideal that permeates his work and that is implied in all of his essays. In "The Collector," for example, the
notion of community is reflected in nearly every aspect of the
text, but perhaps most pointedly in the "philosopher," who has
to open up, has to relinquish his ideal of systematic closure and
certainty in order to participate actively in the conversation. The
advocate in "Truth and Probability" educates the spectator away
from the notion of truth in art in order to help him understand the
purpose behind the painted audience in the theater, which serves
as a reminder that, as a recipient of a work of art, one is always
involved with others, is not a self-identical individual.

In "Diderot's Essay" Goethe transposes that sense of moving
away from the individual and toward community to the realm
of artistic production. He criticizes Diderot for encouraging
young artists to follow their own inclinations without reserve
and thus, paradoxically, in the very attempt to avoid mannerism
instilling in them the notion that "an unconditional path, one
that is taken up by and appropriate to the individual, is the best
and leads the furthest" ["ein unbedingter, dem Individuo ge-
mäßer, selbst ergriffener Weg sei der beste, und führe am
weitesten" (XIII, 226)]. A discussion of the opposition between
"style" and "manner" gives him the opportunity to draw a
more general conclusion about the danger of insistence on individuality. As in other essays, style is treated as an opening up of
the artist's subjectivity to that which is other than itself. Style
describes a mingling of inside and outside (and consequently
also a weakening of the barrier that separates as well as constitutes inside and outside)—a mingling that supercedes the individual and raises the artist "into the realm of the general" ["ins
Allgemeine" (XIII, 244)]. Manner, on the other hand, "even
individualizes the individual" ["individualisiert . . . noch das
Individuum"] and thus distances the artist from that generality,

removes her*him from community: "He [the mannerist] demands nothing from humankind and so separates himself from his fellow human beings" ["Er macht keine Ansprüche an die Menschheit und so trennt er sich selbst von den Menschen" (XIII, 245)]. In then saying that "this applies as much to ethical as to artistic matters" ["dieses gilt so gut vom Sittlichen als vom Künstlichen"] Goethe explicitly ties this opposition of individuality and generality in art to the more general notion of community. In order for community, as well as great art, to come about, subjects must forgo attempts at (or dreams of) achieving self-identity, inner totality, a unified self, and must instead enter into dialogue with that which is other.

Goethe's disclosures of community, as that which itself *is* a dis-closure, diverge from the most prominent description of society in the second half of the eighteenth century—Jürgen Habermas's discussion of the "public sphere" in *Structural Transformation of the Public Sphere [Strukturwandel der Öffentlichkeit]*.[62] There at first appears to be an affinity between Habermas's and my analyses of how community emerges: Habermas postulates *dialogue* as a constitutive moment in the emergence of the public sphere. However, what he discusses in the name of dialogue he actually treats as if it were *monologue*. Letters, for Habermas one of the central dialogic elements in the development of the public sphere, do not represent for him bi- or multidirectional communication that destabilizes the limits of individuals, but rather unidirectional, monologic self-expression—a "soliloquy addressed to others" (67). Their monologic character renders them "experiments in subjectivity" (67). In other words, such "dialogue" is not a means of becoming part of a community, but rather the means of establishing individuality: "In writing letters, the individual develops its subjectivity" (66). This movement toward subjectivity and away from community is reflected in Habermas's concentration on *spoken* dialogue. He discusses conversation as it occurs in clubs, coffeehouses, and reading societies, and even emphasizes the *spoken* aspect of what begins as *written* dialogue—the conversation that occurs *after* the writing in journals, not the intertextual dialogue that takes place there *in writing*. This insistence on speech, and thus on presence and self-identity, allows him to posit the development, not the devolution or deconstruction, of subjectivity as a central characteristic of the emerging public sphere. For Habermas, then, "community" consists in a collection of "private individuals" [*Privatleute*], all developing and claiming their own separate identities, all erecting barriers between them*selves*, rather than storming the walls that separate them.[63]

Habermas would have us think of community as the realm of systematic discourse. It is, for him, the realm of monologic security, but in order for this security to be achieved and in order for the subject to constitute itself and maintain its autonomous individuality, it must also be a realm, like that of the system, of closure and exclusion of the other. In strictly and thoroughly maintaining the boundaries of inside and outside, it supports static hierarchical structures. It is thus the realm not only of a naïve security, but also and at the same time the realm, at least potentially, of tyranny. In "The Essay as Mediator" Goethe also describes systematic investigation in social terms—as the province of exclusionary tactics, of the avoidance of contradiction (and thus the eschewal of a dialogic approach), and of tyranny. After having drawn the connection between a lack of observation and the tendency to overabundant theorizing, to systematizing, he portrays such a systematic scholar at work:

> One notices that the fewer data a good thinker has at his disposal, the more tricks he will employ. As though to demonstrate his sovereignty he even chooses from the available facts only a few favorites that suit him; he skillfully marshals the rest so they do not exactly contradict him; and finally he is able to confuse, entangle, or push aside the hostile facts in such a way that the whole thing then no longer resembles a freely active republic, but rather a despotic court. (XII, 15*)

> [Man wird bemerken können, daß ein guter Kopf nur desto mehr Kunst anwendet, je weniger Data vor ihm liegen; daß er, gleichsam seine Herrschaft zu zeigen, selbst aus den vorliegenden Datis nur wenige Günstlinge

herauswählt, die ihm schmeicheln; daß er die übrigen so zu ordnen versteht, wie sie ihm nicht geradezu widersprechen, und daß er die feindseligen zuletzt so zu verwickeln, zu umspinnen und beiseite zu bringen weiß, daß wirklich nunmehr das Ganze nicht mehr einer freiwirkenden Republik, sondern einem despotischen Hofe ähnlich wird. (XVI, 850)]

In its intolerance of différance for the sake of comfort and security, the *Habermasian* community thwarts the rise of actual community, it resembles more a despotic court than an unbound republic.

Rorty offers a vision different from that of Habermas, a vision of the possibilities that arise when we cease to operate systematically, when we abandon the desire for the certainty and security of universal commensuration: "If we give up this hope [e.g., of finding the a priori structure of any possible inquiry, or language, or form of social life], we shall lose what Nietzsche called 'metaphysical comfort,' but we may gain a renewed sense of community" ("Pragmatism, Relativism, and Irrationalism," 166). We gain that sense of community when we practice what Rorty calls edifying philosophy, when we do all we can to keep the conversation going. This is the view of community that we find in Goethe's essays—in his discussions of dialogue and his critiques of subjectivity—and this *is* community as Goethe *practices* it in the essays. His essayistic writing, in its intertextual dialogism, indeed in its very quality as deconstruction, subverts the exclusionary, hierarchical tendencies of systematic discourse. By attenuating the boundaries between texts and between subjects, by undermining hierarchies, *Goethe's essays write community.* They seek no certainty through final answers, but rather keep the conversation going.

*   *   *

Goethe's novels, plays, and poems repeatedly thematize community and the devolution of individuality and identity prerequisite to its evolution. *Götz von Berlichingen* and *Werther* can both be interpreted not as glorifications of the actions and dispositions

of their heroes, but as *warnings* against the dangers of the hypertrophied subjectivity so thoroughly and catastrophically represented by those two figures; indeed, we could even read the last
and most famous line of *Götz*—"Woe to the coming generations that misjudge you" ["Wehe der Nachkommenschaft die
dich verkennt" (IV, 753)]—as an explicit warning against reading the play as a celebration of its protagonist. *Iphigenia in
Tauris* presents an alternative. The play can be construed as an
attempt to provide its audience—the Germans sitting in the
theater—with an image of the necessity of breaking down cultural and social barriers for the sake of a greater community of
humankind. This image is that of the "German" (the Barbarian
Thoas) giving up what is dearest to himself, Iphigenia, as a
result of the vision of humanity held out to him by Orestes.[64]

Two of Goethe's greatest literary achievements—*Faust* and
Wilhelm Meister—were written in two parts. In both cases the
first part explores the discovery and constitution of individual
subjectivity, whereas the second part can be seen to move in the
direction of self-renunciation [*Entsagung*]; this direction is even
made explicit in the title of the second *Wilhelm Meister* novel—
Wilhelm Meister's Journeyman Years, or: The Renunciants [*Wilhelm Meisters Wanderjahre oder die Entsagenden*]. In both cases,
moreover, the "public" half does not simply balance or comple-
ment the "private" half, but rather supplements it, continues it in
such a way as to call into question its exploration of the possibilities of such subjectivity.[65] Perhaps the fullest articulation of the
theme of *Entsagung*, however, occurs in *Elective Affinities*. Charlotte unsuccessfully tries to convince both Eduard and Ottilie that
this self-renunciation represents the possibility for survival of
their community. We see the danger of excessive individuality in
Eduard, who cares only for himself, even in his love for Ottilie.
His desire for her is not a desire for connection with an other, but
a search for *identity* that simply incorporates the other into the
self and thus subsumes it, as his "reading" of the glass reveals: his
initials, "E.O.," are inscribed on the glass, but he insists on interpreting them not as meaning "Eduard *Otto*," but rather as a
reflection of his identity with *Ottilie*. He is incapable of self-
renunciation, as is Ottilie, who also seeks identity with him, as
the change in her handwriting reveals. Even though she practices

self-renunciation, it is not an *Entsagung* in Charlotte's sense—
not for the sake of community (which Ottilie consistently damns
in her diary entries). Rather, her self-renunciation is for the sake
of *Eduard* and thus implicitly for *herself.* The result of this insistence on identity, on the individual subject, is literally the destruction, the death of the community.

In two other texts, it is dialogue that allows community to
survive. In *Conversations of German Emigrés* the French Revolution is seen to endanger community. Arguments determined by
the Revolution—political discussions in which the participants
insist on their individual positions and refuse to alter their
opinions—cause a crisis in the family and nearly annihilate it.
What saves this community from ruin is a kind of textual dialogue: the narration of stories, of texts, by various members of
the group and the critical reception of those texts. The text then
ends with the "Fairy Tale," and in its portrayal of the snake's
self-sacrifice leaves the reader with an image of *Entsagung* for
the sake of community.

Late in his life, Goethe wrote a poem that, like his essays, calls
our attention to intertextual dialogue and its implicit critique of
systems, and also, through this dialogue, to community. The
poem, "Legacy" ["Vermächtnis"], enters into dialogue with his
earlier poem "One and All" ["Eins und Alles"], which can be
read as an implicit critique of systematic thought.[66] "One and
All" begins with the relinquishing of subjectivity:

The individual will gladly perish if he can find himself
again in boundless infinity, where all vexations dissolve;
where instead of passionate wishes and wild desires, irk-
some demands and stern obligations, the self will delight
in self-surrender. (274)

[Im Grenzenlosen sich zu finden,
Wird gern der einzelne verschwinden,
Da löst sich aller Überdruß;
Statt heißem Wünschen, wildem Wollen,
Statt lästgem Fordern, strengem Sollen
Sich aufzugeben ist Genuß.
(I, 514)]

Goethe advocates, as in the poem "Permanence in Change" ["Dauer im Wechsel"], a process of constant change, of constant activity in order to avoid the stasis that the closure and completion of systems cause:

> And an eternal, living Activity works to create anew what has been created, lest it entrench itself in rigidity. . . . [N]one of it may remain at rest. (275)
>
> > [Und umzuschaffen das Geschaffne,
> > Damit sichs nicht zum Starren waffne,
> > Wirkt ewiges, lebendiges Tun.
> >
> > . . . .
> > In keinem Falle darf es ruhn.
> >   (I, 514)]

He ends the text with a warning that such stasis means the loss of all non-individual existence: "For everything must dissolve into nothingness, if it is to remain in Being" (275) ["Denn alles muß in Nichts zerfallen, / Wenn es im Sein beharren will" (I, 514)]. The fate of these contradictory lines was what later called forth the poem "Legacy."

According to Eckermann, at a meeting of scientists in Berlin, the last two lines of "One and All" were inscribed in gold letters on a plaque (XXIV, 312). By thus giving the statement the quality of truth or absolute knowledge, of permanence, the scientists had violated the sense of the poem. The first lines of the later poem, which parodies "One and All" in its structure and rhyme scheme, then read:

> Nothing that is can dissolve into nothingness! In all that lives the Eternal Force works on: remain, rejoicing, in Being! (276)
>
> > [Kein Wesen kann zu nichts zerfallen!
> > Das Ewge regt sich fort in allen,
> > Am Sein erhalte dich beglückt!
> >   (I, 514)]

For the sake of contradicting what had been taken to be a statement of truth, "Legacy," in its first five stanzas, defends a sense of
existential stasis and presents images and intimations of systems
and systematic thought: the system of the cosmos (stanza 1); the
system and truth of nature ("The truth has long since been
known" ["Das Wahre war schon längst gefunden"]) (stanza 2);
the inner system of the subject—"And then at once turn your
gaze inward: you will find the Centre there within" ["Sofort nun
wende dich nach innen: / Das Zentrum findest du da drinnen"]
(stanza 3); the power of "Understanding" [Verstand] to prevent
falsehood (stanza 4); and the power of "Reason" [Vernunft] to
create stasis and permanence (stanza 5). In the sixth stanza, however, we then discover the reason for this surprising advocacy of
what had been condemned in "One and All":

> And if in the end you have achieved this, and have come
> to feel thoroughly convinced that only what bears fruit is
> true—consider the conduct of the majority, leave them to
> arrange things as they please, and join the smallest
> crowd. (277*)

> > [Und war es endlich dir gelungen,
> > Und bist du vom Gefühl durchdrungen:
> > Was fruchtbar ist, allein ist wahr—
> > Du prüfst das allgemeine Walten,
> > Es wird nach seiner Weise schalten,
> > Geselle dich zur kleinsten Schar.
> > (I, 515)]

Once the statement of the earlier poem, in its critique of systems
and advocacy of self-surrender, had been embraced by the majority and thus itself acquired the quality of systematic stasis—
once it had become *certain*—it was necessary to contradict that
statement in order to keep the debate open. In other words,
Goethe insists that whenever there is a general consensus (and
thus a monologic environment), we must create an opposition;
otherwise the dialogue, the constant activity of which he writes
in "One and All," dies. This opposition ("the smallest crowd"),

even if its philosophical position itself is a defense of stasis, *undermines* stasis by preventing any large crowd from ruling absolutely. By always joining in the opposition, by always keeping open a dialogic space that prevents the certainty, the comfort, and the security of final answers, by keeping the (textual) conversation going, we keep community alive.

* * *

Community, in that it is implied and performed throughout Goethe's oeuvre, might be seen to constitute the final signified of his writing. If so, then the final signified is yet another instance of irony in his work. The irony lies in the fact that community in and of itself cannot *be* a final signified. Like the self-renouncing subjects who comprise it, community is never fully and finally constituted. Rather, it exists only in that it is always becoming, always in the *process* of creation. If we stop at some point and say that "now we have community," it ceases in that moment to be community, because it has fallen into stasis, has posited its own closure and thus countermanded the very openness and difference that make it possible, the uncertainty on which it thrives. Its participants have ceased to clash and now only blend. It has achieved identity, has become an *institution*—with clearly defined boundaries and all the other forms of stasis that term implies. Only in endless process—the process of writing, the process of "de-presenting" and "de-identifying" the subject—does community survive as a possibility.

If community is the goal of Goethe's writing, regardless of genre, then we are again encouraged to see his use of the essay as a genre of genres. Goethe's essayistic writing brings together issues—the breaking of temporal and spatial boundaries, the subversion of identity, the creation of community—that are crucial to all writing. Through their textual self-reflexivity—that is, in both thematizing and performing these activities in their dialogic and anti-systematic process—the essays reveal how writing in general, how texts effect community. And insofar as *we* trace their strategies *in our reading*, insofar as we productively surrender ourselves to their manifold uncertainty, we also perform the community of writing.

And so let this conversation be closed for now. In the meantime may the reader graciously receive what it has been possible to offer in this form.

[Und so sei auch für diesmal diese Unterhaltung geschlossen. Einstweilen nehme der Leser das, was sich in dieser Form geben ließ, geneigt auf.]
— "Diderot's Essay on Painting" (XIII, 253)

Notes

Preface

1. T. W. Adorno, "The Essay as Form," trans. Bob Hullot-Kentor, *New German Critique* 32 (1984): 152; Theodor W. Adorno, "Der Essay als Form," in his *Schriften II: Noten zur Literatur,* ed. Rolf Tiedemann (Frankfurt: Suhrkamp, 1974), 10. Quotations from Adorno will be taken from Hullot-Kentor's translation (which has been altered slightly in this case), but will be documented in the text with page numbers from both editions. For detailed analyses of Adorno's text, see my "Adorno, Goethe, and the Politics of the Essay," *Deutsche Vierteljahrsschrift für Literaturwissenschaft und Geistesgeschichte* 66 (1992): 160–91, and Hullot-Kentor's "Title Essay," *New German Critique* 32 (1984): 141–50.

2. Michel de Montaigne, *The Complete Essays,* trans. Donald M. Frame (Stanford: Stanford University Press, 1958), 3–5.

3. Johann Wolfgang Goethe, *Gedenkausgabe der Werke, Briefe und Gespräche,* ed. Ernst Beutler, 27 vols. (Zurich: Artemis, 1948–71). "The Collector and His Circle" can be found in volume 13, along with all of the essays on art; since Goethe's essays are scattered throughout his work and this edition, I will always document quotations from this edition with both volume and page number. As already mentioned, translations of quotations from Goethe, unless my own (and with the exception of *Faust* and the poems, where I have used other published translations), are from *Goethe's Collected Works,* ed. Victor Lange et al., 12 vols. ([Cambridge], New York: Suhrkamp/Insel, Suhrkamp, 1983–89) and will be documented with volume and page number from this edition.

4. Samuel Johnson, *The Rambler,* ed. Donald D. Eddy, 2 vols. (1753; rpt. New York: Garland, 1978), 1. Quotations from *The Rambler* will be documented in the text with page numbers from this edition; page numbers 1 through 622 indicate volume 1, whereas all numbers beyond 622 are from volume 2.

5. Matthijs Jolles, *Goethes Kunstanschauung* (Bern: Francke, 1957); Hans Joachim Schrimpf, *Goethes Begriff der Weltliteratur: Essay* (Stuttgart: Metzler, 1968); Christoph Gögelein, *Zu Goethes Begriff von Wissenschaft, auf dem Wege der Methodik seiner Farbstudien* (Munich: Hanser, 1972); Heinz Hamm, *Der Theoretiker Goethe: Grundpositionen seiner Weltanschauung, Philosophie und Kunsttheorie* (Kronberg/Ts.: Scriptor, 1976); Victor Lange, "Art and Literature: Two Modes of Goethe's Aesthetic Theory," in *Goethezeit: Studien zur Erkenntnis und Rezeption Goethes und seiner Zeitgenossen.*

Festschrift für Stuart Atkins, ed. Gerhart Hoffmeister (Bern: Francke, 1981), 157–78; *Goethe as a Critic of Literature*, ed. Karl J. Fink and Max L. Baeumer (Lanham, Md.: University Press of America, 1984). Another recent monograph on Goethe's literary criticism is Karin Haenelt's *Studien zu Goethes literarischer Kritik: Ihre Voraussetzungen und Möglichkeiten* (Frankfurt: Peter Lang, 1985).

6. See Gerhard Haas, *Essay* (Stuttgart: Metzler, 1969), and "Zur Geschichte und Kunstform des Essays," *Jahrbuch für internationale Germanistik* 7, no. 1 (1975): 11–39, for extensive discussion and bibliographies of literature devoted to the topic of the essay. Ludwig Rohner published three of the best known pieces in his *Deutsche Essays: Prosa aus zwei Jahrhunderten*, ed. Ludwig Rohner (Neuwied: Luchterhand, 1968): Georg Lukács's "On the Essence and Form of the Essay" ["Über Wesen und Form des Essays"], Max Bense's "On the Essay and Its Prose" ["Über den Essay und seine Prosa"], and Theodor Adorno's "The Essay as Form." Rohner also presented his own introductory "Essay on the Essay" ["Versuch über den Essay"]. I will document quotations from Lukács and Bense with page numbers from this volume. Some of the other treatments of the genre are Dieter Bachmann, *Essay und Essayismus* (Stuttgart: Kohlhammer, 1969); Bruno Berger, *Der Essay: Form und Geschichte* (Bern: Francke, 1964); Richard Exner, "Zum Problem einer Definition und einer Methodik des Essays als dichterischer Kunstform," *Neophilologus* 46 (1962): 169–82; Heinrich Küntzel, *Essay und Aufklärung: Zum Ursprung einer originellen deutschen Prosa im 18. Jahrhundert* (Munich: Fink, 1969); Helmut Rheder, "Die Anfänge des deutschen Essays," *Deutsche Vierteljahrsschrift für Literaturwissenschaft und Geistesgeschichte* 40 (1966): 24–42; Ludwig Rohner, *Der deutsche Essay: Materialien zur Geschichte und Ästhetik einer literarischen Gattung* (Neuwied: Luchterhand, 1966); Klaus Weissenberger, "Der Essay," in *Prosakunst ohne Erzählen: Die Gattungen der nicht-fiktionalen Kunstprosa*, ed. Klaus Weissenberger (Tübingen: Niemeyer, 1985), 105–24; Hans Wolffheim, "Der Essay als Kunstform: Thesen zu einer neuen Forschungsaufgabe," *Euphorion*, Sonderheft: *Festgruß für Hans Pyritz* (1955): 27–30. An interesting essayistic discussion of the essay, and one that suggests some of the points I make, is Michael Hamburger's "Essay über den Essay," *Akzente* 12 (1965): 290–92.

7. Graham Good, *The Observing Self: Rediscovering the Essay* (New York: Routledge, 1988); John A. McCarthy, *Crossing Boundaries: A Theory and History of Essay Writing in German, 1680–1815* (Philadelphia: University of Pennsylvania Press, 1989); John Snyder, "On and of the Essay as Nongenre," in his *Prospects of Power: Tragedy, Satire, the Essay, and the Theory of Genre* (Lexington: University Press of Kentucky, 1991), 149–201. Another related study—Geoffrey H. Hartman's *Minor Prophecies: The Literary Essay in the Culture Wars* (Cambridge: Harvard University Press, 1991)—was about to be released as this book went to press and thus could not be included in my discussion.

8. I will cite the book version of the study: Joachim Wohlleben, *Goethe als Journalist und Essayist* (Frankfurt: Peter Lang, 1981).

9. McCarthy does briefly discuss Goethe's Shakespeare essays within the context of his wide-ranging study of the early German essay (265–73).

10. I use rhetoric here not in the sense of classical rhetorical forms, as McCarthy does (especially at 37 and 136–52), but in the sense it has acquired through poststructuralist theories. For example, in her introduction to Jacques Derrida's *Dissemination*, Barbara Johnson says that "a deconstructive reading . . . assumes: 1. That the rhetoric of an assertion is not necessarily compatible with its explicit meaning" (Jacques Derrida, *Dissemination*, translated, with an introduction and additional notes by Barbara John-

son [Chicago: University of Chicago Press, 1981], xvi). Cf. also Paul de Man, "Semiology and Rhetoric," in his *Allegories of Reading: Figural Language in Rousseau, Nietzsche, Rilke, and Proust* (New Haven: Yale University Press, 1979), 3–19.

11. I do not include Bacon here because his status as an essayist—according to my view of the genre as well as the views of Adorno and others, and despite his own designation of his texts—is questionable. The most recent study of the genre supports me in this: John Snyder says that "not until Rousseau and the Romantics, especially Emerson [and Lessing and Goethe, I would add], did the essay genre burst the strait jacket fabricated by Bacon and return to the unbounded genericity of Montaigne" (172–73) and remarks on "Bacon's reductionism and self-closure" (180)—qualities that, in the course of my study, will come to be seen as incompatible with the essay. For a discussion of Bacon's empiricism and the ways in which it can be seen to be at odds with the essay, see the final pages of my "Adorno, Goethe, and the Politics of the Essay."

12. The Surhkamp edition translates these titles differently—as "Simple Imitation, Manner, Style" and "On Realism in Art."

13. See, for example, David E. Wellbery, *Lessing's "Laokoon": Semiotics and Aesthetics in the Age of Reason* (Cambridge: Cambridge University Press, 1984). Only recently has a study appeared that treats what I would call the essayistic aspects of *Laocoön* and Herder's first "Critical Grove": Eva Knodt, *"Negative Philosophie" und dialogische Kritik: Zur Struktur poetischer Theorie bei Lessing und Herder* (Tübingen: Niemeyer, 1988). For another excellent reading of *Laocoön* that goes well beyond the theoretical content of Lessing's text, see Carol Jacobs, "The Critical Performance of Lessing's *Laokoon*," *MLN* 102 (1987): 483–521.

14. See note 11.

15. See note 6.

16. In the "Epistemo-Critical Prologue" of his *Origin of German Tragic Drama*, Walter Benjamin also explicitly juxtaposes the essay to the systematic "closure" of philosophical discourse: "The alternative of philosophical form provided by the concepts of theory and of the esoteric essay is what the nineteenth century's concept of system ignores" (*Ursprung des deutschen Trauerspiels*, ed. Rolf Tiedemann [Frankfurt: Suhrkamp, 1978], 9).

17. See Friedrich Kambartel, " 'System' und 'Begründung' als wissenschaftliche und philosophische Ordnungsbegriffe bei und vor Kant," in *Philosophie und Rechtswissenschaft: Zum Problem ihrer Beziehung im 19. Jahrhundert*, ed. J. Blühdorn and J. Ritter (Frankfurt: Klostermann, 1969), 99–113; Manfred Zahn, "System," in *Handbuch philosophischer Grundbegriffe*, ed. H. Krings et al., 6 vols. (Munich: Kösel, 1973–74), V, 1458–75; Lutz Koch, "System," in *Wissenschaftstheoretisches Lexikon*, ed. E. Braun and H. Radermacher (Graz: Styria, 1978), 577–78; Niklas Luhmann, *Soziale Systeme: Grundriß einer allgemeinen Theorie* (Frankfurt: Suhrkamp, 1984), 15–91. For a more critical, and more humorous, discussion of systems, see Fritz Mauthner, *Wörterbuch der Philosophie: Neue Beiträge zu einer Kritik der Sprache*, 2 vols. (1910–11; rpt. Zurich: Diogenes, 1980), 251–66.

18. Here I take issue with Good, who says, on the one hand, that "the essay does not aim at system at all" (3), but, on the other, that "the essay's open-minded approach to experience is balanced by aesthetic pattern and closure" (14). Good says he derives his approach mainly from Lukács and Adorno (viii), but Adorno went to great lengths to show that one aspect of the essay's critique of the system is its subversion of closure. And with regard to the more specific issue of "aesthetic closure," Adorno says only that, by producing interpretations that are compatible with the text and with themselves and by

being able to bring all of the elements of the object to expression, the essay *"resembles a kind of* aesthetic independence" (my translation and emphasis), not that it *"acquires* an aesthetic autonomy" (Hullot-Kentor translation, 153; my emphasis) ["Durch diese *ähnelt* der Essay *einer* ästhetischen Selbständigkeit" (11; my emphasis)]. Regarding closure in general, Adorno says the essay is "more closed [than traditional thought] in that it labors emphatically on the form of its presentation" (165; 26); this statement does not, however, imply that the essay ever really *achieves* formal closure. And Adorno also says that the essay "is more open [than traditional thought] insofar as, through its inner nature, it negates anything systematic" (165; 26). In other words, even if we were to attribute to the essay a certain aesthetic autonomy, this autonomy/closure would have to be seen as being attenuated and could not "balance" its fundamental non-closure, its fundamental questioning of the closure of the system.

19. Luhmann, 17 and 35.

20. Zahn, 1473 and 1474.

21. The dialogic aspect of the essay has received extensive attention in the two studies by Haas listed in note 6. Unfortunately, Haas limits his view of what constitutes dialogue to the more explicit and obvious ways in which it can occur, e.g., actual address to the reader, dialogic structuring of the text in the sense of dramatic form, and correspondence. The significance of dialogue is also mentioned briefly by Good (1, 6, and passim) and is discussed at somewhat greater length by McCarthy, who says that "all essayistic writing is marked by an essentially dialogic structure" (39).

22. McCarthy considers the relation of the essayistic text to its reader so important that he elevates "the non-directive attitude of the writer toward her/his subject and audience" (41) to the status of *the* "distinctive trait" of the genre and makes the investigation of that relationship the guiding principle of his study: "[The] common denominator is the writer's invitation to the reader to enter into a collaborative relationship in the method of thinking that lies at the heart of the literary form" (31). I do not argue the significance, only the absolute privileging of this generic characteristic.

23. In the most recent study of the essay, which appeared while the present book was undergoing final revisions, John Snyder portrays textual self-reflexivity as a basic characteristic of the genre (see 153 and 174).

24. The absence of Schiller in this list of essayists is rather conspicuous, and his absence in Part Two, where I will discuss Goethe's essays in relation to those of Lessing and Herder, may be even more conspicuous. Schiller was Goethe's closest friend and is, to this day, far more renowned as a writer of essays than Goethe (we need only consider his inclusion in the many lists of German essayists where Goethe is absent). But I leave him out for a reason. According to my understanding of the essay, Schiller is not an essayist in the tradition that began with Montaigne and that saw its first great efflorescence in Germany with the work of Lessing, Herder, and Goethe. "On Naïve and Sentimental Poetry" ["Über naive und sentimentalische Dichtung"] is an exception that might place him in that company after all, but I would argue that this late text can be considered the product of Goethe's influence as witnessed in their correspondence. To make this argument, however, I would have to enter into a lengthy and complex analysis of the text itself, of the relationship between Goethe and Schiller, and of the effects of that relationship on both writers; such an analysis would take me too far off course in my attempt to understand Goethe's essays and the genre of the essay. Their correspondence and Schiller's essay on naïve and sentimental poetry will, however, be the subject of a chapter in a book I am currently writing, with the provisional title, *Goethe and the Textual Tradition: Readings in Another German Intellectual History.*

Another major issue that requires discussion, but would constitute too extensive a digression here, is the relationship between the essay and the fragment. Jean-François Lyotard points to the difference between them when he says, "It seems to me that the essay (Montaigne) is postmodern, while the fragment (*The Athaeneum*) is modern" (*The Postmodern Condition: A Report on Knowledge,* trans. Geoff Bennington and Brian Massumi [Minneapolis: University of Minnesota Press, 1984], 81). This view, however, is by no means universal. For example, a complex and stimulating study of Roland Barthes recently appeared that asserts the identity of essay and fragment: Réda Bensmaia, *The Barthes Effect: The Essay as Reflective Text,* trans. Pat Fedkiew (Minneapolis: University of Minnesota Press, 1987). Gerhard Neumann also attributes to the aphorism a number of the discursive strategies I will portray as characteristic of the essay in his *Ideenparadiese: Untersuchungen zur Aphoristik von Lichtenberg, Novalis, Friedrich Schlegel und Goethe* (Munich: Fink, 1976). In a chapter on Goethe and Friedrich Schlegel in *Goethe and the Textual Tradition,* I will discuss the divergence of the fragment from the essay that results from their respective stances with regard to systems, but will also discuss ways in which fragments (e.g., Schlegel's *Athenaeum* and Goethe's collections of fragments in such texts as *Elective Affinities* and *Wilhelm Meister's Journeyman Years*) can attenuate that difference and enter the realm of what Lyotard calls the postmodern.

Part One: The Serious Game

1. Herbert von Einem calls it an "art novella," while Hans Rudolf Vaget prefers the term "epistolary novella" (Herbert von Einem, "Kommentar," in Johann Wolfgang von Goethe, *Werke, Hamburger Ausgabe,* ed. E. Trunz, 12 vols. [Munich: dtv, 1981], XII, 603, hereafter cited as "HA" followed by volume and page numbers; Hans Rudolf Vaget, *Dilettantismus und Meisterschaft: Zum Problem des Dilettantismus bei Goethe: Praxis, Theorie, Zeitkritik* [Munich: Winkler, 1971], 112). And Wohlleben, while treating it in the context of Goethe's essayism, first calls it an "epistolary 'novel' " and then an "epistolary treatise" (99), but not an essay. Matthijs Jolles, who throughout his extended study of "The Collector" refers to it as a "narration," begins his book with reflections about what he discerns as the problematic nature of the text's genre: "The narration is thus, so we are at first inclined to say, a kind of hybrid. The theoretical and generally human [whatever that might mean—P.B.] quality of the later chapters prevent us from seeing it as a historical account. It is not a theoretical treatise, since it is too confused and the narrative part, the 'novelistic' formulation, takes up too much room. Finally, it is also not a work of art, for the text seems to point well beyond itself" (10).

2. Johann Caspar Lavater, *Physiognomische Fragmente zur Beförderung der Menschenkenntniß und Menschenliebe,* abridged and edited by Johann Michael Armbruster, 3 vols. (Winterthur: Steiners, 1783), I, 18.

3. Arseni Gulyga, "Goethe als Ästhetiker und Kunsttheoretiker," *Goethe-Jahrbuch* 96 (1979): 111. In a recent study of the essay in eighteenth-century Germany, James Van Der Laan includes Goethe in a list of quotations that explicitly oppose systematic thought (James M. Van Der Laan, "The German Essay of the 18th Century: Mirror of its Age," *Lessing Yearbook* 18 [1986]: 181); he cites a statement from "On German Architecture" ["Von deutscher Baukunst"] concerning the strictures placed on perception and action by "discipline and principle," but does not elaborate on the point.

Regarding the anti-systematic quality of the eighteenth-century German essay, Van Der Laan goes so far as to treat this aspect of the genre as a given, as something that goes without saying and requires no demonstration: "Its [the essay's] authors typically reject a dogmatic and systematic method of writing" (181). However, like others who have written on the essay, he does not go beyond stating that the essay *is* anti-systematic to show *how* it is so.

4. There is a significant connection here between Goethe and the language critics of the late nineteenth century, who also align skepticism about language with skepticism about systems. In Fritz Mauthner's *Dictionary of Philosophy*, for example, we not only find a portrayal of the system as the entirely subjective (Fritz Mauthner, *Wörterbuch der Philosophie*, 251), but we also read that "if there were a natural *ordo* that corresponded to the human *dispositio*, if we were able to create a natural catalogue of the world in an artificial universal language, then something like a thinking machine would be possible. Then a system of science would also be possible" (266). Perhaps an even more important connection is to Nietzsche. In his "On Truth and Lying in an Extra-Moral Sense" ["Ueber Wahrheit und Lüge im aussermoralischen Sinne"] of 1873, he uses his deconstruction of "truth" (and thus of conventional morality), which he had reinscribed as "lie" by arguing the arbitrariness of the socially determined phenomenon of language, as the basis for a critique of systems: "The great structure of concepts displays the rigid regularity of a Roman columbarium and has, in its logic, an aura of that severity and coldness typical of mathematics. . . . Within this dice game of concepts, however, 'truth' means: to use each die as designated, count its spots accurately, forming the correct labels, and never violating the caste system and sequence of rank classifications" (*Friedrich Nietzsche on Rhetoric and Language*, ed. and trans. Sander L. Gilman, Carole Blair, and David J. Parent [New York: Oxford University Press, 1989], 250–51; translation altered slightly).

5. Jacques Derrida, "Structure, Sign and Play in the Discourse of the Human Sciences," in his *Writing and Difference*, trans. Alan Bass (Chicago: University of Chicago Press, 1978), 280–81.

6. Johann Wolfgang von Goethe, *Faust: A Tragedy*, trans. Bayard Taylor (Boston: Houghton Mifflin, 1912), 77. All translations from *Faust* will be documented in the text with page numbers from this edition. The German text of *Faust* is from volume 5 of Ernst Beutler's *Gedenkausgabe* and is documented in the text by part and line numbers only.

7. These views on language might seem to contradict the relationship between language and system that we see in Goethe's remarks on Spinoza. However, what is at issue here is not an intersubjective linguistic context; "words" in this context represent the abstraction of individual subjectivity vis-à-vis the actual experience of the objective world.

8. In etymological terms this might go a bit far, but the words *are* related as a result of their mutual relationship to words having to do with "seeing" and "looking." Cf. articles on "Schein" in Jacob and Wilhelm Grimm, *Deutsches Wörterbuch* (Leipzig: S. Hirzel, 1893), VIII, columns 2419–33, and on "schön" (1899), IX, columns 1464–86, especially columns 1464 and 1476 (vols. 14 and 15 of the reprint edition [Munich: dtv, 1984]).

9. Herbert von Einem has also demonstrated that this remark refers to Kant and his followers (HA, XII, 605).

10. The remark appears in a letter to Ludwig Friedrich Schultz of 18 September 1831: *Gedenkausgabe*, XXI, 1008.

11. Cf. Vaget, 124.

12. Wohlleben has pointed out yet another way in which the philosopher contravenes his own intellectual convictions: "In the sixth letter, in which the idealist philosophy of art is presented, Schiller's speculation on art succumbs to the same irony, since the 'philosopher' presenting that philosophy secretly allows considerations of the most private nature to flow into his theorems: love inspires and overcomes him as well as his speculative thought" (100).

13. In a recent study of Goethe's "theory" of poetry (*Goethe's Theory of Poetry: "Faust" and the Regeneration of Language* [Ithaca: Cornell University Press, 1986]), Benjamin Bennett shows that that theory resides not in explicit theoretical statements, but implicitly *in* Goethe's poetry (here one recalls Goethe's remark on philosophy, which he often equated with "theory," in *Poetry and Truth:* "There was no need for a separate philosophy, since it was already completely contained in religion and poetry" [IV, 171; X, 245]). In his second chapter Bennett adduces the approach to truth advocated in the "Prelude on the Stage": "The truth is formulable, but dangerous for him who formulates it openly" (48). As a result, an ironic attitude toward truth is necessary. Bennett's focus is quite different from mine, but here there is nevertheless a point of contact: systematic inquiry exposes itself to the danger inherent in formulating the truth and thus fails to recognize the necessity of irony; the essay does not make the same mistake.

14. Graham Good, in the context of a closing polemic against deconstruction (*The Observing Self*, 179–82), concludes that the essay "is a democratic form, open to anyone who can see clearly and think independently" (186). This is a surprising conclusion for a study that claims to derive its view of the essay from Adorno, who in "The Essay as Form" can be seen to anticipate deconstructive criticism (see my reading of Adorno's essay on the essay in "Adorno, Goethe, and the Politics of the Essay"). Adorno argues at length that the very possibility of such clarity is precisely what the genre draws into question, and that "independent thought"—that is, the autonomy of the subject—is a claim of systematic thought and discourse which the essay exposes as an impossibility. Goethe's essays demonstrate as well the way in which the essay plays with systematic clarity; they also, as we will see in Part Two, subvert the monologism of "independent thought" in their thematization of the intertextually dialogic nature of all writing.

15. In Nietzsche as well, the combination of seriousness and play constitutes opposition to the systematic:

> There are ages in which the rational man and the intuitive man stand side by side, one in fear of intuition, the other with mockery for abstraction; the latter being just as unreasonable as the former is unartistic. Both desire to master life; the one by managing to meet his main needs with foresight, prudence, reliability; the other, as an "overjoyous" hero, by not seeing those needs and considering only life, disguised as illusion and beauty, to be real. Where once the intuitive man, as in more ancient Greece, bore his weapons more powerfully and victoriously than his adversary, in favorable cases a culture can form and the domination of art over life be established. That dissimulation [dissimulation being a desirable act in Nietzsche's view, since it calls attention to the lie of truth and conventional morality and thus works against their hegemony and the hegemony of the rational, the systematic—P.B.], that denial of poverty, that splendor of metaphorical intuitions and, in general, that immediacy of delusion accompanies all manifestations of such a life. Neither the house, nor the stride, nor the clothing, nor the clay jug betray the fact that need invented them; they seem intended to

express an exalted happiness and an Olympian serenity and, as it were, *a playing with serious matters*. ("On Truth and Lying in an Extra-Moral Sense," 256; my emphasis)

The merging of seriousness and play to combat the rationalistic is thus not unique to Goethe, and within Goethe's work it is not unique to "The Collector and His Circle." It occurs repeatedly in *Poetry and Truth* and it assumes a prominent position in *Faust* by forming the basis for the views of the "Amusing Person" (the player) when arguing with the poet in the "Prelude on the Stage":

> Then pluck up heart, and give us sterling coin!
> Let Fancy be with her attendants fitted,—
> Sense, Reason, Sentiment, and Passion join,—
> But have a care, lest Folly be omitted!
>
> (5)
>
> [Drum seid nur brav und zeigt Euch musterhaft,
> Laßt Phantasie mit allen ihren Chören,
> Vernunft, Verstand, Empfindung, Leidenschaft,
> Doch, merkt Euch wohl! nicht ohne Narrheit hören!
> (Part 1, lines 85–88)]

16. There have been other discussions of the significance of "Spiel" in the essay. However, as in Weissenberger's recent study, "Spiel" is generally not seen as "game" in the sense of *play*, as that which threatens or calls into question the system, but rather, in a limited way, as hypostatized and regulated *game*, as that which would render the essay *systematic*: "The essay fulfills all conditions of the game: from independent domain and the absolute, even if temporally limited, order that constitutes that domain; through rules, which imply an absolute truth; to the aesthetic characteristics of the game, which take on concrete form as 'tension, balance, weighing, replacement, contrast, variation, binding and severing, and resolution,' and which, through their rhythmic meshing, reveal the closure of the game" ("Der Essay," 107–8).

17. Given the deconstructive force of the term "style" in "The Collector," there is a fascinating coincidence in Derrida's work. In *Spurs: Nietzsche's Styles*, we read:

> That Nietzsche had no illusions that he might ever know anything of these effects called woman, truth, castration, nor of those *ontological* effects of presence and absence, is manifest in the very heterogeneity of his text. Indeed it is just such an illusion that he was analyzing even as he took care to avoid the precipitate negation where he might erect a simple discourse against castration and its system. For the reversal, if it is not accompanied by a discrete parody, a strategy of writing, or difference or deviation in quills, if there is no style, no grand style, this is finally but the same thing, nothing more than a clamorous declaration of the antithesis. Hence the heterogeneity of the text. (Jacques Derrida, *Spurs: Nietzsche's Styles / Eperons: Les Styles de Nietzsche*, trans. Barbara Harlow [Chicago: University of Chicago Press, 1979], 95)

We have already seen Goethe's "style" at work in his "strategy of writing" (his parody, however, being more discreet than "discrete"). And in its multiplication of writing voices, to which I will return in Part Two, "The Collector" also employs the kind of "difference or deviation in quills" mentioned here. In both Goethe's text and Nietzsche's text as Derrida reads it, the effect of "style" is to rupture the text, its univocality, its univalence; "style" effects textual heterogeneity, it is the sign of the warring levels of signification within the text.

18. For a discussion of Goethe's later and more extensive essay on Shakespeare— "Shakespeare Without End" ["Shakespeare und kein Ende"]—see my "Literary History and Historical Truth: Herder—'Shakespeare'—Goethe," *Deutsche Vierteljahrsschrift für Literaturwissenschaft und Geistesgeschichte* 65 (1991): 636–52.

19. It at first seems as though the collector is praising this dual—teleological and archeological—tendency on the part of the editors, but the tone of his "praise" attenuates it: seeking the source and the ultimate end, he says, is "commendable" ["löblich"] and "nice" ["schön"] and "cannot be of no use" ["kann nicht ohne Nutzen bleiben"] (III, 133*; XIII, 278). Even if we failed to recognize this ironic tone, the following pages make it clear that the collector is gently attempting to counteract that tendency in his friends: he repeatedly says that he does not wish to criticize them for being too serious in their judgments of art, but at the same time urges them to be more liberal and open-minded in those judgments (III, 133–35; XIII, 278–82).

20. See Rohner's list of essays to be included in the second and third volumes of his collection (*Deutsche Essays*, 671–72).

21. For a detailed discussion of Montaigne's "integration" of his friendship with La Boétie into the *Essais*, see Beryl Schlossman, "From La Boétie to Montaigne: The Place of the Text," *MLN* 98 (1983): 891–909. Schlossman deals not so much with the place of La Boétie's text in Montaigne's essay project as with the extraordinary effect the friend had on his conception of writing in general. La Boétie is disclosed as the absent center of all of Montaigne's writing, his writing itself as the constant attempt to fill that void. As a result, we are encouraged to draw the conclusion that essayistic discourse in Montaigne always moves around an absent center, that that absence itself engenders his essays.

22. Gotthold Ephraim Lessing, *Laocoön: An Essay on the Limits of Painting and Poetry*, trans. Edward A. McCormick (Baltimore: The Johns Hopkins University Press, 1984), 15; Gotthold Ephraim Lessing, *Werke*, ed. Herbert G. Göpfert et al., 8 vols. (Munich: Hanser, 1974), VI, 20. Further quotations from *Laocoön* will be documented in the text with page numbers from the McCormick translation and volume and page numbers from the Göpfert edition. Quotations from other works of Lessing (the translations of which are my own) will be documented only with volume and page number from the Göpfert edition.

In a new study of *Laocoön*, David Wellbery presents a fascinating reading of Lessing's text that explicates the definition of beauty implied in the second chapter ("Das Gesetz der Schönheit: Lessings Ästhetik der Repräsentation," in *Was heißt Darstellung*, ed. Christiaan L. Hart-Nibbrig [Frankfurt: Suhrkamp, 1992]).

23. Carol Jacobs also discusses Lessing's elaborate fictions, although in different terms ("The Critical Performance of Lessing's *Laokoon*," especially 486–89).

24. Edward W. Said, *The World, the Text, and the Critic* (Cambridge: Harvard University Press, 1983), 126–27.

25. One of the innumerable other places in Goethe's work where we find a preference for experience over abstraction is in *Faust*. Mephistopheles promises Faust insight into the meaning of life *through experience*, but first Faust must shed his academic gowns (a symbol for a life lived under the sign of abstraction):

And I advise thee, brief and flat,
To don the self-same gay apparel,
That, from this den released, and free,
Life be at last revealed to thee!
                                    (63)

[Und rate nun dir kurz und gut,
Dergleichen gleichfalls anzulegen,
Damit du, losgebunden, frei,
Erfahrest, was das Leben sei.
                        (Part 1, lines 1540–43)]

In convincing Faust to go out into the world with him, he once again points to the opposition:

I say to thee, a speculative wight
Is like a beast on moorlands lean,
That round and round some fiend misleads to evil plight,
While all about lie pastures fresh and green.
                                                        (73)

[Ich sag es dir: ein Kerl, der spekuliert,
Ist wie ein Tier, auf dürrer Heide
Von einem bösen Geist im Kreis herumgeführt,
Und ringsumher liegt schöne, grüne Weide.
                            (Part 1, lines 1829–32)]

And he concludes his sermon to the student with an even more direct statement of the importance of experience vis-à-vis abstraction: "My worthy friend, gray are all theories, / And green alone Life's golden tree" (81) ["Grau, teurer Freund, ist alle Theorie, / Und grün des Lebens goldner Baum" (Part 1, lines 2038–39)].

26. For further discussion of the correspondence of "theory" and "system," see Adorno's "The Essay as Form."

27. Friedrich Nietzsche, *Sämtliche Werke: Kritische Studienausgabe in 15 Einzelbänden*, 2d ed., ed. Giorgio Colli and Mazzino Montinari (Munich: dtv; Berlin: Walter de Gruyter, 1988). The quotation used in the epigraph is from vol. 6, page 63.

28. Gottlob Frege, "Logik in der Mathematik," in his *Nachgelassene Schriften*, 2d rev. ed., ed. Hans Hermes et al. (Hamburg: Meiner, 1983), I, 261.

29. See my "Adorno, Goethe, and the Politics of the Essay."

30. See note 4.

31. Jonathan Culler, *On Deconstruction: Theory and Criticism after Structuralism* (Ithaca: Cornell University Press, 1982), 149–50.

32. Richard Rorty, "Deconstruction and Circumvention," *Critical Inquiry* 11 (1984): 2.

33. Views such as those expressed here are not uncommon in Goethe's "scientific" writings. In one of his aphorisms, for example, we read "that nothing can actually be proved through experiences and experiments" ["daß sich durch Erfahrungen und Versuche eigentlich nichts beweisen läßt" (XVII, 727)], that one can place experiments in a certain order and thus even achieve certainty and completion in one's own views, but that those experiments can never lead to generally valid conclusions, since "everyone

draws his own conclusions from them" ["Folgerungen hingegen zieht jeder für sich daraus" (XVII, 727–28)]. And in a remark strongly reminiscent of his discussion of Spinoza's system, as well as of Mauthner, he says that "no one comprehends anything but that which is in accordance with himself" ["daß niemand etwas begreift, als was ihm gemäß ist" (XVII, 728)].

34. See Jacob and Wilhelm Grimm, *Deutsches Wörterbuch*, XII, columns 1822–26, especially definitions 2 and 5 (vol. 25 of the dtv reprint edition).

35. In an article published since the completion of this study, James Van Der Laan also calls attention to the double meaning of "Versuch" in Goethe's title ("Of Goethe, Essays, and Experiments," *Deutsche Vierteljahrsschrift für Literaturwissenschaft und Geistesgeschichte* 64 [1990]: 45–53). For a discussion of Goethe's text as an essayistic subversion of scientific discourse as well as of the totalitarian implications of that discourse, see my "Adorno, Goethe, and the Politics of the Essay."

36. Jacques Derrida, "The Law of Genre," *Glyph: Textual Studies* 7 (1980): 206. For a discussion of the "mixing"—i.e., impurity—inscribed in the very notion of genre, see Philippe Lacoue-Labarthe and Jean-Luc Nancy, "Genre," *Glyph: Textual Studies* 7 (1980): 1–14.

Part Two: Talking Pens

The epigraphs to part 2 are quotations from Friedrich Hölderlin, *Sämtliche Werke und Briefe*, ed. Günter Mieth, 2 vols. (Munich: Hanser, 1970), I, 368, and, altered slightly, *Goethe: Selected Verse*, trans. David Luke (Middlesex, England: Penguin Books, 1964), 277.

1. Wohlleben also asserts that "Truth and Probability" is a Platonic dialogue (95), but does not compare the actual process of Goethe's dialogue with the philosophical implications of the form of the Platonic dialogue.

2. Richard Rorty, "Pragmatism, Relativism, and Irrationalism," in his *Consequences of Pragmatism (Essays: 1972–1980)* (Minneapolis: University of Minnesota Press, 1982), 164.

3. In the case of "Truth and Probability" a continuation was actually planned. See the letter to Schiller of 24 May 1798 (XX, 586).

4. Jolles also discusses this "ideal conversation" in his argument that dialogue constitutes a "way of thinking and acting" that informs all of Goethe's work (*Goethes Kunstanschauung*, 54–63, especially 60–61 and 62–63).

5. The Suhrkamp edition translates the title as *Conversations of German Refugees*.

6. I include Storm and Stress here mainly because of Goethe's own views. In *Poetry and Truth* he describes the movement, first, as having arisen out of contradiction to the age that preceded it (IV, 197; X, 285) and, second, as having come about through dialogue (IV, 384; X, 567–68). Even though the writers of the time openly criticized Enlightenment thought and writing, seeing the movement in strict opposition to the Enlightenment remains problematic, since at least one aspect of the movement can be seen as a radicalization of Enlightenment systematics—its glorification of the "Genius," the hypertrophied manifestation of the autonomous subject. In this sense, we might then say that Goethe's own works of the 1770s (e.g., *Götz* and *Werther*), which are generally seen as prime examples of the Storm and Stress movement, actually depart from the norm of the movement (see "The Community of Writing" at the end of this study).

7. Richard Rorty, "Philosophy in America Today," in his *Consequences of Pragmatism*, 226 and 222.

8. Richard Rorty, *Philosophy and the Mirror of Nature* (Princeton: Princeton University Press, 1979), 367.

9. M. M. Bakhtin, "Discourse in the Novel," in *The Dialogic Imagination: Four Essays*, ed. Michael Holquist, trans. Caryl Emerson and Michael Holquist (Austin: University of Texas Press, 1981), 259–422.

10. Tzvetan Todorov, *Mikhail Bakhtin: The Dialogical Principle*, trans. Wlad Godzich (Minneapolis: University of Minnesota Press, 1984).

11. For a discussion and critique of Bakhtin's restriction of dialogue to the novel and his concomitant reduction of poetic/lyric language to the monologic, see Renate Lachmann, "Dialogizität und poetische Sprache," in *Dialogizität*, ed. Renate Lachmann (Munich: Fink, 1982), 51–62. Lachmann also discusses Kristeva's subtly modifying interpretation of Bakhtin and how her notions of intertextuality and "paragrammes" subvert Bakhtin's reduction of poetic language and demonstrate the dialogic quality of language beyond generic boundaries. On the question of speech and its implications for the speaking subject in the dialogic model, see Jürgen Lehmann, "Ambivalenz und Dialogizität: Zur Theorie der Rede bei Michail Bachtin," in *Urszenen: Literaturwissenschaft als Diskursanalyse und Diskurskritik*, ed. Friedrich A. Kittler and Horst Turk (Frankfurt: Suhrkamp, 1977), 355–80.

12. The philosophical implications of dialogue and monologue were not, of course, the sole province of Goethe. They are at issue, for example, in one of Lessing's early plays, *Philotas*, where we see the opposition between radical subjectivity and the social inscribed in the drama's use of dialogue and monologue. See my "Lessing's Tragic Topography: The Rejection of Society and Its Spatial Metaphor in *Philotas*," *Deutsche Vierteljahrsschrift für Literaturwissenschaft und Geistesgeschichte* 61 (1987): 441–56. On the impossibility of contradiction in monologic discourse, see Volker Nölle, *Subjektivität und Wirklichkeit in Lessings dramatischem und theologischem Werk* (Berlin: Schmidt, 1977).

13. Heinrich von Kleist, *Sämtliche Werke und Briefe in vier Bänden*, ed. Helmut Sembdner (Munich: Hanser, 1982), III, 319.

14. The last words of Kleist's text are "the continuation is forthcoming" ["Die Fortsetzung folgt" (III, 324)]. He thereby opens up his text to a potential dialogue of texts, but the text that could soonest be considered the continuation would be his "Letter of a Young Poet to a Young Painter" ["Brief eines jungen Dichters an einen jungen Maler"] of 1810, where he repeats his defense of the autonomous subject, describing art as the expression of such autonomy, and thus continues to oppose dialogue: "The task, for God's sake, is not to be an other, but rather to be yourself and to reveal yourself, your innermost self and that which is most truly your own, through outline and colors!" ["Denn die Aufgabe, Himmel und Erde! ist ja nicht, ein anderer, sondern ihr selbst zu sein, und euch selbst, euer Eigenstes und Innerstes, durch Umriß und Farben, zur Anschauung zu bringen!" (III, 336)].

15. In his very useful chapter on the significance of dialogue in "The Collector" and in Goethe's work in general (44–63), Jolles makes what seems to be a similar point about the dis-integration of the subject in dialogue. However, he then attempts to rehabilitate the subject by claiming that the "subordination of the I" (a phrase that itself maintains the subject as part of a hierarchy) occurs only for the sake of eliminating "arbitrary absoluteness"; in the place of that individual subject he posits a more general subjectivity that results from dialogue's combination of elements—what he calls "a

higher dignity" (53). The image of a unity, a totality, remains in his insistence on the prerequisite for dialogue of a "common center" (53). Furthermore, in his discussion of Goethe's "ideal conversation" he claims that this dialogue leads not to a *problematization* of the self's presence, but rather to a "timeless presence" (61); in other words, while he seems to say that dialogue undermines the absoluteness of the self, he ends up positing dialogue as a means of achieving the subject's absoluteness—its complete presence.

16. Barbara Johnson, *The Critical Difference: Essays in the Contemporary Rhetoric of Reading* (Baltimore: The Johns Hopkins University Press, 1980), xi.

17. Jacques Derrida, "Differance," in his *Speech and Phenomena and Other Essays on Husserl's Theory of Signs*, trans. David B. Allison (Evanston, Ill.: Northwestern University Press, 1973), 129.

18. Here there is an affinity to Bakhtin's work (which Holquist alludes to briefly in his introduction to *The Dialogic Imagination* [xxi]). Bakhtin, however, mitigates his own subversion of the notion of a unitary language by reinstating such language as a quality of poetic genres other than the novel.

19. Jolles makes the general statement that "dialogue is the content and form of the 'Collector' " (54), but concentrates only on the more obvious manifestations of dialogue—that of the correspondence with the editors and that between the members of the collector's circle. And although he discusses the essay's unsystematic quality and attempts to show that its dialogic character interferes with any theoretical intentions, he undermines this argument by positing dialogue itself as a kind of system when he calls it "a higher lawfulness" (53) and claims that it, even more than a systematic treatise, leads to closure (47).

20. In *Werther*, Goethe had practiced a similar textual strategy. We find essentially the same situation in the novel: we have only one side of the correspondence and must thus "supply" the other side. For a discussion of this aspect of the text and of its implications for the novel as a whole, see Benjamin Bennett, "Werther and Montaigne: The Romantic Renaissance," *Goethe Yearbook* 3 (1986): 1–20, especially 12–13.

21. When Goethe discusses, in *Poetry and Truth*, the lively dialogue that brought about the Storm and Stress movement, he refers as well to a dialogue of texts in that he speaks of literary communication as having taken place in the pages of the journals and "poetic almanacs" ["Musenalmanache"] (IV, 383–84; X, 567–68).

22. Julia Kristeva, "Word, Dialogue and Novel," in *The Kristeva Reader*, ed. Toril Moi (New York: Columbia University Press, 1986), 36–37.

23. See also Jochen Schulte-Sasse, "Poetik und Ästhetik Lessings und seiner Zeitgenossen," in *Hansers Sozialgeschichte der deutschen Literatur vom 16. Jahrhundert bis zur Gegenwart, Band 3: Deutsche Aufklärung bis zur Französischen Revolution, 1680–1789*, ed. Rolf Grimminger (Munich: Hanser, 1980), 315–88.

24. In a conversation with Eckermann (11 April 1827) Goethe mentions this passage from "A Counter-Riposte" in a reference to the unsystematic quality of *Laocoön* (XXIV, 247).

25. A central point in the argument of "Pope, a Metaphysician!" is the critique of the questionable translation of Pope's "Whatever Is, is Right" as "Tout ce qui est, est bien" (III, 649). The Royal Academy in Berlin had formulated its 1753 prize topic in French and in the wording of the topic had even shortened this misleading translation to read "Tout est bien" (see III, 787).

26. Mendelssohn's reactions to Lessing's drafts are quoted from volume 6 of Lessing, *Werke*.

27. Roland Barthes, "From Work to Text," in his *Image—Music—Text,* ed. and trans. Stephen Heath (New York: Hill and Wang, 1977), 160.

28. Roland Barthes, "The Death of the Author," in his *Image—Music—Text,* 146.

29. Johann Joachim Winckelmann, *Gedanken über die Nachahmung der griechischen Werke in der Malerei und Bildhauerkunst,* ed. Ludwig Uhlig (Stuttgart: Reclam, 1969).

30. *On the Origin of Language: Two Essays,* trans. John H. Moran and Alexander Gode (Chicago: University of Chicago Press, 1986), 128*; Johann Gottfried von Herder, *Sämtliche Werke,* ed. Bernhard Suphan, 33 vols. (Berlin: Weidmann, 1877–1913), V, 47. Quotations from Herder's works will be documented with volume and page numbers from the Suphan edition and, in the case of the treatise on the origin of language, with page numbers from the Gode translation.

31. Klaus L. Berghahn, "Von der klassizistischen zur klassischen Literaturkritik," in *Geschichte der deutschen Literaturkritik (1730–1980),* ed. Peter Uwe Hohendahl (Stuttgart: Metzler, 1985), 54.

32. For an excellent, detailed analysis of the relationship between *Laocoön* and the "First Grove," see Eva Knodt, *"Negative Philosophie" und dialogische Kritik.* Also, *Laocoön* is implied in the opening lines of the *Treatise on the Origin of Language* where Herder begins his argument with a discussion of *screams:* "While still an animal, man already has language. All violent sensations of his body, and among the violent the most violent, those which cause him pain, and all strong passions of his soul express themselves directly in screams, in sounds, in wild inarticulate tones. A suffering animal, no less than the hero Philoctetus, will whine, will moan when pain befalls it" (87) [*"Schon als Thier, hat der Mensch Sprache. Alle heftigen, und die heftigsten unter den heftigen, die schmerzhaften Empfindungen seines Körpers, alle starke Leidenschaften seiner Seele äußern sich unmittelbar in Geschrei, in Töne, in wilde, unartikulirte Laute. Ein leidendes Thier so wohl, als der Held Philoktet, wenn es der Schmerz anfället, wird wimmern! wird ächzen!"* (V, 5)].

33. The idiosyncrasies in the French are Goethe's.

34. For a more extensive discussion of the relationship between *Clavigo* and *Emilia Galotti,* see my *"Emilia Galotti und Clavigo:* Werthers Pflichtlektüre und unsere," *Zeitschrift für deutsche Philologie* 104 (1985): 481–94.

35. Aloys Hirt, "Laokoon," *Die Horen: eine Monatsschrift* 12, no. 10 (1797): 1–26.

36. The Suhrkamp edition translates the title as "On the *Laocoon* Group."

37. For an enumeration of many of the points of contact between Goethe's essay and Hirt's study, some of those I discuss and others that I do not include, see Wohlleben, 94.

38. See Jolles, 32–43.

39. See *Poetry and Truth,* IV, 371–72; X, 548–50.

40. Curiously, Goethe, in the essay, only *implies* that this is why the father does not scream; he never discusses the point explicitly. The explicit connection between the description of Laocoön's physical state (nearly identical to that in the essay) and the impossibility of screaming is made, however, in Book 11 of *Poetry and Truth,* where Goethe recalls his reactions to seeing the statue in Mannheim in 1769 (IV, 371–72; X, 549).

41. For example, in Siegfried Seidel's notes to the essay in the *Berliner Ausgabe: Goethe, Werke, Berliner Ausgabe,* ed. Siegfried Seidel (Berlin: Aufbau, 1973), XIX, 787.

42. In another essay, Goethe similarly poeticizes a work of art; in "Rembrandt the Thinker" ["Rembrandt, der Denker"] he creates a narrative to accompany Rembrandt's *The Good Samaritan* (III, 66–68; XIII, 1080–82).

43. See Wohlleben, 95.

44. The "Translator's Confession" recalls, again, Kleist's "On the Gradual Completion of Thoughts While Speaking." In both cases, the arrival of another person and the ensuing conversation help the writer out of the dilemma caused by their attempt to formulate their thoughts clearly (although in Kleist the composition of a treatise is only implied). But Goethe's confession also recalls the extreme divergence between his views and those of Kleist. In the case of Kleist, that conversation turns out to be more a monologue, the goal of which is then to be able to complete the thought logically and solve the problem. In "Diderot's Essay," on the other hand, the conversation undermines the very possibility of such completion, leads to the abandonment of the plan to write a treatise and then to an open-ended dialogue of texts, neither of which makes claims to a "completion of thoughts."

45. See also Jolles, 56–60.

46. Jacques Derrida, "Speech and Phenomena: Introduction to the Problem of Signs in Husserl's Phenomenology," in his *Speech and Phenomena*, 78. Derrida describes how speech came to indicate presence as follows:

> In order to really understand where the power of the voice lies, and how metaphysics, philosophy, and the determination of being as presence constitute the epoch of speech as *technical* mastery of objective being . . . we must think through the objectivity of the object. The ideal object is the most objective of objects. . . . Since its presence to intuition, its being-before the gaze, has no essential dependence on any worldly or empirical synthesis, the re-establishment of its sense in the form of presence becomes a universal and unlimited possibility. But, being *nothing* outside the world, this ideal being must be constituted, re-peated, and expressed in a medium that does not impair the presence and self-presence of the acts that aim at it, a medium which both preserves the *presence of the object* before intuition and *self-presence*, the absolute proximity of the acts to themselves. The ideality of the object, which is only its being-for a nonempirical consciousness, can only be expressed in an element whose phenomenality does not have worldly form. *The name of this element is the voice.* (75–76)

47. Cf. Derrida in "Speech and Phenomena": "Every nonphonic signifier involves a spatial reference in its very 'phenomenon,' in the phenomenological (nonworldly) sphere of experience in which it is given. The sense of being 'outside,' 'in the world,' is an essential component of its phenomenon. Apparently there is nothing like this in the phenomenon of speech" (76).

48. Cf. my discussion of this passage in the first section of Part One.

49. This is a "quotation" from "Speech and Phenomena," 86.

50. It should, of course, be noted that many contemporary theorists, such as Derrida in *Glas*, do attempt to move beyond explicit theoretical statement into the performative dimension that Goethe's essays already inhabit.

51. Hugo Friedrich, *Montaigne*, 2d ed. (Bern: Francke, 1967), 28.

52. It should be noted that this uncertainty about the number of addressees does not come to light in the translation, since the collector's use of the address "gentlemen" ["meine Herren"] is omitted (III, 123 and 130).

53. Quoted from HA, VI, 639.

54. Ibid., VI, 640–41.

55. Roland Barthes, *S/Z*, trans. Richard Miller (New York: Hill and Wang, 1974), 4.

56. See also Barthes's essay, "From Work to Text": "The Text (if only by its frequent 'unreadability') decants the work (the work permitting) from its consumption and gathers it up as play, activity, production, practice" (162); "The reduction of reading to a consumption is clearly responsible for the 'boredom' experienced by many in the face of the modern ('unreadable') text, the avant-garde film or painting: to be bored means that one cannot produce the text, open it out, *set it going*" (163).

57. The Suhrkamp edition translates the title as "On Interpreting Aristotle's *Poetics,*" which does not sufficiently capture the sense, conveyed by the word "Nach*lese,*" of returning to the text and rereading it.

58. Wilkinson and Willoughby, although they do not develop the point as a general quality of *texts* or deal with reading as rewriting, recognize the proximity for Goethe of production and reception: "To Goethe, being receptive means: to discover by creative effort" (Elizabeth M. Wilkinson and L. A. Willoughby, "*Wandrers Sturmlied:* A Study in Poetic Vagrancy," in their *Goethe: Poet and Thinker* [London: Edward Arnold, 1962], 44).

59. Barbara Johnson, "The Critical Difference: BartheS/BalZac," in her *The Critical Difference,* 3–12.

60. Jacques Derrida, *Of Grammatology,* trans. Gayatri Chakravorty Spivak (Baltimore: The Johns Hopkins University Press, 1974), 150.

61. In the critical commentary to the autobiography (HA, IX, 764).

62. Jürgen Habermas, *Strukturwandel der Öffentlichkeit: Untersuchungen zu einer Kategorie der bürgerlichen Gesellschaft* (Neuwied: Luchterhand, 1976).

63. It is here that I take issue with Van Der Laan's study of "The German Essay of the Eighteenth Century" (diss., University of Illinois at Urbana-Champaign, 1984). He calls the essay "a form of independence and self-assertion. Indeed, it expresses individualism and individuality" (237). In its intertextuality the essay implies non-independence, and in its deconstruction of subjectivity it undermines the very notion of autonomous individuality and unique self-expression. Van Der Laan, despite having discussed dialogue in the essay, concludes his study with statements that the essay is "a search for identity and meaning" and "a harbinger of the solipsistic philosophy of a subsequent generation [Romanticism]" (239). This conclusion can be seen to follow from a view of the essay as the genre of the subject—a view that has its foundation in the "personal," autobiographical quality of Montaigne's essays. But in considering Montaigne's "self-expression" it is crucial that we also consider the particular quality of that expression, namely the skepticism that always accompanies it. Michel Beaujour calls our attention to this quality of Montaigne's writing when he describes how Descartes "centered his own method around his *ego,* thereby systematizing and normalizing Montaigne's sceptical invention of a subjective method" ("Genus Universum," *Glyph: Textual Studies* 7 [1980]: 27). Beaujour describes what he calls "genus universum" as the Renaissance discourse of "fragmentation, open-endedness, neoteny, and serious playfulness" (29); this could also be seen as a partial description of what I discuss under the name of "essay" and call a "genre of genres."

64. For a detailed discussion of the performance of cultural and social boundary-breaking in *Iphigenia,* see Benjamin Bennett, "*Iphigenie auf Tauris* and Goethe's Idea of Drama," in his *Modern Drama and German Classicism: Renaissance from Lessing to Brecht* (Ithaca: Cornell University Press, 1979), 97–120, especially 102–8 (my formulation is borrowed from page 106).

65. For a detailed discussion both of the problematics of that constitution of subjectivity and of the subversive rewriting that occurs in the continuation of *Wilhelm Meister,*

see Sylvia M. Schmitz-Burgard, "Vorschriften: Geschlechterdiskurs im europäischen Roman des 18. Jahrhunderts (Richardson, Rousseau, Goethe)" (diss., University of Virginia, 1992).

66. The two poems can be found in *Goethe: Selected Verse*, 274–75. Luke's translations, while in "plain prose," seem to capture best the sense of Goethe's poems.

Index